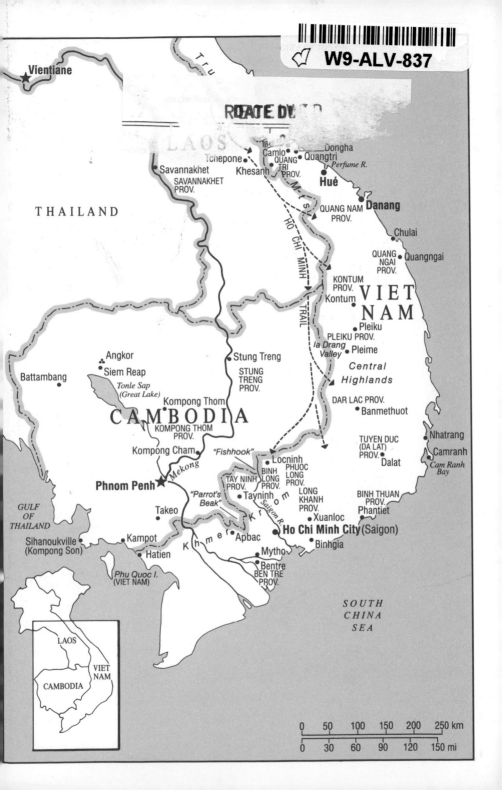

BITTER VICTORY

Other books by Robert Shaplen

A Corner of the World
Free Love and Heavenly Sinners
A Forest of Tigers
Kreuger: Genius and Swindler
Toward the Wellbeing of Mankind:
    50 Years of the Rockefeller Foundation
The Lost Revolution
Time Out of Hand: Revolution and
    Reaction in Southeast Asia
The Road from War
The Face of Asia (Introduction)
A Turning Wheel

BITTER VICTORY

Robert Shaplen

1817

HARPER & ROW, PUBLISHERS, New York
Cambridge, Philadelphia, San Francisco, Washington
London, Mexico City, São Paulo, Singapore, Sydney

For Jayjia

Major portions of this work originally appeared in somewhat different form in
The New Yorker.

FIRST EDITION

Designer: Jénine Holmes
Copyeditor: Mary Jane Alexander
Map by George Colbert
Index by Anne Holmes for Edindex

Library of Congress Cataloging-in-Publication Data

Shaplen, Robert, 1917–
  Bitter victory.

  Includes index.
  1. Vietnam—Description and travel—1975–
2. Cambodia—Description and travel—1975–
3. Vietnam—History—1975–   4. Cambodia—History—1975–
5. Shaplen, Robert, 1917–   —Journeys—Vietnam. 6. Shaplen, Robert,
1917–   —Journeys—Cambodia. I. Title.
DS559.912.S52   1986   959.704′4   85-45661
ISBN 0- 06-015586-8

---

86 87 88 89 90 HC 10 9 8 7 6 5 4 3 2 1

Contents

Acknowledgments   vii

Introduction   1

CHAPTER 1
Ho Chi Minh City—or Saigon?   5

CHAPTER 2
Compromise and Reform   47

CHAPTER 3
The Proud Center   117

CHAPTER 4
The War Through Vietnamese Eyes   142

CHAPTER 5
Cambodia in Captivity   196

Epilogue   299
Index   301

Acknowledgments

I would like to thank those who made my trip possible, including Tran Trong Khanh, second secretary in charge of press affairs of the Permanent Mission of the Socialist Republic of Vietnam to the United Nations; Duong Minh, the deputy chief of public affairs in Hanoi, who was my host during my visit and who arranged my schedule; and Nguyen Dinh Phuong, an experienced diplomat I was most fortunate to have assigned as my interpreter. The hundred or more Vietnamese I interviewed, and who were generous with their time and patient, are too numerous to mention, but I thank them all. I am grateful for the encouragement and sound advice given me by my editor at Harper & Row, Buz Wyeth. And, as always, my thanks go to William Shawn, the editor-in-chief of *The New Yorker*, who supported me in my long efforts to return to Vietnam and who published three articles in the magazine that furnish a considerable part of this book.

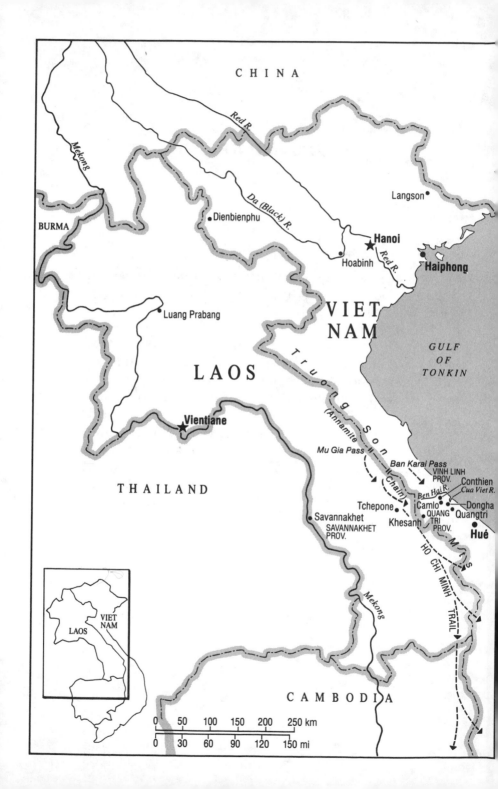

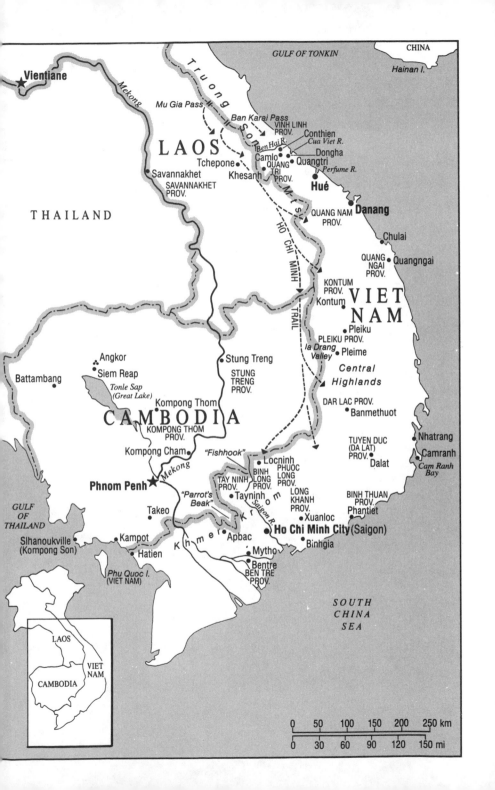

CHINA

GULF OF TONKIN

Hainan I.

Vientiane

Mekong

Mu Gia Pass

Truong Son Mts.

Ban Karai Pass

VINH LINH PROV.

Conthien

Cua Viet R.

Ben Hai R.

Camlo

QUANG TRI PROV.

Dongha

Quangtri

Tchepone

Hué

Khesanh

Perfume R.

Savannakhet

SAVANNAKHET PROV.

LAOS

HO CHI MINH TRAIL

QUANG NAM PROV.

Danang

Chulai

THAILAND

QUANG NGAI PROV.

Quangngai

KONTUM PROV.

Kontum

VIET NAM

Pleiku

PLEIKU PROV.

Ia Drang Valley

Pleime

Central Highlands

Angkor

Stung Treng

Siem Reap

STUNG TRENG PROV.

Battambang

Tonle Sap (Great Lake)

DAR LAC PROV.

Banmethuot

Kompong Thom

CAMBODIA

KOMPONG THOM PROV.

TUYEN DUC (DA LAT) PROV.

Nhatrang

Kompong Cham

"Fishhook"

Dalat

Camranh

Cam Ranh Bay

Mekong

Locninh

BINH LONG PROV.

PHUOC LONG PROV.

TAY NINH PROV.

Phnom Penh

"Parrot's Beak"

Tayninh

LONG KHANH PROV.

BINH THUAN PROV.

Takeo

Saigon R.

Xuanloc

Phantiet

Slhanoukville (Kompong Son)

Kampot

Apbac

Ho Chi Minh City (Saigon)

Binhgia

GULF OF THAILAND

Hatien

Khmer Krom

Mytho

Phu Quoc I. (VIET NAM)

Bentre

BEN TRE PROV.

SOUTH CHINA SEA

LAOS

VIET NAM

CAMBODIA

| 0 | 50 | 100 | 150 | 200 | 250 km |
| 0 | 30 | 60 | 90 | 120 | 150 mi |

Introduction

Vietnam has been a large part of my life for forty years, since I first arrived in Saigon in June 1946, shortly after the French had regained control of the southern portion of the country. By the end of that year, when the first Indo-China war started, they had recaptured Hanoi from the Communist Vietminh as well, but they never did recover all of their former colonial empire in Asia, including much of Laos and Cambodia and the northern tier of what became Vietnam, major areas of which were held throughout the war by the Vietminh guerrillas. Eight years later, in the spring and summer of 1954, came the climactic French defeat at Dienbienphu, followed by the French surrender and the Geneva Conference that perpetuated two antagonistic Vietnams and set the stage for another disastrous war.

Between 1962 and 1975, the years of United States involvement, I spent about a third of my time in Vietnam, and on April 29, 1975, I was among those who fled Saigon by helicopter as North Vietnamese troops were about to seize the city. Thus ended a sorry chapter in American history, a prolonged but futile effort to shore up a series of South Vietnamese governments none of which ever proved themselves politically or militarily capable of withstanding the zealous and dedicated Communist forces determined to unify the nation. As I rode to the airport along streets crowded with hostile and panicky South Viet-

1

namese, and then flew safely to an aircraft carrier in the China Sea, I felt more remorse and shame than anger. It was not that we had let down the South Vietnamese and deserted them—they were as much or more to blame for their defeat—but that we had played our role so poorly for so long. We had never properly defined our original commitment, had become overinvolved militarily, had misconstrued our political aims, and then had angrily fought a bootless and cruel war ineffectually. And we had paid heavily for our blunders while all but destroying a once beautiful country.

At first I had no desire to return. It was over and done with, I felt, and like so many other Americans, I wanted to forget—or try to forget—what had happened in Vietnam. But after some time I became curious. I wondered why the Vietnamese, so indomitable in war, had been unable to benefit from their remarkable victories, why their economy was such a mess, why they had let themselves become bogged down in another conflict, in Cambodia, and why they had become so isolated and ostracized in Southeast Asia and in the world. Were they, after all, compulsively self-destructive, like lemmings? Were they so addicted to violence and struggle that they were simply incapable of adjusting to peace? Was this part of their innate character, or due to some quirky geopolitical trick of fate? Or had they simply made some bad mistakes and suffered more than their share of bad luck?

It took me nearly ten years to find out some of the answers. Despite repeated requests for a visa, and one or two promises, I ran into a brick wall of being ignored or rejected. Finally, in the spring of 1984, with the help of the Permanent Vietnamese Mission to the United Nations in New York, I received permission to travel to Hanoi via Bangkok. I arrived there in September and, to my pleasant surprise, was allowed to remain five weeks in Vietnam and a week in Cambodia. Virtually all my requests to see people and visit places were met, though there were a few important exceptions, notably two or three old friends in Saigon who, I was told, were "unavailable" for one reason or another. The high point of my visit was an illuminating four-hour talk with Le Duc Tho, the number-two man in the political hierarchy after Le Duan. It turned out that I had come at a good time, when the Politburo was just beginning to rethink the Vietnamese role in Cambodia and when the abysmal failures of the national economy and halfhearted attempts at reform had finally led to an earnest effort to set things right. Above all, though the options were not only theirs, they were finally trying to escape their long years of isolation and diminish their overreliance on the Soviet Union. But their success or failure depended not only on a resolution of the Cambodian war, which was primarily their decision to make, but on a willingness on the part of the People's Republic of China and the United States to negotiate equitably on a number of other issues as well.

My trip was rewarding and, in most ways, gratifying. Though I did not obtain all the answers to my questions, I came away with a better understanding of why and how the North Vietnamese won the war, and why they have had so much trouble winning the peace. They have a long way to go before they come to terms with themselves, let alone with other nations, but they are making progress and they remain infinitely patient and doggedly determined to survive.

CHAPTER ONE

Ho Chi Minh City—or Saigon?

(1)

I had last seen Trinh Cong Son a few days before the end of the war, in a small garden filled with azaleas and frangipani next to the house where he was staying, not far from my hotel. He was with his brothers and sisters and a few friends when I arrived, about dusk that evening in April 1975, and he was strumming his guitar and singing some of his sad antiwar songs that had made him famous and had been banned by the government for the past five or six years. This had not kept them from being played on pirated cassettes by thousands of young Vietnamese all over the country; they could occasionally still be heard in some nightclubs in town, particularly one on Tu Do, or Freedom Street, where a young girl named Khanh Ly, who had a strong, resonant voice, sang them by popular demand to large audiences that included many members of the armed forces, who applauded her wildly. I remembered one song in particular called "A Lullaby of Sounds of Cannon Fire in the Middle of the Night," and in the garden that evening I asked Trinh Cong Son to sing it again. The first part went:

> *Every night the sounds of cannon fire*
> *reverberate through the city*
> *A city sweeper stands still in the*
> *street, a broom in his hands.*

*The sounds of cannon fire wake a
    mother from her sleep,
Fill the heart of a baby with
    poignant sadness . . .
Shelters are being destroyed, laid in
    lifeless ruins,
Yellow skin, yellow flesh—what a
    tragedy being blown to pieces.*

At this time, Trinh Cong Son was thirty-six years old, a thin, intense man with deep-brown eyes and a small, wispy beard. His voice was soft and melodious, and it seemed to hover in the heavy pre-monsoonal atmosphere—full of foreboding, for North Vietnamese troops were drawing closer to the city almost hour by hour. We Americans still there had already been given our designated points of departure by helicopter, and had done what we could to arrange for Vietnamese friends and associates who wanted to leave to depart by transport planes. None of us, however, could have predicted the pandemonium and panic of that final day—April 29, 1975—when the last fourteen hundred Americans were airlifted out of the country and a hundred thousand Vietnamese fled, some of them by helicopter but many more by boat. I had asked Trinh Cong Son if he would remain, and he had replied, "Yes, I will stay here—we are all Vietnamese. But if the Communists don't offer me inspiration, I won't write."

Now here he was again, nine and a half years later, walking toward me through the glare of the late afternoon sun on the rooftop dining room of the old Majestic Hotel, overlooking the river. He looked much the same, except he had shaved his beard and he wore horn-rimmed glasses, which he pointed to as soon as he sat down, to acknowledge the passage of time. "I am still a bachelor," he began, and he went on to tell me he was mostly writing songs for documentary and feature films. He summarized the themes of several of the films. One was about a group of girls on a state farm near the Cambodian border who were captured and beheaded by the Khmer Rouge troops of the murderous Pol Pot, who between 1975 and 1979 ordered the killing of at least a million of his fellow Cambodians. Another was about a woman doctor who had fought against the Americans and had been killed by bombs in the jungle when the war was almost over. A third film told the story of a group of teenage boys and girls who had been corrupted by the insidious life of Saigon but had been "reeducated" and were leading productive lives in the city.

"I have a wider audience now," he said, "workers and peasants as well as students—and I travel about and sing for them too. Vietnam has not lost its taste for song and melody. In fact, there is a mass audience today, and there wasn't before." I asked him if there is less sadness now that the war is over. "There is no sadness the way there was," he said. "If there is any, it is a private sadness of pathological people—people who hug it in their hearts and don't accept the fact that society has changed. They haven't changed, and they blame society. They don't share the common cause, they don't mix. Frankly, there are fans of mine who blame me now for changing. They wanted to keep me a prisoner of their own feelings of sadness, to retain my old image, but I wanted to free myself in new sentiments and aspirations. My philosophy is that if a man doesn't change day by day he's a dead man."

I asked him if he would sing me one of his new songs, and he said he would sing "Myth About Mother," and explained that Mother was Vietnam, who had protected her children during the war and sacrificed herself in every way for their benefit. He wrote it, he added, for the tenth anniversary of the liberation of Ho Chi Minh City (Saigon's new name). As he sang, he tapped out the rhythm with his fingers on the tablecloth. His voice was as vibrant and clear as ever, and the tune was evocative and haunting. It brought me back to that scene in the garden, but neither of us referred to it, and in a few moments, after I had thanked him for taking time off on a busy day, he excused himself, explaining that he had an appointment to finish some recordings.

Trinh Cong Son was one of the few old friends or acquaintances I was able to see during my four days in Ho Chi Minh City, which was part of my six weeks' return to Vietnam in the late summer and fall of 1984. Another was an American-trained economist who had gone through a short period of reeducation and was now working as an adviser for the new government, which had recently introduced a series of liberalizing measures designed to encourage farmers and workers to surpass their production quotas in return for the right to sell their surplus output on the free market. But I was unable to see most of the people I inquired about, either because there was not enough time—the government information office tends to hurry one through Ho Chi Minh City—or because, I was told, they were "out of town." I tried to get in touch with several former Buddhist leaders, including Thich Tri Quang, the best-known bonze, or priest, of the sixties, who had led the revolt against President Ngo Dinh Diem that culminated in the coup of November 1963, during which Diem was assassinated. I had met Tri Quang a number of times in the old days, though he had always been elusive and, even when I finally would catch up with him, he would be cryptic and evasive. He had kept up his political activities—he was anti-Communist, anti-American, and anti-war—until 1975, moving back and forth between Saigon and Hué, in central Vietnam. After the war, he was reported to have been held under house arrest for a year and a half and then set free. Whether voluntarily or otherwise, he has since been "in seclusion" at his old pagoda, An Quang, in Ho Chi Minh City, and has apparently refused to see any visitors. Another Buddhist leader I had known was Bui Tuong Huan, a layman who had been active in Buddhist politics and close to Tri Quang. I learned that he was about to join his family in America, and then I heard that he was having second thoughts about leaving Vietnam. I was unable to locate him and no effort was made to help me.

A most unusual case was that of Tran Van Giau, now in his early eighties. Giau was one of Ho Chi Minh's earliest and closest associates, having been trained as a Communist with Ho in Moscow in the early thirties. During the Second World War, he had returned to Cochin China—the southernmost part of French Indo-China and the area that became South Vietnam—and had become the leader there of the Vietminh, the revolutionary front Ho had formed. This was at a time when the Communists in the south were undergoing one of their bloodiest and most violent periods of internal and anti-Trotskyist struggle, and Giau was in the middle of it. Subsequently, his independent attitude and his alleged failure to prosecute the revolution against the Japanese and the French led to his political decline and eclipse. He became a historian, occasionally meeting with visiting foreign scholars. Not long before my visit, however, he briefly reemerged by making known his belief that socialism in the south should develop in its own way, reflecting the basic differences between the two parts of the country. He had chosen the wrong time to raise this touchy subject, for the new measures providing individual incentives for farmers and workers all over the country and some degree of controlled free enterprise had just been worked out as a kind of compromise. When I requested to see Giau, I was told he was in the southernmost part of the Delta "writing a Party history." Later, in Hanoi, I asked Prime Minister Pham Van Dong about him, and my question was politely brushed off. "Yes, I know him," Dong replied, and that was all.

Besides Tran Van Giau, who had obviously become

something of a non-person, it was also hard to see any of the more recent wartime southern leaders of the old Provisional Revolutionary Government or the National Liberation Front, such as Nguyen Huu Tho, the former head of the NLF, who is chairman of the National Assembly, essentially a high ceremonial post. The men who run things in Hanoi, even though some of them were born in the south themselves and have retained strong revolutionary roots there, have never come to trust these southern wartime figures, with a few exceptions—Nguyen Huu Tho being one, and another being Mme Nguyen Thi Binh, who was the PRG's foreign minister and chief negotiator in Paris for a time and is now minister of education.

My biggest disappointment in Ho Chi Minh City, though not an altogether unexpected one, was being unable to see a former prominent Vietnamese journalist who had been one of my closest friends for a dozen years. He had solicited and accepted my advice to send his wife and children to the United States in April 1975, but had decided to stay on himself, "at least for a while," he told me, in part because of his mother, who was old and ill. Some time later, though, he had arranged for his family to return to Vietnam, and we correspondents subsequently heard that he had secretly been a Communist intelligence agent all through the war and was rewarded afterward with the rank of colonel and a new car—the one he had was about twenty years old and we had always wondered what kept it running. He was now a ranking official of the export trade office. One of my guides during my visit, who had also been a journalist before he joined the Vietcong in the jungle, corroborated this story and added that my friend had a new name. I had no reason to doubt the account, but I felt, as I had all along, that it was not the whole story. I wondered, for example, why he had bothered having his family moved back and forth in the first place, with the help of the American publication he had worked for. Had he really been a Communist all along, or had he decided to become one only after April 30, 1975, for one reason or another? For "survival," perhaps? That had always been a favorite word of his, and he had often expressed his philosophy that all Vietnamese were "survivalists." Could he have been working as a double agent, or even a triple agent, and before throwing in his lot with the Communists had he wanted to make sure that he had covered all his tracks? There was some reason to believe that this was possible. Moreover, there were certainly many Vietnamese I knew who were nationalists first and foremost—who had disapproved strongly of what the South Vietnamese government and the Americans were doing to the country, and felt that the alternatives, including a takeover by the Communists, who were also nationalists, could be no worse and might be better. Perhaps my friend was simply in this group; I recalled that he had expressed little doubt in the final two or three years that the Communists were winning the war. At the same time, he was surely one of the best-informed men in town and had countless news sources that no one else seemed to have. In our conversations over the years, often lasting for hours, I discovered that the facts and opinions he furnished about the Communists, the government, and the many contending individuals and groups—including Buddhists and Catholics who opposed both sides in the conflict—were more on the mark than anything I could obtain from other sources, not excluding the American Embassy, which often knew surprisingly little about what was going on among the non-establishment Vietnamese. Some friends of my friend who also stayed behind but who have left Vietnam since have repeated the story that he was a Communist all along. But others who knew him at least as well have denied it, and have added that he became increasingly critical of the regime after 1975, and had told them he was sorry he had stayed. In any event, in response to my repeated inquiries, I was told that he, too, was "out of town," somewhere deep in the Delta, but I suspect that, even if he really was around, he would not want to see me.

Later, as I thought more about it and debated what my friend's status really had been and was, I remembered some of his cynical and bitter comments about the impact the Americans had made on Vietnam, beyond the sheer physical destruction. And as I went back over my notes, there was one passage in particular that leaped out at me and set off a fresh spate of uncomfortable feelings and doubts. "You Americans think you have given the Vietnamese a better material life, but it's not true," he had said. "Most of the equipment you poured in here will end up as scrap. Perhaps the situation will have to disintegrate further before something new can be built. The only hope is that a new, younger group, with ideas of its own, will emerge, and that these young people will understand that both the old prewar society and the American superimposed one are finished. If we don't go Communist, it may take twenty years, or even longer, to bring about a new synthesis, but it will happen. First, though, we must undo the damage we have done. The Vietnamese like to raise monkeys. You have seen them in the animal markets, in homes, in the parks. What you have done here in Saigon is create a monkey climate. The only Vietnamese you really know—the ones you have dealt with—are monkeys. Why don't you at least help us get rid of the monkeys before you go?"

Despite the rebuff in my efforts to find my friend, I kept searching for him, hoping I might bump into him on the street or find him in one of the cafés or restaurants he used to frequent. This feeling that he and others I had once known who, willingly or unwillingly, had stayed behind were somewhere about the city, were watching *me* even if I couldn't see *them*, kept bothering me through my stay. It was part of the strangeness, the eeriness, of being back in a place I had known so well for more than forty years—a place that looked the same in many ways and yet wasn't the same anymore. Or was it—or part of it, anyway? Trinh Cong Son, singing his song for me, talking about his new life, had obviously changed, but had he really changed very much? Had his old sadness about the war been altogether replaced by the euphoria he had expressed? Or did those old fans he had mentioned, who were his age, haunt and torment him more than he cared to admit? If this was so, and if his new fame and good fortune while in many ways surpassing his earlier success had, in fact, left him less of a hero or a martyr, he was obviously determined to stick to his new career and reap its rewards. Since he had never made any money before from his old pirated cassettes and had been officially ostracized, he was obviously better off now under the Communists than under the old regime, but it was hard to tell if he felt more gratification; it would have taken far more time than the hour or so we spent together even to begin to scratch that slippery surface.

There were many such anomalies as I wandered around Ho Chi Minh City. The Saigon past indeed hangs over the place, and I found it difficult, as many Vietnamese do, including government officials, even to call it by its new name. Gone was the mad bustle of the old days, the sense of a city constantly on the make, scrounging, cheating, stealing, pushing and jostling, pimping and whoring, full of discordant sounds and multiple smells, always bursting at the seams by day and seething through its pores at night. What was left, it seemed at first glance, was a dormant mollusk, its shell closed, waiting for the weather to change or the tide to come back in. There was something terribly tentative about that city, something untold and untellable, not because of any dark secret but because the plot was obscure, the future still unclear. Moreover, for someone like myself, who had first visited Saigon in the mid-forties when it was still radiant and softly verdant, and who had seen it change so drastically during the two long wars against the French and the Americans, to return now for even a short visit was in itself a jarring and in some ways a grotesque experience.

One incident, for example, that had taken place in 1972 when the American troops were just beginning to leave, kept coming back to me. I was having dinner with some friends at a restaurant in Cholon, the Chinese section of the city, when there was a sudden howl of sirens outside. After years in Saigon, I had become used to sirens, whose throbbing *wow-wow-wow* breaking through and above the usual roar and rumble of army trucks and the staccato sound of motorbikes and sputtering taxis was heard regularly. We paid no attention at first and went on enjoying our fried crab. But then it became apparent that some emergency vehicles had come to a stop directly in front of the restaurant. I went out to find the block cordoned off, while Vietnamese and American military police carried out a house-to-house search in the glow of rotating red-and-white searchlights from the tops of jeeps. I approached a young American MP who was waving his M-16 rifle like a fishing rod. He couldn't have been more than nineteen years old, and he looked as if he might have arrived in Vietnam the day before. Showing him my press credentials, I asked him what was going on, but he replied only, "Sir, you'll have to go back into that restaurant." A Vietnamese MP—an older man—muttered something in broken English about "students" and "more riot." The Saigon University residential compound, Minh Mang, was only a block away, and for the past week the students had been demonstrating against too rigid police controls. Pointing to the roof of one of the buildings across the street, the Vietnamese policeman said something about "terrorists." I again tried the young American, who was now ducking in and out of doorways and pointing his gun at anyone still on the street. He was so jittery that I was afraid the weapon would go off at any moment, and it was obvious he was in no mood to listen to further questions from me. "Sir," he finally spluttered, "have you got a disaster pass?"

I had never heard of a disaster pass—and, as I subsequently found out, there was no such thing (the young MP was probably referring to a special pass entitling a small number of officials to go anywhere at any time)—but the phrase stayed with me, and I later reflected that, in a manner of speaking, I had had a disaster pass for Saigon for what was then more than a quarter of a century and, when I left the country under rocket fire of the North Vietnamese at the end of April 1975, would be almost thirty years. Those broken years in Saigon had been filled with disaster of one sort or another, though interspersed with many tranquil periods too. It was inevitable that, now in 1984, as I wandered about—I may have been followed by plainclothes police, as friends had warned me I would, but my hosts allowed me to go pretty much where I wished—I would reflect back on the whole crowded panorama of years with mixed and conflicting feelings as I tried to sort out myself as much as the Vietnamese.

It was difficult to do this without an almost constant sense of revived sadness and guilt, not only for war itself and the vast loss of life and tremendous destruction it had caused, but for the decline and degradation of Saigon as a city, at least from 1965 on, when the Americans began arriving in strength. The first Indo-China war, between the Vietminh and the French, from the end of 1946 to the middle of 1954, had affected Saigon, but not nearly as much as the second one, between the Vietnamese Communists of both the north and south and the Americans and those South Vietnamese who fought with them. The major impact of the first war had been felt in what was then North Vietnam and the northern parts of South Vietnam. Moreover, having ruled Indo-China for a century, and the south in particular as a colony, the French had always felt more at home in Saigon than the Americans, who seemed out of place and ill at ease there, like bulls in a China shop, which perhaps is why they wreaked so much damage beyond the ravages of war alone. Among other things, they had turned the city into a monstrous urban sprawl, full of ugly, squalid slums in which crime abounded and violence was endemic. During the French period, to be sure, Saigon had in some ways been a more dangerous place than later, chiefly because of the young men on bicycles hired by the Vietminh to throw grenades into cafés in the heart of the city, usually around eleven in the morning or five in the afternoon. But after a while the cafés and restaurants on the side of town put up protective metal screens, and despite some deaths and injuries caused by the grenades, the easy way of life the French had established went on in the city until after the fall of Dienbienphu in May 1954 and the subsequent French total defeat. Until then, as I looked back, I remembered the constant feeling of excitement, of a genuine sense of adventure one felt in the city. Clandestine meetings with Vietminh agents in teahouses on the outskirts of town could be fairly easily arranged, to which one traveled by cyclo—pedicab—and where one sat and sipped tea or apéritifs and discussed the theory and practice of revolution. Some assassinations and political murders took place, but by and large in those days, which seemed very far off, there was none of the tawdriness and none of the dementia the Americans brought with them.

All of this came to an ugly head, of course, on April 29, 1975, when we fourteen hundred remaining Americans fled Saigon so ignominiously—and, as it turned out, so luckily (only four lives were lost during the day-long evacuation), but not so fortunately for those Vietnamese we left behind. This was the climactic disaster that was hard to forget, that has haunted all of us ever since. And as I reexplored Saigon, searching in vain for faces I knew, I suddenly realized that, consciously or subconsciously, I was looking for other faces too, for Vietnamese who had been strangers but had come up to me on the street that last day to beg for help in getting out of the country. There were some faces among them I was certain I would never forget. A number of these people had clung to the sides of the bus as it slowly made its way through the panic-stricken streets in midafternoon to Tan Son Nhut airport, where, if they had not already lost their hold, they were brushed or batted away like flies by club-swinging Vietnamese police. Thousands of others simply ran hysterically through the streets, asking any Occidental they saw to help them escape. In the last two hours before I left my room at the Hotel Continental, the old colonial hotel where I had always stayed, two Vietnamese friends who had previously told me they were electing to remain had come to say that they had changed their minds. One of them, a longtime political leader whom the Communists would surely have killed, subsequently appeared one evening two weeks later at the door of my high-rise apartment in Hong Kong; he had managed to climb aboard the last helicopter to leave the roof of a six-story building two blocks from my hotel where I had suggested he go, and after being flown to the deck of an aircraft carrier had gone by ship to Guam and then back to Hong Kong, where he eventually obtained a visa to go to England. The second man, a longtime journalist friend who was antigovernment but even more anti-Communist, failed to get out and, I later heard, died in prison.

During the last two or three years of the war, when the possibility of a Communist victory became apparent, many South Vietnamese I knew used to debate the question of how the north would ultimately deal with the south. Some

—especially northerners who had fled south after the nation was divided in 1954—firmly believed that the Communists would take over quickly, completely, and ruthlessly, with an administrative machinery that would be the equal in efficiency of the North Vietnamese Army. These people fully expected a bloodbath. Others were more hopeful; they included true believers in southern nationalism, which, though it was then weak compared with that in the north, had often demonstrated a vibrancy and momentum of its own. There were some people who were simply wishful thinkers and romantic liberals, and there were significant numbers of so-called third force elements, who included many professional, religious, and intellectual leaders and groups with plenty of ideas but no cohesion and no troops of their own. Most of these people and scattered southern Communists, Socialists, and former Trotskyists, including members of the old National Liberation Front and other front organizations, firmly believed in some form of southern "exceptionalism." They felt that socialism in the south, even under the banner of a united Communist nation, had to follow its own course and develop in its own way, and that the north would permit this to happen. The fact that the north proved to have no intention of allowing the south to do any such thing does not mean that the northerners, despite their harsh regimentation, succeeded in transmitting their Spartan precepts to the more easygoing southerners. On the contrary, a good many northern cadres, especially in the first few years, succumbed to the easy life of the south and were overwhelmed by the rich variety of things available there, though they had no money to buy them. Moreover, after a decade of trial and error and of experimental failures, it has been the south that has helped persuade the north to adopt some basic economic compromises, which the pragmatists in the Politburo and the Central Committee have introduced in the guise of a more moderate approach to socialism.

The question of recrimination and revenge in dealing with members of the former regime, and of meting out punishment on a large or lesser scale, remains obscure and has been the subject of considerable speculation and guesswork. It should be considered apart from the economic and social problems the national government faced in trying to bring the north and south together—an area where the north made obvious mistakes in trying to move too quickly in the south during the immediate postwar period. Of the scores of thousands of Vietnamese who stayed on in the south, including many who had worked for the Americans and who might have left in time had they solicited help sooner, others who were sadly overlooked or forgotten by their American employers or counterparts in the mad rush to get out of the country at the end, and countless additional thousands who simply never had a chance to escape, many were eventually sent to reeducation camps or prisons. The estimates range as high as several hundred thousand. The majority remained in the camps for periods ranging from a few weeks or months to three years, but some have been held for a decade. Of the total subjected to reeducation or political imprisonment, according to a comprehensive study among refugees in the United States and in France conducted by two University of California scholars, Karl D. Jackson and Jacqueline Desbarats, at least sixty-five thousand are alleged to have been executed primarily for political crimes between 1975 and 1983. (This figure does not include those who died by accident—as a result of clearing minefields, for example —from malnutrition, disease, or exhaustion, or who committed suicide or simply disappeared.) The survey, involving 831 respondents, took three years to complete. Thirty-seven percent of those questioned knew or had heard of one or several persons who were executed for political reasons, according to the authors. Most of these deaths allegedly took place in 1975 and 1976 in the Saigon and the Mekong Delta areas. The most common victims, the respondents claimed, initially were field-rank military officers of the old regime, and then people who resisted the new government one way or another. Thousands of others were said to have died "slow deaths" in camps, jails, and in the so-called New Economic Zones, where urban residents from overpopulated cities, especially Ho Chi Minh City, were sent.

Even if one accepts the sixty-five thousand figure, it does not constitute a bloodbath in comparison to what happened in Cambodia between 1975 and 1979 or in Nazi-controlled Europe before and during the Second World War. It nevertheless contradicts some of the claims of Western observers that no recriminatory deaths occurred in Vietnam, and also refutes Vietnamese government denials of any political killings. While accounts of refugees can be questioned, the survey did employ careful scientific methods; and the inability to obtain direct verbal, documentary, or photographic evidence in Vietnam makes it the best source of data available so far. During my stay in Vietnam, I found no one who would discuss such matters openly, though officials acknowledged that, beyond the fact a good many had undergone reeducation, an estimated seven to ten thousand persons are still being held in camps or prisons for political crimes. State Department and other official sources maintain that this figure is too low and that the number of political prisoners still held is at least forty thousand. As for those scores of thousands who chose to stay in Vietnam in 1975 knowing that their lives might be imperiled, most did so because they preferred to take that risk rather than live as destitute aliens in some strange, faraway country. Whether they ended up in camps or jails, or miraculously managed to stay free, virtually all of these people have remained outcasts in the new society and have survived at the mercy of relatives or friends. Additional hundreds of thousands eventually made the decision to flee abroad in small boats, but not all were successful; at least half as many as escaped were caught and jailed, or died at sea, or were killed by pirates.

My head spinning with all these recollections and conflicting feelings, it was impossible, as I walked around town, readily to separate the past from the present, to try to regard Ho Chi Minh City as a place in its own right, with a character and quality of its own, entitled to be considered as a brand-new entity. Where did it actually fit into the new Vietnam, where did it belong? These were the very questions the Politburo and the members of the Central Committee of the Communist Party of Vietnam had been debating for a decade, and had only begun to deal with in practical terms. Once the fact had been accepted, belatedly, that the south, and especially Ho Chi Minh City, had a different "mentality" from that in the north, as a high official in Hanoi reluctantly admitted to me, it was one thing to approve of the city's remaining a hub of commerce and light industry and a production center for consumer goods as it moved gradually toward socialism—in the words of Le Duan, the Party's secretary general,* an "export city"—but another thing to change people's habits, customs, and attitudes, and slowly reshape the whole way of life of the place. Despite a number of outward manifestations of change—in how the Communists organized the city's administration, for example, and established control over the press and religious institutions—it seemed highly doubtful that they would manage to achieve such a subjective reshaping for many years, if ever. The south was bound to remain "different," in more ways than one: beneath its new, almost smug exterior, its pretended antiseptic cover, I felt lurked the same cynical sneers and self-deprecating smiles as in the past, and the same latent sense of rebellion against the status quo.

* Le Duan died in Hanoi on July 10, 1986, of kidney disease. His demise may signal the passage of a number of the old guard's leaders. The forthcoming Sixth Party Congress is expected to name his successor and also appoint new younger men to other top Party posts.

Perhaps there could be no better demonstration of this than the trials that began in the city late in 1984 of more than one hundred persons arrested on charges of sabotage, espionage, and plots to kidnap foreign diplomats for terrorist effect. At the first such trial, of twenty-one people, held in December of that year, it was charged that the conspiracy was the work of an organization called the United Front of Patriotic Forces for the Liberation of Vietnam, which allegedly included some Vietnamese who left the country after 1975 but returned clandestinely over the past several years carrying counterfeit money. The Chinese were said to be supporting the scheme out of Thailand, with the approbation of the Americans. After the first trial, three persons were sentenced to death and the other defendants to long jail terms. The government, although highly security conscious as always, gave the case considerable publicity, even inviting a group of foreign correspondents over from Bangkok to witness the opening days of the trial. This was in sharp contrast to previous examples of resistance activity, including plots ostensibly led by a number of former regime soldiers and tribesmen in the Central Highlands mountain chain, and by Chinese espionage and sabotage agents accused of operating below the northern border with China, where sporadic violence has continued since the brief Sino-Vietnamese war early in 1979. The case, however, failed to cause much of a public sensation, and there was only scant information about follow-up proceedings. But news of other spy allegations and reported crimes against the nation or society has appeared regularly, and it is apparent that eternal vigilance is one of the permanent shibboleths of the new regime.

Refugees abroad, especially in the United States, maintain that internal opposition in Vietnam has grown steadily, and that all sorts of schemes are regularly hatched to overthrow the government. Many of these reports and rumors are exaggerated but some have had a basis in fact.

Vietnamese security officials show enough concern about them, in what undeniably has remained a highly disoriented southern society, to give credence to the more serious reports of active dissent and alleged plots of treason and rebellion. It is apparent that, in the restricted political and social climate of the Socialist Republic of Vietnam, where the police are usually discreet but ubiquitous, the situation is kept under extremely firm control. There is no way that foreign visitors, in a short time, can tell what really goes on beneath the surface. But it was obvious that the old days when one would hear a dozen reports a week about coups and plots to overthrow the government were obviously gone—it was a relief not to have to listen to how it was all up to the Americans "just to give the go-ahead" for this or that scheme to succeed. Finally, after forty years, the Vietnamese are completely on their own. They have won their revolution, deservedly so, though they have only begun to consolidate their victory. This is particularly so in the south, and in maverick Ho Chi Minh City, or Saigon, or as a friend of mine, another returning correspondent, aptly calls it—Hoville.

(2)

Not many foreign visitors, other than those who have some official business to conduct, such as representatives of international agencies and occasional private businessmen on scouting trips, travel to Ho Chi Minh City. Vietnam's domestic airline, which flies small Russian Tupulov transports, runs a dozen or so flights a day in and out of Tan Son Nhut airport, which during the American war was one of the two or three busiest in the world. The exception to the now quiet routine is Thursdays, when Air France 747s take out the weekly allotments of the several thousand Vietnamese allowed to leave each month under the Orderly Departure Program arranged between the

Vietnamese government and the United Nations High Commissioner for Refugees. One thousand a month are permitted to leave for the United States. These are mostly middle-class people, including many Sino-Vietnamese, who either have relatives in America or have received visas as a result of some association with the United States prior to 1975. (As many as twice that number of refugees—two thousand in some months—are still fleeing Vietnam in small boats.) In addition 250 Amerasian children, the off-spring of American fathers and Vietnamese women, leave monthly, most of them with their mothers and other relatives; only a small percentage of these children, a majority of whom are teenagers, have identifiable fathers, so most are resettled by voluntary agencies once they reach the United States.

One afternoon I watched one of these departure scenes, which included both Amerasian young people and Vietnamese emigrants. Many of the latter, especially older people, were in tears as they were about to leave their country forever. They were being seen off by hundreds of friends, who crowded the second-floor pavilion of the departure lounge, rebuilt since the war's end. The emigrants had arrived at the airport early in the morning, hours before takeoff, to line up for an elaborate customs and immigration procedure, during which customs agents went through every piece of baggage, opening sealed crates and roped-up suitcases, searching through all pockets of clothing, the pages of books and magazines, and even ripping the soles off shoes and the heads off dolls looking for money or jewels that may not be taken out. The Amerasians were more bewildered than emotional, though most of them seemed happy to be leaving, which is not surprising since they are generally regarded as outcasts in Vietnam—they are called *con lai*, or half-breeds. Downtown, in the blocks around my hotel, I was constantly accosted by numbers of them during my stay, asking for money or wanting to know if I could help them get to the United States. "My name Mary, my daddy American," was the typical greeting, in English. But none of them knew who or where their father was. I was taken aback for a moment by one tall, striking-looking young woman who was about thirty years old and whose skin was blacker than that of most black Amerasians. Then I realized that her father was probably Senegalese—that she had been born toward the close of the French war, in 1954, during which many colonial soldiers from Africa had fought in Indo-China. She confirmed that she was half-Senegalese, and said that she and her mother were trying to obtain visas for France; like the others, she didn't know what happened to her father, whether or not he was even still alive.

By the end of 1985, about eight thousand Amerasians and their relatives had left Vietnam, out of a total of thirty or thirty-five thousand, according to Nguyen Phi Tuyen, a Vietnamese Foreign Service officer in charge of the Orderly Departure Program in Ho Chi Minh City. Until 1984, when the special quota of 250 Amerasian youngsters a month was approved by the United States, they were included in the general thousand a month quota for Vietnamese refugees allowed to leave for America under the ODP, and processing was very slow. The Vietnamese welcomed the new quota but have kept requesting that the United States take all the youngsters out as quickly as possible—at the present rate, they point out, it will take a decade for all of them to depart with their designated relatives. "These people are not refugees," Nguyen Co Thach, the foreign minister of Vietnam, has insisted. "These are your children, they are your responsibility. I would welcome anyone to come and take them away, such as private American groups." What worries the Vietnamese, as Tuyen emphasized when I spoke with him, is that many of the Amerasians are already approaching the age of majority, which is eighteen, and they will then be eligible for citizenship, including conscription, all of which will create new problems of trying to fit them into a society that has already ostracized them and has more than its share of unemployed young people.

The four thousand or so Amerasians on the streets of Ho Chi Minh City—one sees them all over the country, but they are not as conspicuous elsewhere—are perhaps the most striking and conscience-stirring phenomenon of postwar Vietnam, particularly since they so undeniably are part of the American heritage. The degradation of the past, the thousands of beggars and swarms of pimps and prostitutes who roamed the streets, and Saigon's horde of wild street boys, many of whom were orphans, are less in public evidence now, though one still sees them; but they no longer follow foreigners up and down the streets, soliciting tirelessly in monotones, and shouting Vietnamese curses when ignored or rejected. The Amerasians, on the other hand, are invariably gentle; they know how to utilize their blood ties when accosting Americans in subtle ways, throwing out whatever names or associations they can cull out of their experience or imagination, or pointing to their faces and particularly their eyes to provoke sympathy and response. The inclination is to give them a few dong—it is illegal to give the youngsters or their mothers dollars. The mother of one twelve-year-old girl had been arrested for accepting dollars from "a fat American," the girl told me, and she was distraught because they were scheduled to leave on the next flight and her mother was still in jail.

A few other glimpses of Ho Chi Minh City: The waterfront along the Saigon River was not as active as it used to be, but there were a dozen or more freighters alongside the docks or anchored in midstream flying Vietnamese flags and a few flying Russian and Eastern European ones. Groups of unemployed youth (the national unemployment rate is as high as 20 percent) lounged along the harbor rails, and each morning scores of men and some women gathered in the narrow park areas by the river to exercise together. Vendors were offering cigarettes individually or by the pack, lottery tickets, and ice cream on sticks. The old floating restaurant, the My Canh, was still open for business. At the central bank, where I changed some money at the official rate of a little over eleven dong to one dollar (the black market rate was then two hundred to one, and a year later, just before the dong's devaluation, it went as high as a thousand to one), it took a half hour and fifteen giggling girls to complete the transaction. I was the only customer. One of the girls, as she handed me back my passport, said, in English, with a laugh, "Too many girls here, yes?"

Several of my favorite restaurants in the center of town that used to be run by Corsicans had been turned into coffee shops—most restaurants, which the government considers undesirable, are being taxed out of business. Two of the old ones on Dong Khoi (Uprising) Street, which is Tu Do's new name and in the French days was called Rue Catinat, were primarily cafés that sold pastries and sandwiches and soft drinks and beer. They were both packed at noon and in the evening with crowds of young men and women. At one of the places, a small band, including a saxophone and a trumpet, played out-of-sync jazz interspersed with Western rock, and at the other a man at an ancient piano tinkled a mixture of Vietnamese ballads and old American popular tunes. The government now reluctantly concedes that, even after a decade of attempted reforms, the south—particularly Ho Chi Minh City—remains "culturally decadent." An article a year or so ago in *Tap Chi Cong San,* a magazine devoted to Party theory, criticized southerners for "not attending the recommended cultural things but the ones that are not recommended." It admitted that "not too much progress had been made in eradicating all this," and bemoaned that "twenty years of U. S. puppet regime rule has left its impact." Specifically condemned were "no-holds-barred comedians" and films showing "kung fu scenes, knife fights, pistol scenes, car-motorcycle chases, bedroom scenes, drunkenness and revelry, improper bathing, off-color songs, and lewd styles of performance such as senseless gyrations." The article went on to lament that, despite cleanup campaigns to get rid of half a million copies of undesirable magazines and newspapers, mostly Western publications that had been smuggled in sporadically, a black market still existed for such undesirable material. "Whether we like it or not, it's a fact of life that incorrect aesthetic tastes are still widespread," the article said, and concluded, somewhat lamely, "So we must wipe out decadent works and create good works."

In the center of Nguyen Hue, the broad avenue that runs up from the waterfront for several blocks to the City Hall, flowers and a random array of clothes, watches, utensils, plastic toys, and trinkets were still sold at the old kiosks, but no one seemed to be buying anything. However, I was told that, undercover, refrigerators and stereo sets and other such expensive goods were still available. Faded English-language signs saying "Arts and Handicrafts" remained up. Traffic was far less than it used to be, but a score of old Chevrolets, once black and now repainted red, were for rent at the curb. "Sometimes they are used for weddings," one of my guides told me. A large bookstore seemed to be more popular than it had been in the past. Ho Chi Minh City is a better place to buy books than Hanoi, and I bought several English translations of things I had wanted, while my interpreter, a diplomat named Nguyen Dinh Phuong, who had just returned to Vietnam after five years in Japan—I had been fortunate to have him assigned to me because of the Foreign Ministry's desire to have him reacclimate himself to the country —was overjoyed to find the second volume of a Vietnamese history he had been avidly searching for.

Phuong had two sisters living in the city whom he had not seen for twelve years, and he spent as much time as he could visiting them. But one evening the two of us went to Cholon to have a Chinese dinner. It was as crowded as ever, much more so than Ho Chi Minh City proper, and the streets were dangerously packed with bicycles and three-wheeled cyclos—laden with goods more than with passengers—but despite this bustle it seemed run down, gray and dusty. Apparently it was true that, as I had heard, most of the wealthy and middle-class Chinese had left, either under the departure program or as "boat people," and that the lower middle class had taken over. We ate at a restaurant I remembered, which had been famous for its crabs and shrimps, but the food wasn't nearly as good as it used to be. The place was just as noisy, though, and the owner, bare from the waist up, was just as fat, and still operated the fastest abacus in the East.

We had a much better dinner one night across from the old red brick Cathedral, at a French restaurant called La Bibliothèque. It was run by a lively Vietnamese woman, Mme Nguyen Phuoc Dai, who was a lawyer and had been a vice-chairman of the former National Assembly. Mme Dai owned a dozen cats, of every conceivable size and color, and they seemed to possess the two and a half rooms, one of which was lined to the ceiling with dusty legal tomes. She told us that there were no longer any lawyers in private practice in Vietnam, but that she conducted "adjudications for the city's people's committees," helping settle personal disputes. That may have been one of the reasons she was allowed to continue running her restaurant. She served us a delicious dinner of onion soup and fresh crabs, which she cooked herself on a small oily stove, surrounded by her cats. The only other guest except for Phuong and myself and Bob Minnich, an American who worked for the Orderly Departure Program, was Tim Page, a British photographer I had known in years past, who was back in Vietnam on his second trip since the war, and who knew Mme Dai well. He had just returned, exhausted, from several days in the Delta and all of us reminisced at length with Mme Dai, who wouldn't let us pay for our meals.

After dinner we walked over to the former Rex Hotel nearby, to stop in at a dance held once a week by the city tourist association. The dance floor on the roof was dimly lit, with rotating disks of red, blue, green, and yellow that cast eerie shadows over the scene. A surprising number of attractive young hostesses were on hand, and there were a score or more foreigners, mostly East Germans, Hungarians, and Poles and a few Russians. The orchestra played old dance tunes and the big, lumbering East Europeans, most of whom were working on construction projects, filled the small floor with their diminutive Vietnamese partners in low tow. Two Vietnamese singers, a man and a woman, were much better than might have been expected—especially the man, who gave a good rendering of "Star Dust," though it was apparent he had memorized the English words without understanding them. The evening, including eight orange drinks, cost me seven hundred dong, plus two hundred dong for a hostess who had apparently assigned herself to me. At ten forty-five the lights came on and at eleven sharp the crowd dispersed.

The following morning I dropped in at one of the ubiquitous handicraft shops on Dong Khoi Street that sold the same shabby collection as before—garish landscapes and portraits, lacquerwork, and stuffed animals and snakes. It was run by a Chinese, who told me, in a low voice, that business was bad and that his taxes were rising. While I was there, one of the Russians who had been at the dance the previous night came in to pick up a painting he had ordered made from a photograph of his wife and himself. He was unhappy with his wife's likeness in the painting, and as an argument seemed to be brewing I decided to leave.

One of the persons I had asked to see was a novelist now in his mid-fifties named Nguyen Khai, whom I met by appointment one morning in the offices of the Writers' Association, a quarter of whose national membership of four hundred is southern. Khai's family, though originally from the north, has been living in the south for decades, and he is the only member to have fought with the Communists, joining them in the fifties toward the end of the French war, in the U Minh forest, which was one of their strongest southern jungle bases. In 1955, he went to Hanoi, and he did not return to Ho Chi Minh City until 1979, when he brought his wife and son with him. "When we arrived, my son was older than I had been when I left," he said. His reunion with his parents and sisters and brothers is the theme of one of his books, but his best-known novel is entitled *The Last Meeting in the Year.* Its setting is Ho Chi Minh City several years after the war, during the annual year-end Tet festivities. In the novel, a Mrs. Hoang, the mother of an extended family, has invited some friends as well as family members to dinner. A number of the guests belong to the old Saigon intelligentsia, and a lively discussion takes place about a wide variety of things, including the social degradation caused by the war, diplomatic and military gossip about the old regime, maneuvers going on between the Chinese and the Americans, and the virtues and drawbacks of the new regime. Where there used to be a case of champagne opened for Tet, the family now has only one bottle to serve, and everyone takes a sip. Mrs. Hoang is caustic and bitter about the Communist government, even though two of her sons are working for it, but the other guests mostly agree that it is best to take life as it comes and accept their role. An hour or so before midnight, Mrs. Hoang disappears into her room, and when she doesn't return for some time there is concern that she may have decided to take her life. But at midnight she reappears and serves dinner, though she announces, with regret, that she has been unable to obtain her favorite dessert. Thus she expresses her decision to go on living and make the best of things.

A number of postwar novels and short stories deal with similar themes of adjustment and readjustment to life, and, according to several critics as well as writers I spoke with, many of these new works, by authors now in their thirties, make up for lack of style and imagination "by being more matter of fact, more realistic in confronting everyday hardships and problems," as Khai said, adding, "My generation was more romantic; the new one, you might say, is more existentialist." The evils of bureaucracy and poor management are dealt with openly, frankly, and often dramatically. One best-seller called *Facing the Sea,* written by a young southerner named Nguyen Manh Tuan, is about the quarrels that take place in a fishing enterprise, first between representatives of the old and new management and then between the Communist management and the workers. Problems of corruption, pillaging, and laziness are described in vivid dialogue and in angry but sometimes humorous scenes of confrontation. "In the years just after the war," Khai told me, "there was a lot of writing about the differences between the north and the south, but now there is more awareness of common problems and difficulties, and especially about the bureaucracy." The interest in this subject, which has been reflected in recent short stories, seems no accident, for it has been repeatedly and forcibly stressed as a major problem by Party leaders. In an important speech at the Party's Fifth National Congress, in March 1982, Le Duc Tho, generally considered to be the most influential member of the Politburo after Le Duan, declared: "It is necessary to put an end to a situation in which every unit head is voicing his complaints about the cumbersome nature of the organization but readily sets up more offices for his own service and either expands or maintains its table of organization. It is necessary to eliminate the practice by certain localities of granting party membership only to yes-men. District and precinct party committees and basic-level party committees must find outspoken people who have, out of their concern for the common good, dared to denounce shortcomings and defend the truth."

In Hanoi, before I went south, I had a long talk with Nguyen Dinh Thi, the head of the National Writers' Association, who is four years older than Khai—it was at his suggestion that I looked Khai up. Thi, a swarthy northerner with an engaging sense of humor and an urbane manner, fought with the Vietminh against the French and admits to representing "old-style romanticism," saying, "You might call me a sad optimist." He is one of Vietnam's best-known authors, having written novels, plays, poems, and essays. "My friends call me a duck because I swim a little, fly a little, and walk a little," he said. "I'm now writing my first novel in ten years. Writing about the war is not an easy nut to crack—not if you want to write about it seriously. It's easy to be shallow about it, but it was such a trial for everyone. We all struggled with the idea of survival and then with the founding of a new society. They go together, but to determine the link between the shape of the new society and the old everlasting problems that have to be confronted is difficult—it's hard to write about true socialism, for example, in a genuine sense that doesn't sound unreal or distorted."

I asked Thi whether he thought there was a significant generation gap in Vietnam and whether this was detectable among writers. "There is no conflict but there are differences between the generations," he replied. "The older generation has a wider cultural canvas. Many of them know French and English, and they have read more. They have a broader education—they know about the past as well as the present. The younger generation is more narrow in its outlook, but it has the advantage of fighting and working for the future. Relatively few of the soldiers and workers today can be called intellectuals. The new writers are mostly grass-roots types. Their weak point is that they have no perspective, no background, no basis of comparison. Their spectrum of life is more limited and narrow. But they benefit from considering the new regime as their own, so in some ways they feel more free to criticize it frankly, and to attack its weaknesses. They have no complexes or hang-ups, so they show a greater freedom of spirit."

Correspondents who visit Ho Chi Minh City are invariably taken on a hospital tour, and I was no exception. I was fortunate, or perhaps unfortunate, enough to go to Tu Du hospital, where Dr. Nguyen Thi Ngoc Phuong, one of Vietnam's foremost gynecologists, gave me an hour's tour and talk on what she maintained were the effects of toxic sprays, including Agent Orange, on women who became pregnant. Dr. Phuong, an energetic and impassioned person who has devoted most of the past ten years to this subject, methodically puts her foreign visitors through a wringer. Both Tim Page and myself, who went there separately, left wet-eyed after witnessing her "exhibits" and listening to her well-planned presentation. The exhibits consisted mainly of deformed fetuses, including some without brains (examples of anencephaly) and some with enlarged heads (or hydrocephaly), and of samples of hydatiform moles, which are clusters of abnormal tissue formations that appear in the placenta in place of normal fetus forms. Dr. Phuong, who told me she had lectured at a number of international forums but has been unable to obtain a visa for the United States, also led me through the hospital rooms, including a ward for young girls, all of whom had hydatiform moles. Some were sharing beds, because the hospital was overcrowded. The rate of choriocarcinoma cases, in which the mole becomes a malignant tumor, Dr. Phuong said, is still increasing in Vietnam, ten years after the war, and she showed me a series of statistics to demonstrate that the incidence of such cases and other defects has been highest in southern provinces such as Ben Tre, where the Vietcong were most active, and which therefore were most heavily sprayed with toxic substances. For example, one set of figures shows a rate of 7.4 percent incidence of birth defects among pregnant women in a heavily sprayed village, against less than half of one percent in a village in another province which wasn't sprayed at all. The choriocarcinoma patients we saw, most of whom were in their twenties, were receiving chemotherapy treatment after having had hysterectomies. "Ninety percent of them will recover," Dr. Phuong said, "but, of course, they will never be able to have children." She gave me a hard stare and added, "That means a lot to Vietnam." On the way out she asked me to sign her visitors' register, which contained an impressive list of names. The formidable Dr. Phuong had obviously left her impact, and it was also apparent that she regarded her campaign against this sort of chemical warfare, which she described as "a more silent form of genocide than nuclear warfare," as an important part of her work.

(3)

From Dr. Phuong's hospital I drove a mile or so to Ham Tu Street in an old part of town that, during the French days and the early days of Diem, was the headquarters of an armed gangster sect, the Binh Xuyen, that conducted extortion and gambling rackets and dominated the local Saigon government. It was run by an old scoundrel named Le Van Vien, known as Bai Vien, who fled to Paris with sufficient spoils to live comfortably—I met him there in the early seventies, not long before he died. Diem eventually defeated and dispersed the Binh Xuyen, and thereby eliminated the earliest major threat to his regime. The area had afterward been taken over for military training and had then become residential and commercial.

I remembered that the river ran through it and that it had often been flooded. It was now primarily commercial, and I was visiting the Second September Engineering Cooperative, which has won a record number of national and local awards as a model of its kind. Owned by the workers rather than by the government, the cooperative has been recognized by Hanoi for having initiated a new system of ownership and management that falls between state and private ownership. "We operate according to production contracts," I was told by Vo Sau, a quiet man with a warm, creased face who lost part of an arm in the French war and was a political worker in the Vietcong during the American conflict. "That is, our engineers go out and look for our own customers. We go down into the Delta and up into the high plateau and ask the people what they need —what kind of water pump, for example. Then we draw up the blueprints, get the approval of the local people's committee, and buy our raw materials from the city. It really is free enterprise and I personally think this contract system will last a long time, especially now that the Party has approved it. Not to be boastful, but we originated it, several years ago, and it is now being copied by cooperatives all over the country."

The youngest of six children of a well-off Mekong Delta family, Sau was the only one who fought on the Communist side. After the last war, he started the co-op with ten workers, including some who had fought with the South Vietnamese and were unemployed and a few former small factory owners who had access to some sort of equipment. The co-op now employs eighty people, and among them are two graduate engineers with degrees from Canada and Sri Lanka. Run by a council of workers, which elects three persons from its members as directors—Sau is one—it manufactures engineering tools of all sorts, agricultural implements, threshing machines, and small tugs and barges, including dredges specially designed for drawing the silt out of the shallow Delta canals. Most workers' salaries at the factory range from fifteen hundred to twenty-six hundred dong a month—the average factory worker's salary in Vietnam at this time was only three or four hundred dong monthly, though what a man makes depends on the amount and nature of his work. The two top engineers at the factory were earning five thousand dong a month, and Sau and the two other directors were getting thirty-six hundred. Of the factory's total income, which in 1984 was about twenty million dong, a third went to the government for taxes, a third for repairs and expansion, and a third for wages. The co-op works closely with seventeen satellite production groups in the same ward, including some that are government owned. "Our workers participate actively at all levels—in management, production, and the distribution of income," Sau said. "They make the decisions. They are their own masters." Before I left, Sau showed me the co-op's latest major project, a large flat-bottom barge and a tugboat with a Russian engine, being built in the Saigon River alongside the factory. The barge was to be used for carrying tractors and the specially designed silt excavation equipment. "There's no limit to the kind of things we can make," Sau said. "All we need is ideas from people who know what they want."

Sau's Second September Engineering Cooperative is a particularly successful example of the kind of compromise between private initiative and state supervision of the means and mechanism of production that the national government is now trying to formulate and develop. A factory that establishes its own system of work rules and wages, arranges its own production contracts, buys raw materials through district or city committees, and devises its own methods of management, with the state effectively serving as a monitor or watchdog, can be described as quasi-capitalist. Government officials accept the definition but insist that the ultimate aim remains "the steady socialist transformation of the economy by gradually increasing the socialist sector and reforming the capitalist one."

This is how the objective was described to me by Le Quang Chanh, who has been vice-chairman of the People's Committee of Ho Chi Minh City since 1975. Chanh, a plump, bespectacled man with the quiet confidence of a veteran Party cadreman, pointed out that in the south today the economy has five different sorts of components: state owned, collective, combined privately owned and state owned, small-capitalist, and individual entrepreneur. (In the north, there are only three—state owned, collective, and private—though there are some examples of combined state-and-private enterprises.) "At the moment," Chanh said, "as we concentrate on agricultural production and light industry, including more consumer goods, while at the same time developing our heavy industry in a reasonable and rational way, depending on the availability of raw materials and machinery, we are adopting a gradualist approach to socialism. Small traders will slowly turn into producers for the government, while others will be agents for government-owned enterprises, or we will make them that. Small producers can be organized collectively." He went on to say that the government will diminish the number of entrepreneurs through taxation, by registration, or by supervising bank accounts. "We want to move the best skilled people into the state-owned sector, but we will not interfere with those whose production doesn't affect the spiritual life of the people—shopkeepers who are traditional traders in fine arts or handicrafts, for example. This sector will last a fairly long time. What we are doing is in conformity with the specific concrete conditions in Vietnam. It can't be dogmatically defined, and it's not based on what other countries do."

Technocrats and economists I spoke with in both Hanoi and Ho Chi Minh City all emphasized, as did political leaders like Chanh, that cooperatives working under production contracts would become the backbone of Vietnamese socialism. Joint ventures with foreign companies, such as those in Japan and Singapore, and in some Western as well as Eastern European nations, would greatly benefit Vietnam, in the opinion of reform-minded economists like Vo Van Kiet, a southerner by birth and the nation's top economic planner. In fact, preliminary discussions were held soon after the war with France and Singapore to start such ventures in tourism, the production and distribution of frozen seafoods, and development of agro-industrial products. There has even been some bold, if premature, talk about setting up free trade zones and writing new investment codes. The Vietnamese actually introduced such codes in the early postwar years when exploration of offshore oil deposits in cooperation with the West, begun under the old regime, seemed likely to be continued. The invasion of Cambodia in December 1978 and the break with China that followed put an end to all that and resulted in the almost complete cutoff of Western and Japanese assistance and the isolation of Vietnam, which then became almost totally dependent on the Soviet Union and the Eastern bloc nations.

(4)

The problem of stirring up enthusiasm for the new reformist programs outlined by Vo Van Kiet and others among the sluggish and often cynical youth while offering "social direction" to all elements of the population is recognized by the Vietnamese leaders as perhaps their greatest challenge nowadays. This is especially so in the south, where the impact of the long French and American presences is still keenly felt and where, traditionally, the easier way of life compared to central and north Vietnam is another important factor. Not only were consumer goods always more readily available in the south, but the climate has always been more conducive to growing rich and abundant crops of rice and other grains, and fruits and vegetables, while fish have been more plentiful in the Mekong Delta rivers and canals as well as the ocean. The struggle for existence has never been as difficult in the south as elsewhere in the country, and the peasants of the Delta, consequently, never worked as hard or as many hours a day as those elsewhere. Although it produces half the nation's rice, its overall agricultural potential has only begun to be tapped, according to a recent article in *Nhan Dan,* the Vietnamese Communist Party newspaper, written by Tran Bach Dang, a veteran southern Party cadre who, in 1985, was once again in favor after five years in disgrace as a result, apparently, of his veiled criticism of a number of senior Party leaders and his protection of several independent newspapers and magazines. Although Dang, in his article, defended Delta residents from the charge that they were corrupted by many years of non-Communist rule and by lavish American aid programs, it has been no secret that their independent ways and reluctance to be organized and forced into cooperatives proved one of the first big failures of the new regime after 1975. After much debate and numerous experiments—which will be discussed more fully in the following chapter—the production contract system adopted in its current form in 1983–84 is now proving more successful. In his article, Dang disclosed that the further development of the Delta is being studied by a group of "talented scientists," most of whom are non-Communists, under the direction of Vo Van Kiet, for whom Dang used his underground pseudonym—"Comrade Sau Dan."

The task of fostering support for the Party's programs

in the south is undertaken primarily by the Fatherland Front, a national body composed of more than a score of mass organizations, which was initially established in the north in the fifties but after the war was reorganized to include the south's National Liberation Front. The new Fatherland Front has an increasingly important function as an internal propaganda and proselytizing machine, reaching into all phases of public life. In Ho Chi Minh City, for example, it is active in all the seventeen wards and reaches down into the 342 communes and the thousands of block committees and households below. The deputy secretary general of the Front in charge of the south is Mme Nguyen Ngoc Dung, a pleasant diplomat with a motherly air who for a while had the rank of ambassador in the Vietnamese delegation at the United Nations, and whom I first met in Havana, in 1979, during a conference of the nonaligned nations. "When they gave me this new assignment, I asked myself at first if I was being demoted," Mme Dung told me over cocktails and dinner on the roof of the Majestic Hotel. "I wondered if I had done something wrong. I didn't understand the challenges and difficulties. But now I find that the Front is becoming more appreciated as an important instrument in the education of the people. The people have very different levels of understanding and consciousness. We can divide them into three groups: those who are enthusiastic and progressive; those who are indifferent and skeptical; and those who are opposed to the regime or have doubts about many of its programs. Our basic purpose is to make people grasp the content of the socialist revolution, and to do that through the mass organizations of peasants, youth, workers, women, scientists and technicians, Catholics and peasants, writers and artists, and so on. In a way, I guess I'm suited to the job, because my family is a small Fatherland Front. My mother is a Buddhist, my brother was a member of one of the religious sects, my husband fought in the jungle and his ideas were different from those of my daughter, who was an activist in the city. We used to have heated discussions, and if I succeeded in uniting my family, I can unite various mass groups."

Mme Dung, having cited the importance of teaching the masses ideology and getting them to understand and adapt to the new resolutions and reform measures introduced in the past two years, placed equal or greater stress on the impact that the Fatherland Front has on the daily living conditions of the people. "Our job is to teach them how to combine theory and practice," she said, "to explain the new resolutions in concrete, everyday terms." She cited as an example getting all the communes and districts in the city to eliminate their own slums, to build new houses where they could, to put in new drainage pipes. "The government can supply the material, and the work and the money can come from the households themselves, except those that are too poor," she said. "We learned from experience, when the reforms failed several years ago, that we can't be too rigid or dogmatic. By getting people to work together in the right way, we can help them overcome their hostilities. We're still finding things out about economic efficiency—what works and what doesn't— through trial and error. All this is not made easier by our many shortages and scarcities, but it's all part of the transitional period to socialism." Mme Dung spoke enthusiastically of a plan devised by Mme Ba Thi, the director of a company that was supplying rice on behalf of the government to a million people of Ho Chi Minh City—the remaining two and a half million were getting their rice on the free market. When government procurement was lagging because the peasants refused to accept the low prices that the government offered, Mme Ba Thi created a new group of purchasing agents who, in effect, acted on a commission basis: the more rice they were able to obtain, at somewhat higher prices—which Ba Thi arranged to pay

—the more they got paid. "People thought at first she was destroying the socialist way of life," Mme Dung said. "Some even wanted to put her in prison. But now she is being awarded a medal, simply because she decided that solving the problem was the most important thing. This is an example of how we inevitably run into contradictions in carrying out our reforms under difficult circumstances that are unique to us. We don't want to take unorthodox measures, but sometimes we are forced to do so."

(5)

Before leaving Ho Chi Minh City, I visited the district of Cu Chi, to the north, which is now a suburb of the city but used to be part of another province. It was believed to be the most destroyed district in Vietnam as a result of constant bombing and shelling, gassing and defoliation, most of which took place in the mid-sixties during several large search-and-destroy operations conducted by the United States. Despite losing twelve thousand soldiers and civilians killed during these campaigns in Cu Chi alone, the Communists remained entrenched in the area until the end of the war. They survived mainly because of an astonishing complex of underground tunnels that extended for miles beneath the entire district, and connected with others that reached all the way from the Cambodian border to the outskirts of Saigon. Part of this elaborate web consisted of three levels and occasionally four that were as deep as twenty meters and contained elaborately constructed conference halls, food, storage, and work depots, hospitals, and kitchens with vents that led to smoke outlets several hundred yards away. A portion ran underneath a riverbed. Some of the tunnels were dug by the Vietminh during the French war, but most were built by their successors, the Vietcong, in the sixties.

American and Australian troops that regularly attacked the area once it was detected suffered heavy casualties from booby traps and mines, let alone hand-to-hand combat that was often conducted at close range with knives, grenades, and pistols. The Americans tried all sorts of specially designed devices and experiments to drive the Communists out of the tunnels, but they never succeeded —largely because the tunnel compartments were separated by trapdoors which effectively sealed the sections off from one another. It was not until the end of the war, when B-52 bombers leveled the whole area, that the tunnels were largely destroyed; by that time the major battles that took place, including one code-named Cedar Falls in January 1967, were over, and the Americans had left Vietnam.

From the outset of the American combat participation, in 1965, and even prior to that, the tunnels served as one of the major headquarters of the Vietcong and later of the North Vietnamese in the south; the Tet campaign in February and March of 1968 was planned in and partly launched from the tunnels, a portion of which came to be called the Iron Triangle because it was so heavily fortified and impregnable to attack. On a number of occasions, unable to discover where the the camouflaged surface outlets were or led to, the Americans built their own headquarters directly on top of parts of the tunnel complex. In a book written about the Cu Chi tunnels by two British correspondents, John Mangold and Tom Penycate, published in 1985, which graphically describes the heroics both of the Vietnamese tunnel fighters and the "tunnel rats," as the Americans, usually small Hispanics, were called, they relate the story of how, on Christmas Day, 1966, Bob Hope was entertaining the troops of the United States 25th Infantry Division above ground at Cu Chi while directly underground, at the same time, a Vietnamese entertainer named Pham Sang and his group were entertaining the Communist guerrillas. Vietnamese soldiers often spent weeks and sometimes even months in the tunnels under the most adverse conditions. I tried crawling through the passageways during my visit, but I was too tall to maneuver them, though I got as far as one of the underground chambers. One of the former defenders of the complex who was acting as my guide watched my clumsy efforts with obvious amusement. "The Americans even brought dogs to detect the tunnels," he said, "but we used pepper to keep them away."

Before the war the district of Cu Chi was peaceful farmland, mostly rice fields and orchards, and rubber plantations. But the war turned it into a barren chemical wasteland, denuded of trees and foliage, and it seemed to me doubtful, when I saw it, that it would ever again be green and bountiful. I spoke with Cao Van Nghiet, the Party secretary of Cu Chi, who told me, "There isn't a square meter here that doesn't show the effects of the war. There is a lack of reconciliation, partly because there are so many people who were badly wounded and who are blinded or maimed." Nghiet, a lean, hard-looking man in his fifties with a pockmarked face, added that so much of the ground had been torn up by bombs and artillery shells or been rendered useless by chemical sprays that crop production was still poor, despite some improvements, a decade later. "Living conditions remain bad," he said. "Things are better than they were during the war, but as revolutionaries we are not satisfied. Many houses have not been rebuilt yet. We're building new canals for irrigation so we can have two rice crops a year instead of one. We also hope to raise tobacco, soya, sugarcane, and pharmaceutical plants. Cu Chi is supposed to be a breadbasket for Ho Chi Minh City, though we hope to process some of our crops, and eventually to develop light industry. Half the communes are now cooperatives, but that's not enough—the target is at least seventy-five percent of the land and eighty-five percent of the households."

I remarked that this would be far in excess of the average among farmers in the Mekong Delta, only a third of whom have joined cooperatives to date, and Nghiet smiled his only smile of the day and replied, "We'll do better here because we remain revolutionary fighters and we know more than some of the others what it is to struggle."

Pride and martyrdom still run deep in Cu Chi and its neighboring districts. In June 1972, just across the boundary in the district of Trang Bang, in Tay Ninh province, a famous photograph was taken of a twelve-year-old girl running down the center of Highway 1 immediately after a napalm attack. She was naked. Her hair and part of her neck and arms had been burned, and she was flailing her arms and crying, and she had no idea where she was running, except away. I remembered the girl not only from the picture but because I had met her one morning in my hotel dining room in Hanoi before I came south. Her name is Kim Phuc, and she was twenty-one years old in 1984. She was on her way back home to Tay Ninh from a burn center in Germany where she had been treated and had some skin grafts. I mentioned this meeting to Nghiet, and he nodded and said he recalled the girl, too. Then he said he wanted me to meet "another famous woman," who lived nearby. On the way back to Ho Chi Minh City we stopped off in her village. She is almost seventy and is known as Ma Bap. She lives in a thatched one-room hut with double mud walls and hidden spaces in between, and a secret cellar, where she used to hide Vietcong soldiers. She showed me all her hideouts and told me, with a toothless grin, how her activities were stopped when two soldiers were caught by South Vietnamese government troops and made to confess where the hiding places were. Ma Bap was arrested and tortured but then let go. Her punishment did not seem to have diminished her satisfaction and pride. "There were dozens that I hid," she said, triumphantly. "I considered them all my sons."

CHAPTER TWO

Compromise and Reform

(1)

A door opened at the far end of the room, and a Vietnamese of medium height with a glistening shock of white hair walked briskly toward me, smiling broadly. He was wearing an open-necked blue-gray cotton shirt and trousers to match, and after we shook hands he beckoned for me to sit down beside him on an overstuffed couch. We were in the capacious salon of the former French High Commissioner's palace in Hanoi, which is now used by the Socialist Republic of Vietnam for receiving guests. Le Duc Tho, seventy-three years old and a senior member of Vietnam's Politburo, gave me a reflective and quizzical look, almost as if he were refreshing his memory of an unfamiliar type of being. "You are the first American I have seen since Paris," he said, with another smile.

I murmured my thanks for his hospitality, expressed my gratification at having this chance to return to Vietnam for the first time in more than nine years, and reminded him that we had met in Paris in the fall of 1972, during the peace talks he had conducted with Henry Kissinger. I complimented him on how well he looked, for he gave every appearance of being as physically strong and alert as when he craftily outnegotiated Kissinger and, by ultimately gaining permission for North Vietnamese troops to remain in South Vietnam after the Americans withdrew, in effect set the stage for Hanoi's final stunning victory two and a half years later, in April 1975.

My reminiscent appraisal of Tho's sharpness of mind was thoroughly borne out in the next four hours, at the outset of which he summarized a number of questions I had sent him before we met: comparisons of the two historic wars of resistance waged by the Vietnamese, first against the French and then against the Americans; comments on the long, difficult relationship between Vietnam and China, which was once described by both countries as "like lips and teeth" but since 1979 has degenerated into open hostility and sporadic violence along their common border; the continuing war waged in Cambodia by the Vietnamese, which has exacerbated the Sino-Vietnamese dispute; and, finally, the internal situation today in Vietnam.

As Tho spoke—without interruption except for the expert translations of my interpreter, Nguyen Dinh Phuong, who had been a member of Tho's staff in Paris and is fluent in French, English, and Vietnamese—I was astonished at the clarity and precision of his replies, and at the astute way in which he marshaled them. From time to time, we sampled bowls of nuts and fruits that had been set out on a low table in front of us and sipped tea or coffee, but this did not impede the calculated flow of Tho's thoughts. What struck me most as he went on, almost in the manner of a professor delivering a perfectly planned lecture, was his combination of cold, tough, doctrinaire Communist reasoning, ideologically pro-Soviet and anti-Chinese, with a sustained note of rectitude that had in it elements of zealotry and of reproach to Vietnam's enemies. This is not untypical of Vietnamese leaders, especially when they are explaining and defending their goals and accomplishments while engaging in carefully structured self-criticism or suggesting possible solutions to difficult problems. Given Tho's position as the most experienced and respected member of the Communist Party of Vietnam after Secretary General Le Duan, his answers seemed particularly significant. Absolute belief in the validity of the Vietnamese revolution—which, he stressed, was still unfolding and was unique—and in the principles guiding it was the keynote of Tho's recitation; but something else that came through, especially toward the end, offered a clue to why he had agreed to see me.

After reiterating the oft-repeated distinction the Vietnamese make between the American people and their government, Tho said, with emphasis, "We do wish normalization of relations will come sooner rather than later." He professed inability to understand United States policy since 1975, especially under President Reagan. He was also particularly emphatic in his comments on the future of Cambodia (the initial invasion of which by Vietnam, late in 1978, he had directed) and of a possible solution there. A settlement could best be achieved, he said, "through bilateral negotiations of the sort I conducted in Paris with Kissinger." In this case, he apparently meant talks between, on the one hand, the Vietnamese and the Thais, or possibly the Vietnamese and the Chinese, and, on the other hand, the various Cambodian factions, including the Vietnamese-installed-and-supported government of Heng Samrin and political groups in a coalition that opposes him. He did not mention Prince Norodom Sihanouk, the former chief of state of Cambodia and the formal head of that coalition, or Son Sann, the other non-Communist leader. But he made it clear that such talks could not include Pol Pot, the head of the Khmer Rouge, which was responsible for murdering a million or more Cambodians in the course of the four-year reign of terror following the Communist takeover in 1975; Pol Pot's troops today provide a majority of the sixty-thousand-man army that is fighting two and a half times as many Vietnamese and thirty thousand of Heng

Samrin's inexperienced soldiers in the areas along the Cambodian-Thai border and in some inland regions of Cambodia. "I can definitely say our troops will not remain in Cambodia," Tho added. "In a word, we want to pull out, but our withdrawal depends on the adversaries of the Kampuchean people." He implied that the United States could play a useful role by persuading the Chinese to cease assisting Pol Pot, and he did not rule out the possibility, once bilateral agreements were reached, of international guarantees to support a settlement, including free elections.

My interview with Le Duc Tho (which proved prophetic, and to which I shall return) was one of the high points of my six weeks' visit to Vietnam, with several days in Cambodia. I traveled over much of the country south of the seventeenth parallel and visited places I had once known well and had particularly wanted to see after a decade's absence, including Hué, Danang, and Quangtri, as well as Ho Chi Minh City. I had not been in the north since 1951, when it was still in French hands, and I was surprised to find Hanoi essentially unscarred by American bombing, and, though run-down and shabby, still beautiful architecturally and gracefully landscaped, with rows of flowering tamarind trees along most avenues and streets, and with well-tended public parks and gardens. Many of the old cracked stucco colonial buildings, both public and private, were being repaired, despite an obvious shortage of cement, paint, and other materials. Potholes in the streets were being filled by teams of women who passed by wearing kerchiefs over their mouths and pulling carts of tar and sand. Since there were relatively few cars and trucks, the potholes were mainly hazards for the thousands of bicycles that provide Hanoi's primary means of transportation and are a constant threat to pedestrians, who have to duck in and out among the swarms of hurtling bikes and the occasional motorized vehicles that are the sworn enemies of the cyclists. Moving tranquilly and neutrally in the center of the main streets, like tired cater-pillars, are a few fifty-year-old French orange-and-yellow trolleys, two or three cars linked together. Foreigners are not permitted to ride these, but I was free to walk through the streets of the city and stop off in shops or markets as I wished, and I had no sense of being followed or observed except by ordinary people. Somebody would occasionally ask if I was Russian, and when I replied, "No, American" —the Vietnamese word for "American" is *My*—would smile or nod and hurry on. Vietnamese are not supposed to talk to foreigners except under specific authorization or to help direct them if they are lost, and my efforts to strike up conversations in French or English were usually cut short after a few minutes. Western diplomats and others in the country, even those who speak Vietnamese, told me that this happens all the time. "The best I can do is ten or fifteen minutes at a stretch," one of them said. "Then my companions always find an excuse to leave. It's not that they don't want to talk, but that they're afraid. You may not notice it, but the police, in uniform or civilian clothes, are everywhere, and so are informers."

During the month I spent in the north, I was able to meet most of the top officials I had asked to see and also experts in various fields that I was particularly interested in, ranging from economics to military history to writing and the state of literature. In these interviews, which sometimes were followed by informal lunches, I encoun-tered no reluctance on the part of my host or guests to converse freely, which is not the usual experience of the handful of foreign correspondents, whether Communist or Western, who have been stationed regularly in Hanoi. Indeed, I detected a hunger for communication on the part of most Vietnamese I met officially; they seemed eager both to listen and to expound on topics of common concern. Beyond that, they frequently reached out to establish rapport with me as an American. Time and again, I was pointedly reminded that around the corner from my hotel—an old dilapidated place called the Thong Nhut, which means "reunification"—was a newly painted green stucco building that had formerly been the American consulate and that stands ready for reoccupancy as soon as the United States government decides to establish some sort of relations with Vietnam. Between the spring of 1977 and the fall of 1978, a series of preliminary talks between the two countries came close to tentative agreement, but they fell apart over the demands by Hanoi (finally withdrawn) for more than three billion dollars in reparations to "heal the wounds of war"; over the Vietnamese military buildup along the Cambodian border; over heightened Soviet influence in Vietnam; and over the growing exodus of refugee boat-people. Moreover, Congress was showing itself to be strongly against any move toward recognition. Then the Carter administration decided to recognize China, and the whole subject of Vietnam was relegated to the far back burner. The Vietnamese thereupon signed a treaty of friendship and cooperation with the Soviet Union. Since then, the Cambodian war, the still unresolved question of finding and identifying the remains of as many as possible of the nearly twenty-five hundred missing Americans in Vietnam, Laos, and Cambodia considered to be identifiable, and a number of other matters have led to little progress.

It is difficult to persuade Hanoi's leaders that they no longer occupy the diplomatic limelight in Washington. Whatever sympathy they might have enjoyed has been thoroughly dissipated as a result of the long war they have waged in Cambodia. The major dry season Vietnamese offensive there, which began in November 1984 and continued until May 1985, was the fiercest in the six years of fighting. It was initially directed against the non-Communist forces of the opposition and then against the stronger Khmer Rouge elements, and it demonstrated that the Vietnamese are determined to crush as much resistance as possible before agreeing to any negotiations. Their troops succeeded in destroying all the major base camps of the opposing coalition along the Thai-Vietnamese border—about twenty—but this may have proved a blessing in disguise for the coalition, forcing it to fight a guerrilla war. When the wet season began, in the late spring of 1985, resistance increased over a wider area within Cambodia. Almost all the fighting, however, was done by the Khmer Rouge. A thousand or so of Sihanouk's troops took part, but those of Son Sann, for the time being, remained in Thailand, and there was growing friction among the leaders of the Son Sann group and between Son Sann and Sihanouk over establishing a joint command and over political matters as well. There were also reports of Pol Pot's retirement as the active commander in chief of the Khmer Rouge, but there seemed little doubt that even if this was true, his influence remained paramount. By November 1985, with the onset of another dry season, the fighting within Cambodia stepped up; it was spread out over a wider area than in 1984, and partly because it was difficult or impossible for correspondents to cover, news of the tide and pace of battle was hard to obtain or verify. But the Khmer Rouge seemed to be inflicting considerable damage on the Vietnamese lines of communication, along both the roads and rivers of Cambodia. The Vietnamese and Heng Samrin fores were said to be suffering serious morale problems—Samrin himself accused his fledgling army of lacking "attack initiative." The spirits of the guerrilla troops, on the other hand, particularly those of the Khmer Rouge, seemed higher, despite the superiority of Vietnamese weapons.

Notwithstanding the apparent stalemate in Cambodia, when I left Vietnam at the end of September 1984, I was convinced, on the basis of what Le Duc Tho had told me and what was beginning to occur on the larger diplomatic front, that the Vietnamese had come to realize the Cambodian issue would have to be settled if they wanted to achieve their two major objectives: an accommodation with the United States that would diminish their military and economic dependence on the Soviet Union, and a mending of their destructive breach with China. In subsequent conversations at the United Nations in New York, with Foreign Minister Nguyen Co Thach and other Vietnamese and Asian diplomats, and with Prince Sihanouk (with whom I will deal more extensively in a separate chapter), it seemed to me that, for the first time since the Cambodian war began, serious efforts were under way to reach some sort of political compromise. At the same time, it was more apparent that the issues, regarding not only Cambodia itself but Vietnam's relations with the concerned Southeast Asian nations and, perhaps most vitally, with the major powers, precluded any quick or easy solutions. The special importance of Cambodia as the linchpin of peace in the region had become clearer.

In some ways, the Cambodian question represented "unfinished business" of the Vietnam war; but in other respects it had become a separate and more fundamental question of the survival of a small nation whose fervid aspirations to independence and neutrality symbolized the struggle of other nations similarly caught in the swirling tides and currents of a new phase of international politics, one that was ever more complex and often more violent and disruptive than anything seen before. Unique and more fierce incidents of terrorism were, of course, a part of this, as were such things as the politics of food and famine and militant manifestations of religious extremism, as well as subtle changes in the role and nature of diplomacy, which had become more complicated and convoluted, and frequently more unprincipled and duplicitous.

The long and often painful history of Sino-Vietnamese relations serves as a classic example of both the old and new methods of warfare and diplomacy. For a thousand years the Chinese had dominated Vietnam, and the Vietnamese had fought back bravely and from time to time had managed to free themselves from the Chinese yoke, only to succumb again. Finally, in 1945, Ho Chi Minh had established an independent Vietnam in the northern half of the country and had instituted his own brand of nationalist communism—four years prior to the Chinese Communist takeover of all of China. In 1954, as a result of the Geneva Conference after the defeat of the French in Indo-China, the Vietnamese felt that collusion among the major powers, notably China, France, and the United States, had cheated them of their chance to unify Vietnam legally through a plebiscite, which, though promised, never took place. The second Indo-China war, against the South Vietnamese and the Americans, followed. The Chinese supported the North Vietnamese with generous supplies of food, weapons, and other war matériel, though Russian aid was even more substantial, but it was not all smooth going. On numerous occasions, the Chinese held up the transport of Soviet aid shipments across China, and Peking tried unsuccessfully to hold the North Vietnamese back from pushing on to victory in South Vietnam, urging protracted guerrilla warfare instead, which would have tied the north down for a longer period; a united Vietnam under the banner of Hanoi didn't suit Peking's long-term geopolitical or revolutionary purposes. Then, in 1978, three years after the Communists captured all of Vietnam, came the break between Peking and Hanoi. After the failure that same year of the brief effort to establish a relationship with the United States, Hanoi moved more completely, albeit with some reluctance, into Moscow's camp. Ideologically, the Vietnamese had always been closer to the Russian Communists than to the Chinese, but at this juncture Moscow undoubtedly took strategic advantage of the vacuum that existed in the region, due chiefly to the swift departure of the United States, to gather Vietnam into its fold and make it as dependent as possible on Soviet aid. Early in 1979, following Vietnam's invasion of Cambodia and the overthrow of the tyrannical Pol Pot regime, the Chinese attacked across the Sino-Vietnamese border "to teach Vietnam a lesson," but withdrew after seventeen days during which they probably suffered more casualties than the Vietnamese; neither side was able to claim a clear-cut victory.

From the start of the war in Cambodia, it was clear that the Chinese were backing Pol Pot and the Khmer Rouge and, in fact, had probably urged him to bring the issue of conflicting border claims with Vietnam to a confrontational head. Thereafter, the longer the war went on, the more apparent it became that it was, in truth, a larger conflict between the Vietnamese and the Russians, on the one hand, and the Chinese and the Thais, supporting the Khmer Rouge and then the coalition government including Sihanouk and Son Sann, on the other. On the sidelines, designating Thailand as its "frontline state," but divided over the role and objectives of Vietnam and over the threat posed by China, was the Association of Southeast Asian Nations (ASEAN), composed of the six nations of Indonesia, Malaysia, Thailand, the Philippines, Singapore, and, most recently, Brunei. Without the involvement in the war of the two Communist powers, it is doubtful that the conflict would have lasted so long. The Soviet Union, while continuing and, in fact, increasing its direct aid to the Heng Samrin regime in Cambodia and also maintaining its military and economic aid to Vietnam, has lately begun to express a more benign interest in Southeast Asia, and to speak of peace. But it is China that remains the real key to the situation.

Sooner or later, most observers believe, the Vietnamese

and the Chinese will reach some sort of agreement. ("It will happen not in twenty years but within five years," Nguyen Co Thach confidently predicted, when I spoke with him in Hanoi.) Thach was fully aware that Cambodia remained the stumbling block and that there were differences within the top Vietnamese hierarchy over the war, with the military, led by Defense Minister Van Tien Dung, intent on prosecuting the offensive and defeating the Khmer Rouge and the coalition forces on the ground. But the 1984–85 Cambodian campaign directed by General Le Duc Anh, like Dung a member of the Politburo, while successful, had not proved decisive, and the guerrillas had emerged no weaker and perhaps stronger than before. The offensive also elicited fresh aid from China to the Khmer Rouge, and, significantly, an increase in assistance, though in lesser amounts, to the Son Sann and Sihanouk troops. Throughout most of 1985 and early in 1986, as the fighting in Cambodia continued, both the Chinese and the Vietnamese stepped up their exchanges of artillery fire across the Sino-Vietnamese border, which reached record proportions, and this was accompanied by a fresh positioning of troops on both sides. There was growing talk of a new attack by Chinese forces—"to teach the Vietnamese a second lesson," as the Chinese put it. But no such ground attack took place. The Chinese were obviously aware that, this time, the Vietnamese were far stronger and better prepared to meet any such assault and that another border war would prove even more costly than the one in 1979. Secondly, China was deeply involved in its much debated economic reform and modernization programs and could ill afford another military diversion that could prove politically divisive. And, in the third place, the climate in Southeast Asia had changed; where, in 1979, ASEAN as a whole had welcomed the Chinese attack, now Indonesia and Malaysia were less willing to support a second effort and were actively seeking a peaceful solution to the Cambodian problem. A fourth factor may have been most important: the Chinese had been conducting talks with the Russians on and off for more than a year, and by 1985 some progress had been made, particularly on trade exchanges. Both Peking and Moscow were seriously interested in continuing the discussions and creating some sort of rapprochement. And Mikhail Gorbachev, the new Soviet chief, has gone so far as to suggest to Peking and Hanoi that they try to resolve their differences in the overall interests of peace and harmony in the area.

Realizing that improved relations with China would require time and patience, and that the Chinese could not be cajoled into surrendering their stake in Cambodia through their support of the Khmer Rouge, the Vietnamese adopted a fresh approach in their efforts to resolve or ameliorate some of their differences with the United States besides those over Cambodia. A precipitating factor was their growing concern about being further isolated, as a result of the Sino-Soviet talks as well as ongoing discussions between the Chinese and the Americans over establishing closer military, economic, and cultural ties. As China thus emerged in the strongest position it had enjoyed to date as a balancing force between the two superpowers, the Vietnamese responded with deep consternation and then altered their course. After months of high-level debate, culminating in a meeting of the Politburo held in Hanoi in mid-December 1984, a decision was taken to adopt a more "flexible" foreign policy, aimed especially at improving bilateral relations with the United States and persuading the Americans to play a larger role in the region and perhaps eventually to help promote a settlement of the Cambodian problem. In this new policy, the Vietnamese had the backing of a sometime friend, or neutral party—Indonesia. The Indonesian foreign minister, Mochtar Kusumaatmadja, acting as an interlocutor in behalf of ASEAN, helped persuade Hanoi to make some concessions on the issue of the missing Americans from the Vietnam war, one of the principal reasons for the stalemate with Washington. Once that was accomplished, Kusumaatmadja maintained, a larger dialogue between the Americans and the Vietnamese might follow, beginning with the opening of a full-time technicians office in Hanoi and paving the way for a "special interests section" and eventual diplomatic exchanges.

In February 1985, responding to repeated requests from the Americans, the Vietnamese agreed to permit an American identification team to inspect a site near Hanoi where a B-52 bomber was known to have gone down during the war. The inspection, which did not take place until July, was fairly casual, and it wasn't until November that Hanoi permitted a full team of technicians, with heavy excavation equipment, to accompany a Vietnamese team to another site near the city where a bomber was shot down in December 1972. Thirteen days of digging produced very litttle evidence of possible human remains, but at least the first thorough joint attempt had been made and the "atmosphere" between the Americans and Vietnamese participants was described as "good." It was later agreed that additional joint searches would be conducted. During the year, Hanoi also returned the remains of more than thirty airmen who had been shot down in Vietnam, raising the total since the end of the war to about a hundred and thirty listed initially as prisoners of war or missing in action, or, more recently, as probably killed in action but whose bodies were not yet recovered. Altogether, the United States now lists nearly eighteen hundred Americans as unaccounted for in Vietnam— eleven hundred in the south and seven hundred in the north. In addition, more than five hundred and fifty are unaccounted for in Laos, eighty-two in Cambodia, and six in China. Of the total, half are assumed to have been killed in action but their bodies are not yet recovered, and the other half, about whom there is little or no information, are regarded as probably killed, though the Pentagon and the State Department do not rule out the possibility that some may still be prisoners of war or may be hiding out somewhere in Vietnam or Laos.

The matter of remains is still an extremely touchy one. Hanoi has not yet accounted for the bodies of some four hundred and fifty Americans which, according to testimony before a congressional committee in 1980 by a one-time Vietnamese mortician now a refugee in the United States, are being held in a warehouse in Hanoi. American officials who have been most closely involved in the issue of missing Americans believe this story to be true, whether or not the exact number is as high as the mortician said. When I asked Vietnamese officials about this, they either denied or were evasive about the charge that they are doling out stored remains at stated intervals—in August 1985, twenty-six containers of remains, the largest amount at once so far, were returned, which prompted renewed speculation that the Vietnamese were indeed holding more than they had admitted. But officials in Hanoi reiterated that they were doing what they could to find all missing bodies, and they emphasized that, given the continuing anti-American feelings and bitterness of Vietnamese villagers who were the chief victims of bombing attacks, plus the fact that tens of thousands of Vietnamese war dead are still missing, it was not easy to go out into the rural areas and look for evidence of dead Americans.

A month after the release of the twenty-six remains, at a meeting of technicians and some middle-rank diplomats of both sides in Hanoi, the Americans submitted a plan to resolve the issue of those still missing within two years. The Vietnamese responded with a plan to solve the problem "in as short a time as possible." The meeting was described by American officials as "the most positive" in twelve years, and it set the stage for the first joint search of a crash site in November. Then, in January 1986, at a higher-level meeting in Hanoi attended by assistant secretaries of the State Department and the Pentagon, further progress was made. The Vietnamese said they were conducting an "educational" or "informational" campaign among villagers to track down fifty reports of missing Americans. Some of the specific information was provided by the Americans, but the Vietnamese were also becoming more cooperative and had apparently determined to help solve the issue on a humanitarian basis. Though nothing was said openly, there were implications that the more information about leads the Americans submitted, the more likely it would be that additional remains would be released, including those in all likelihood being secretly held. Hanoi now seemed more eager to get rid of the whole issue, which had become an embarrassment to them, and the Americans, in turn, were willing, as one of them told me, "to help take them off the hook." It was agreed that the issue would no longer be a major one in any decision to establish relations with Vietnam. This left the withdrawal of Vietnamese troops from Cambodia as the chief remaining condition for recognition. The Vietnamese also seemed more eager to solve the question of missing Americans on their own insofar as possible, although more technical meetings than before will henceforth be held. The possibility was left open for the use of American helicopters and other technical instruments to facilitate the search. The United States told the Vietnamese that they were especially concerned about thirty-one so-called discrepancy cases, involving war prisoners who were known to have been in contact with other POWs while in captivity but about whom nothing was known after the return of the POWs following the American withdrawal from the war in 1973.

A considerable number of relatives of missing men, and

several technicians who have served regularly on the identification teams that now visit Hanoi at least six times a year, believe it is possible that a few Americans—perhaps as many as a dozen—may still be alive in Vietnam and are either being held in remote places or, as seems more likely, are hiding out and living there with Vietnamese or Lao women. The possibility that some POWs are still being kept, though considered unlikely by United States officials, is not ruled out in principle, and the idea has gained fresh hold in the past two years as a result of the Rambo films and the private activities of a number of former American Special Forces men who have conducted forays into Laos and are busily conducting "Rambo campaigns." Although there have been almost eight hundred reports or "sightings" of "white Occidentals" since 1975, including several in the past two years, there has been no confirmation of any American living in Vietnam—the Vietnamese denied three specific reports in 1985, including one of a black man who turned out to be a large "dark Khmer," presumably from one of the mountain tribes. The Americans are determined to resolve the issue of live Americans once and for all and have reduced the list of alleged sightings of live persons to ninety-five, which the Vietnamese have also promised to follow up on. Most of these have resulted from reports of refugees, and a few have come from members of international aid groups working in Vietnam or Laos. The ninety-five figure is simply based on the fact that the information obtained cannot be ruled out as a fabrication. This whole issue was brought to a head in 1979 when Private Robert Garwood, a marine turncoat, left Vietnam voluntarily after having stayed behind at the war's end and was repatriated to the United States. Garwood claimed to have personally seen or heard of about sixty resident Americans, but he has refused to testify before a congressional committee and his accounts are not regarded as trustworthy by American officials.

Another still unresolved issue is that of freeing the remaining eight to ten thousand inmates of reeducation camps—those are the Vietnamese figures—and allowing them to go to the United States. In 1982, at a meeting in Geneva, the Vietnamese suggested the Americans take the inmates, since most of them had United States connections of one sort or another. Washington responded positively but demanded that a census and screening process be established to determine their bona fides and to avoid having ordinary criminals, who are also kept in reeducation camps, sent to the United States. The Vietnamese then began to renege on the whole idea, expressing the fear that, if released, many of the prisoners would take part in anti-Vietnam activities in the United States, and they demanded guarantees that no such activity would be permitted, which the Americans said were impossible to give and would be a violation of the freedom of the ex-prisoners once they were in this country. It was apparent that there were differences within the Politburo about the whole question. Although Prime Minister Pham Van Dong and Foreign Minister Thach originally favored it, by April 1985, Le Duc Tho peremptorily declared, "We cannot turn them [the inmates] over to the American side for one simple reason: these people were guilty of war crimes." Since the 1982 Geneva meeting, the Vietnamese have refused to meet again on the question, though the Americans have repeatedly brought up the matter. In November 1985, the United States asked Vietnam once more to allow the prisoners to leave, but there was no immediate response. Tho and others have indicated that they want some sort of diplomatic recognition to precede any release, while the United States considers the question, like that of the missing Americans, to be a humanitarian one that should be settled separately and not as a condition for recognition.

(2)

The more I talked to foreign diplomats in Hanoi about Vietnam's relations with the outside world, and particularly with the United States and China, and the more I learned about the precarious internal economic and social condition in which the Vietnamese still find themselves ten years after the war, the more persuaded I became that if they are to solve their internal and external difficulties they will first have to come to terms with their situation in ways they have not yet attempted. This will mean making adjustments and compromises that are as deeply psychological and emotional as practical and political. The problem is historical, in that it requires a distillation to separate the past from the present, to bring about a catharsis that will lessen the almost mythical burden of an era that created incredible victories in war but left the Vietnamese unprepared to deal with the tasks of development in peacetime. This failure derives in large part from a confused identification of military victory with political stability and legitimacy. In fairness to the Vietnamese, some of the problems stem from forces beyond their control, including traditional Chinese expansionism and antagonism; an abysmal colonial heritage from the French, which left them almost totally unprepared to assume the responsibilities of governing themselves; and a degree of calculated indifference since 1975 on the part of the United States, which is still experiencing the guilt and shame of having met its first defeat in war. Much of it, however, has been the fault of the Vietnamese, who have demonstrated their share of hubris and a crippling inability to create unity among themselves and to reach out to others, including their neighbors in Southeast Asia, in a spirit of friendship and compromise.

Finally, part of the problem is a generational one, of

which the Vietnamese are very much aware, for they see the older revolutionary leaders, in their seventies, who have dominated the scene for half a century, confronting the stark reality of their mortality. When I brought this up with Prime Minister Pham Van Dong, who is seventy-eight and somewhat physically enfeebled, he replied that it was a matter he thought about constantly. Of the men still alive, he was closest to the legendary President Ho Chi Minh, who died in 1969, and his answer revealed how thoroughly the hallowed memory of Ho endures yet also indicated growing awareness that memory is not, in changing times, enough of a guide. "How to make all the generations go forward with the flame that has been handed down from President Ho, that is the main thing," Dong said, with passion. After a moment's pause, he went on, more quietly, "As the head of a commission on educational reform, I attach great importance to this question. I believe that the younger generation will do better than we have. We shall avoid what you call the generation gap. We shall see that our youth and the generation in the middle will go forward and deal with new tasks and challenges with intelligence, understanding, and creativity." Having said this, with what seemed to me more hope than conviction, he touched on a matter that has aroused particular concern among the older leaders. "We know that young people have their own aspirations—that they want better clothes, some up-to-date fashions, a richer culture. These things should be welcome. That's progress, and we're not fighting it. But their minds and spirits are important. We must keep them Vietnamese, and their achievement will then be great. In ten years' time, we will see."

It was the last part of Pham Van Dong's answer that seemed to reveal the primary source of concern among those who are grappling today with the problems Vietnam is facing. Not the least of these is keeping a large army in Cambodia at a time when the country needs manpower for reconstruction and production at home, but when years of poor planning and bad management have held back progress and have exacerbated many of the basic differences between the northern and southern halves of the nation. Mismanagement has been partly responsible for undue poverty and a steady 15 or 20 percent rate of unemployment, and this has helped produce a growing malaise and has provoked a mood and condition of bureaucratic stasis. In this context, the long Cambodian war —though it has been the main reason for the almost complete cutoff of more than two hundred million dollars a year in Western and Japanese aid, and was a principal factor in China's curtailment of a five-year aid program worth almost a billion dollars—has become a treadmill: the country's leaders are almost afraid to stop and get off, because the economic consequences of withdrawal and demobilization might be greater than the relatively low cost (about twenty million dollars a year in wages, clothes, and medical care) of keeping so many men occupied at a distance from the uncertain situation at home. Moreover, while there are recent signs that some of the major problems in agriculture and other aspects of the economy are finally being confronted and are being dealt with pragmatically, if not yet satisfactorily, there remain larger and far-reaching ideological differences about the future course of the country. After so many years of dislocation, the pattern of overall production and distribution is extremely uneven, and this adds to the confusion over planning and implementation.

Though Vietnam is blessed with unusual natural resources, it remains shockingly poor and undeveloped today, with an annual per capita income of about one hundred and fifty dollars. Differences in living standards are wide, and to a considerable extent the nation survives on "the second economy"—moonlighting. This has provoked increasing friction between emerging elements of haves and have-nots—elements that include the troops fighting in Cambodia and living off the land there in strange and often unfriendly surroundings, and people back home, particularly in the south but also in parts of the north, for whom life has become easier largely because they have benefited from the new economic incentives created by the government over the past few years. In fact, the military, being traditionally conservative, is especially suspicious of the liberal agricultural reforms initiated and refined in the past five years by the so-called pragmatists, who, in the current political dialogue, are opposed by the Old Guard "ideologues." For the moment, under the leadership of Le Duan, who is seventy-seven years old, and the majority of the Politburo (it numbers fourteen, including two alternate members), the pragmatists appear to be firmly in control, but the issue is by no means settled, and probably won't be for several years. Ironically, at this time of bitter conflict with China there are similarities between the goals of the Vietnamese pragmatists, who condone a limited free market, individual incentives, and greater management autonomy, and the objectives of those directing China's far more extensive program of modernization, including the institution of a broader market economy and a return to some capitalist practices. The irony is compounded by the fact that both the Chinese and Vietnamese insist that their respective systems do not digress from Marxism but denounce each other's as having strayed far from the Marxist-Leninist fold.

The argument, except among scholars and theoreticians, has to all intents and purposes become moot, for both countries are one-party authoritarian states with their own dogmas, which they alter and adjust as they see fit, and with little leeway for free discussion or tolerance of public dissent. Observers who have studied China and Vietnam over the past decade, however, agree that there is far more "socialist dynamism" today in China, and certainly more enthusiasm.

"There is no incentive in Vietnam except on the black

and gray markets," one Western diplomat in Hanoi commented to me in the fall of 1984, despite the introduction of the new economic reforms. "Everything since the war here has been anticlimactic. What kept people going for so long, against the French and then against the Americans, was the siege mentality, and it provided a remarkable drive and force. But now that the big wars are over there is no substitute for its élan, and this accounts for the malaise—for the lack of ambition, ingenuity, and imagination. And for something that may be more dangerous in the long run—for an unfocused discontent among the younger cadres, both those who are serving their three years in the army and those who have been discharged. They're missing something, but they don't know what it is or how to get it. Cambodia is not enough of an inspiration. Those who go abroad to Russia or to Eastern Europe to study, or to work, return with their experience and degrees, or some money, but no one knows what to do with them once they're back. Their knowledge is useless, because there has not been enough development in Vietnam to prepare the way. What they really need is a basic education in job-related skills—in vocational training—but there's very little of that. They don't know how to do the simplest jobs, and the expertise they've acquired abroad means nothing in a society where industrial growth has scarcely begun. So they hang around cafés or act as interpreters, or simply disappear into the woodwork."

Vietnam has long prided itself, justifiably, on eradicating illiteracy in the country, but it has only begun to come to grips with the more difficult problem of relating and adjusting educational opportunities and expectations to economic conditions—particularly to the slow pace of development. About 95 percent of ethnic Vietnamese and 70 percent of the minority population (about a million) are literate. The growth of education as prosecuted after the 1945 revolution was phenomenal. Fewer than two hundred thousand students were attending primary schools in 1945, and in the colonial period under the French there were only five secondary schools. By 1980, according to government figures, approximately twelve million students in the Socialist Republic of Vietnam were attending primary and secondary schools; in 1982, seven hundred thousand who had completed the secondary level of general education (grades ten, eleven, and twelve) had applied to universities, but of those only 10 percent were accepted. The trouble has been finding jobs in an economic system that is not only underdeveloped but unenterprising. Vietnamese estimates show that of the eight hundred thousand students leaving school each year —either after completing the first nine grades divided into levels of five and four, or the secondary level—at least a third have no immediate prospects of work. To complicate matters, although the standard of living is generally higher in the countryside, most young Vietnamese, like their counterparts elsewhere, want to go to the cities, where life is more exciting and "civilized," with more opportunities for entertainment, sports, and cultural activities of one sort or another.

As reported by Sophie Quinn-Judge, in a recent survey in *Indochina Issues,* not enough is being done, despite some attempted reforms in 1979 and the early eighties, to create vocational opportunities and to increase the teaching of science and technology geared to current national needs. Vietnamese officials themselves admit that there is too much stress on theory rather than practice, and not enough concentration on producing low- or medium-level technicians or better-skilled farmers. In a speech late in 1984, Prime Minister Pham Van Dong warned that traditional outlooks on education, including the idea that gaining entrance to a university is the only worthwhile goal of education, must be changed. He said: "The goal of general education, as of the entire educational system, is to create patriotic people with socialist ideals; with the qualities, knowledge, and skill to do a job well, in accordance with the division of labor at the local level and in the whole country, appropriate to the level of economic and social development at a given period." Unfortunately, these goals aren't being met, and the system is not sufficiently geared to meeting them. Students are being taught some trades, and in the past five years more than four hundred job-training schools or so-called study-and-work schools, as well as factory-sponsored classes in 250 trades, have been started up throughout the nation. But there is an admitted lack of good teachers, and a dire shortage of equipment; perhaps hardest of all to contend with, too many students remain dispirited and uninspired. The best ones still want to go on to universities, while the majority lose interest because of lack of progress, lack of work that is challenging, and the paucity of good teachers, many of whom have to moonlight in order to compensate for low salaries. The result is that, without opportunities, students in their mid and late teens fall into moods of apathy and ultimate alienation.

Even in Hanoi, where one feels a greater sense of discipline and control—during most of my stay in the city the police were regularly checking identity cards on the sidewalks by blocking off one street at a time—each day I noticed groups of idle youth, mostly boys, lounging on corners or sitting in cafés and coffee houses, where on weekend nights there was music, both Vietnamese and Western. By and large, though, there was relative freedom to congregate and move about.

The area around the picturesque Hoan Kiem Lake in the center of the city—surely one of the loveliest spots in any capital in the world—was always crowded with youthful couples strolling or resting on the grass and with children playing, and the outdoor cafés rimming the lake were full of customers and sightseers. On weekends and holidays, the atmosphere was positively buoyant—most notably during the Independence Day period early in September and the annual Children's Festival later in the month, when many of the streets were all but awash with spinning plastic toys. On both occasions, the crowds were so heavy around the lake and in other parts of town that it was hard to make one's way about. Both Vietnamese and Westerners told me that the mood of the city had changed greatly in the past five or six years, and that some of this is undoubtedly due to the influence of the south, partly because so many northerners had served in the army or as government cadres down south or had begun to visit relatives and friends there regularly. Bui Tin, an amiable man who is deputy editor of *Nhan Dan*, the Party paper, which is the country's largest, and who was a military hero in both the French and American wars, said that he first noticed the change about 1977, in habits and modes of dress. "It began when both girls and boys started wearing elephant-ear pants" (similar to bell-bottoms), he said. "They're still worn today but the newer fads are jeans and close-fitting linen or cotton shirts, as well as T-shirts with American names on them. For a while in 1978, the police would stop youngsters on the streets and tell them to go home and change their clothes and cut their long hair, but by now the new styles are pretty much accepted. It's been several years since the girls started wearing more colorful clothes and jewelry and lipstick. There's an increase in consumer goods, despite many shortages. Television now comes right into the bedroom. Where do people get the money? By and large, farmers have done well, and the workers in light industry around Hanoi are beginning to enjoy some benefits, too." Bui Tin, who has a twenty-six-year-old son and a twenty-one-year-old daughter, went on to discuss the attitudes of today's youth. "It's hard to explain to them what our generation went through—to get them to understand that during the war just for us to have meat was a rare treat," he said. "It's only natural that they're interested in getting some enjoyment out of life— taking pleasure from fresh air and sunlight, and going out on picnics. But this makes it hard for them to grasp the idea of the problems we face in the nation. They have become too impatient for the good things of life."

Later, when I talked to Hoang Tung, the former chief editor of *Nhan Dan,* who is now the chief of propaganda and a member of the ten-man Party Secretariat, which ranks just below the Politburo, he acknowledged that youthful unrest indeed exists and is serious. Like Bui Tin, Hoang Tung is a veteran of both resistance wars and, despite a rather flat voice and a gloomy appearance, he, too, has a frank and open manner, with a touch of the common man about him. "During the revolution, at every turning point, we have been able to obtain good partici- pation by the youth, although not all of it was voluntary and youth had to be mobilized," he said. "At the outset, in the forties, some responded to Ho's call, but it was foreign aggression that really brought them around. The French used every ploy and stratagem to gain their support, but colonialism remained colonialism, and youth joined our cause. When the American war started, we had to mobilize the youth all over again, and in many respects it was harder. After a revolution, it is always difficult to maintain the support of youth. We are now facing that challenge once more—especially in the south. The billions of dollars the Americans poured into the country and the habits of living they introduced naturally had a strong impact, and, in fact, there are still enemy forces today that are trying to undermine our society. We are trying in many ways to persuade young people to give up their selfish individual- ism and their fast way of life. We have to work as never before to educate a new generation. These selfish individ- uals you see in the big cities are not all over the country. Young people are still joining the army and are fighting and dying. And others, in schools throughout the country-side, are studying hard to understand the progressive nature of society and the value of productive work. So we feel that we can still win our youth over, in spite of the problems that always exist in a postwar generation."

As I listened to Hoang Tung and Bui Tin, and others, trying to weigh what they said against some of my own observations and what Westerners living in Hanoi told me, I was reminded in strange ways of the past and of the endless discussions about the same sort of subjects that my Vietnamese friends and I used to have in Saigon and elsewhere before and during the war. Certainly the South Vietnamese government faced many of the same problems that the northerners face now in trying to win the support of youth, and it fared even more poorly. But beyond the youth question and other matters of morale and popular response, I was struck by the fact that after only a few days back in the country, and in unfamiliar Hanoi rather than in Saigon, I felt truly at home among the people I met. And the longer I stayed and traveled about, the more I realized that some of things I felt and observed before were still very much the same—or, at least, my reaction to them was.

As I thought about this, seeking to put my long absence in focus and to separate my responses from nostalgia, it seemed to me that Vietnam and the Vietnamese, in the many years I have known the country and the people, have always been, and still are, possessed of far more than the customary quota of national anomalies and contradictions. Because of the stresses they have had to contend with in defending themselves against foes almost constantly throughout their turbulent history, they have paid an extreme emotional, psychological, and intellectual price. Xenophobia runs deep in them, and suspicion and mistrust have become part of their normal attitude. Ambivalent and unpredictable, they can be devious, calculating, self-driven, abrasive, and exasperating one moment, and amenable, sympathetic, generous, and gracious the next. Charm for charm's sake is not one of their prime attributes, but they can be disarmingly—or sometimes brutally—open and frank. Also highly secretive at times and given to clandestine approaches, they are adept at guile and machinations, yet they can be naive, artless, and ingenuous to the point of self-delusion. Their humor is often black—sardonic, wicked, macabre—but it can be playful and childlike, too. Their capacity for cruelty is matched by their high threshold of pain, but torture and suffering, particularly over the war years, have inspired compassion and solicitude, while also enhancing their belief in fate. The sharing of hardship, in battle or behind prison bars, creates permanent bonds. Sentimental and romantic, as reflected in their poetry and prose, they can be unresponsive, distant, and uncaring. Such qualities as loyalty and treachery, sacrifice and betrayal have special, often convoluted meanings for them, whose origin seems deeply imbedded in their long and violent history of dynastic and familial disputes, of fighting against heavy odds to defend their sense of self and national identity. Heroes and heroines abound in their rich heritage, but so do villains and scoundrels, and the shrines of their memory are crowded with more victims than victors. They have more pride than humility, and more cunning than caution. I often felt, during the years of the war, and especially during the American war, that they exhibited what was almost a compulsion for self-destruction, while at the same time they demonstrated—as they are still demonstrating—a unique capacity for survival. Their determination and their belief in themselves are extraordinary, as was proved dramatically by the tougher and infinitely more clever and patient northerners in their long fight to defeat the French and then the Americans and also their southern compatriots, who lacked their physical stamina, emotional willpower, and passionate conviction.

What I found most interesting during my visit to Vietnam was that many if not most of these characteristics and contradictions are still confounding Westerners, and other Asians, too, who try to follow the elusive course of the Vietnamese revolution and to understand why the Vietnamese act as they do, ostensibly to their own continuing disadvantage. One of the anomalies of the national character that Americans in South Vietnam used to comment and complain about was the stubborn sense of individualism among Vietnamese, which often made it difficult to negotiate and compromise with them on military and political matters or on any others. The southerners, with their inclination for being disputatious and disunited, seemed to demonstrate this to a destructive degree. There was no doubt that, in contrast, the sense of unity and discipline that the Communists engendered and enforced in the north were prime reasons for their success. Once differences were resolved at the top, and the policies and programs decided by the Politburo were explained at meetings held at regional and local levels down the line, there was no divergence from the course established: it was carried out with dedication and zeal. The southerners, on the other hand, fought among themselves and with the Americans throughout the war, sometimes about inconsequential things.

Now that the war is over, the conflict between individualism and regimentation remains peculiarly unresolved, and this may provide a key to many of the troubles the Vietnamese are experiencing. The difficulty that the north has had in creating a real, workable unity between the two parts of the country is only one of the more visible manifestations of this profound problem, which extends to all spheres of national life. It was summed up for me by a man who spent nearly four years heading one of the principal international aid agencies in Vietnam, who was based in Hanoi but spent much of his time traveling around both the north and the south. "Socialism simply doesn't work for the Vietnamese," he told me one day, almost despairingly. "They are far too individualistic. The state can run the railways and the utilities, but it's got to get out of the retail trade, including marketing and distribution. Despite the heavy influence of the Soviet Union here, no Vietnamese I know has any interest in a system as a system. They all search for ways to get around any system—to cock a snoot at authority. This is true from the government level all the way down to the moonlighting worker. And yet, and here is where it gets to be complicated, they still want to be highly centralized and even state run, to mobilize all forces of the country, to make the cooperatives an organized success, and so on, while at the same time compromising with free enterprise and private gain. The question is: Can they have it both ways? Can they mix heresy and orthodoxy and get away with it?"

Clearly, the Vietnamese are determined to have it both ways, but whether they can get away with it remains the big question. Although the north has been a Communist state for forty years, and underwent some of the classic crises of communism, including a bitter struggle over radical land reform in the mid-1950s, the nation has been so taken up with waging war that organizing and running an economy and a social structure are challenges it has only started to deal with. Introducing and applying Communist or Marxist-Leninist theories and practices on a broad scale and a nationwide basis are actually a relatively new experience. The basic role models of the Soviet Union and the People's Republic of China, with their historic ups and downs and separate inconsistencies, to say nothing of their periods of hostility and probably permanent ideological breach, have confounded and disturbed the Vietnamese far more than helped them in formulating their own concepts for solving the problems of a much smaller and far less developed nation, and one that was so devastated in the recent war. On top of that, the Vietnamese have been confronted with their own peculiar condition of what Marxists like to describe as "inherent contradictions" to an extent that transcends theory or dialectics, and in practical or realistic terms is almost schizoid. The vast differences in all respects, including cultural ones, between the north and the south, which are only now being partially acknowledged by some top Vietnamese leaders (but which others still dogmatically refuse to accept), have made it virtually impossible to introduce national economic and social programs that are consistent, coordinated, and workable.

After visiting both parts of the country, I was left with the feeling that the circumstances and ways of life—and perhaps more significant, patterns of thought—of the two regions remain as fundamentally different as ever. And it is hard to see how, given their separate historical development, things could be otherwise. While all Vietnamese have always been stubbornly independent-minded, the northerners were never as thoroughly subjugated as the southerners were by the French during the century-long existence of Cochin China—roughly what became known as South Vietnam—as an outright colonial domain. Tonkin in the north and Annam in the center were made protectorates rather than colonies, and though they were also under complete French domination and rule, they were not as economically important to the French as Cochin China, with its lush Mekong Delta ricelands (much of which the Catholic Church owned, along with wealthy Frenchmen and a few well-off Vietnamese), its rubber plantations, its shipping and other assets. Cochin China, with Saigon as the famous "Pearl of the Orient," was the linchpin of the French empire, the true "jewel in the crown." To the *colons*, the people of Cochin China were subjects and servants, to be used in any way the masters saw fit—the men as clerks or workers and the women as maids and, if so desired, as formal mistresses, or lesser sexual partners; the French were considerably more tolerant of such liaisons, and also of mixed marriages, than either the British or the Dutch.

What the French did not do, in contrast to the Dutch or British, was give their Vietnamese civil servants any notion of independent decision making or any responsibility or freedom of action. And any Vietnamese, in the central and northern parts of French Indo-China as well as in the south, who risked engaging in underground nationalist activities and were captured, were subjected to imprisonment and torture far exceeding anything sanctioned by the British or Dutch. When the French left, in 1954, and the South Vietnamese took over on their own under President Ngo Dinh Diem and his malevolent family, these punishments continued to be meted out, and this went on right up to the end of the South Vietnamese regime, in 1975. The Americans, for their part, remained oddly aloof from such matters, but made their own contribution to the spiritual and moral debilitation of the southerners: they introduced consumerism, and by flooding the economy with commodities ranging from refrigerators and stereos to motorcycles, trucks, and jeeps, and from fast food to millions of PX items and gimmicks and gewgaws of every conceivable variety, they created a vast free and black market that provided hundreds of thousands of Vietnamese with their only source of income. The remnants of this ubiquitous and corrupt economy are still everywhere to be seen in Saigon and, to a lesser extent, elsewhere in the south, and even in the north. The Americans, it should also be said, did far more than the French ever did to introduce modern machinery and technology into the south, and to train the Vietnamese to use it; but not much of this has survived or been utilized, although American-trained Vietnamese mechanics and other specialists have gradually been allowed to apply their knowledge and use whatever machines and tools are still functioning in the absence of spare parts and raw materials that the United States used to supply.

In many sections of Ho Chi Minh City, one still sees small machine shops buzzing with activity, but such sights are rare in downtown Hanoi. The sidewalks there are crowded, however, with men working to repair ancient bicycles by hand, and it is easy to trip over a loose wheel or a handlebar. At night, when streetlights are out and there are not many pedestrians, one may come across small groups tinkering by flashlight on a car engine or some other piece of broken machinery, but the larger machine and tool shops are on the outskirts of the city and are government run. Vegetables, fruits, fish, meats, and poultry, though, are sold everywhere in Hanoi on a free enterprise basis—not only in the half-dozen large public markets but also all over the sidewalks, by women from the nearby countryside, and this unofficial sector of the free market provides the bulk of the city's trade and commerce in food. The open market in food is just as active in rural areas, as I discovered during a day-long trip to the Chinese border and back, and also on a shorter trip to the harbor of Haiphong. This one started with an early-morning stop on a small, verdant street famous for its outdoor soup-and-noodle shops, where my interpreter and I had delicious bowls of the soup the Vietnamese call *pho.* As we rode through town on our way to the two-and-a-half-mile Long Bien bridge over the Red River, which was repeatedly bombed and constantly repaired during the war and is still undergoing extensive reconstruction, we passed through a commercial section, where Phuong pointed out the old streets, dating back to precolonial days, that still bear names based on what they have always sold—silk, dyes, soap, cake, sugar, tin, paper, and so on. Some of these products are now distributed by cooperatives and others are marketed by individual traders.

In most parts of the city, and also in the outskirts, coffee shops still abound, but there are very few restaurants left as a result of the heavy taxes on unwanted luxury establishments. Tailors, barbers, women's hairdressers, and other individual entepreneurs offering services of one kind or another seem to keep busy, but numerous shops stocked with private art objects and government handicrafts have few customers. Bookshops are well patronized. They sell mostly government and Party publications and scientific or educational books, along with some fiction and poetry. Translations from Russian are plentiful, and there are some from French, but not many from English. During several visits I paid to a government-run department store three blocks from my hotel, the place was fairly crowded with people looking over the drab goods on the counters and commenting on their prices, but there were not many buyers. Some of the prices I noted, which I rated in accordance with the then average worker's monthly salary of three or four hundred dong (roughly a dollar and a half to two dollars at the prevailing black market rate, and thirty to forty dollars officially—salaries have since been raised, and so have prices) were three hundred and eighty dong for an embroidered girl's blouse, two hundred and forty-five for a simple girl's dress, a hundred and fifty for a child's shirt, and two hundred and fifty to four hundred for men's trousers. Guitars sold for three or four hundred dong, but combined tape recorders and radios ranged from fifteen thousand to thirty thousand. Bicycles averaged from fifteen thousand to twenty-three thousand dong. In the street shops, a cup of coffee sold for seven dong, a glass of weak Vietnamese beer for twenty dong, and a pack of local cigarettes twenty dong. In order to get by, even with what, at the time of my visit, was a modest ration system for basic necessities, and with low government-controlled rents, I was told, one needed at least a thousand extra dong a month, which accounted for the fact that just about everyone was moonlighting in one way or another, or buying and selling or bartering goods on the side.

In the decade since the end of the war, the Vietnamese,

particularly those in the larger cities, have gone through
so many economic ups and downs that they have become
more than ever accustomed to doing what comes naturally
to them—surviving at any cost and in their own determined way, hoping for the best but expecting the worst,
and effectively living from day to day. The worst period
was not, as might be supposed, immediately after the war,
but some years later. A Frenchman named Jean Pierre
Dubris, who has lived in Vietnam much of his adult life
(he was arrested as an antiwar activist in Saigon at one
point during the war, and is now a government translator
in Hanoi), told me, "In those early days after 1975 in the
north, everyone—men, women, and children—wore
green fatigues and huddled together to keep warm. We
were all shivering. Whole families slept together in one
bed. But the spirit of victory was in the air, and everyone
pitched in to help repair the damage done by the bombing
and to get things started again. There was enough food,
because the Chinese were still sending us rice and other
things—all in all about a third of our requirements. The
really hard time began in 1978, after China cut off aid,
and then attacked us across the border. Russian aid had
hardly begun, and the Chinese thought they had us on the
ropes. To make things worse, the weather was very bad—
we had typhoons, droughts, and floods—and the harvests
were poor. The army was already in Cambodia, and the
heroes of the war in the north were the regional and local
forces, who turned back the Chinese and eventually
forced them to retreat, despite their false claims of victory."

Just how bad conditions were in 1978–79 is shown by
the figures on total food production, which in 1978 hit a
record national low of 12.9 million tons, of which grain
production was 12.2 million. This meant that the average
Vietnamese was receiving only 251 kilograms of food that
year. In contrast, between 1965 and 1973, the northerners

themselves grew enough to supply each of their citizens with 312 kilograms, and since the Chinese were donating about half a million tons of rice annually, the actual per capita figure was 324 kilograms. The 1978–79 crisis was so bad, in fact, that for the first time in two decades, since the mid-fifties land reform struggle, defiance of the government was openly expressed—this time there were hunger riots. In 1979, to wage their two-front war, in Cambodia and against China, the Vietnamese were forced to keep more than a million men under arms. The army is still that size, and has regularly consumed between a third and a half of the budget. The Chinese invasion, though it lasted less than three weeks, destroyed half a dozen cities, a railway line, a power station, and a number of factories—most serious, perhaps, an apatite (phosphate) mine that was the country's main source of fertilizer; even today, six years later, the mine is operating at less than half its capacity. As a result of the troubles with China, thousands of Chinese workers and experts in both light and heavy industries, including textile and coal mining, fled Vietnam, seriously affecting production. The same was true of operations at the port of Haiphong, where the Chinese had traditionally held key jobs.

In the south, with American aid of more than a billion dollars a year cut off after the war and no more raw materials being imported, industry and virtually all business except black marketeering came to a standstill and unemployment soared. Light industry, which had always been extensive in the southern area, particularly suffered. The north, which had also been almost totally dependent during the war years on outside aid, mostly food and military supplies from the two Communist powers, the Soviet Union and China—practically all of which had been in the form of outright grants—failed to grasp the significance of how complete the dependence in both parts of the country had been. Although they still had Soviet support and assistance, the northerners now faced new and tremendous challenges with limited help. The further fact that the south had collapsed so swiftly and that Saigon had been taken without a fight increased the sense of euphoria and omnipotence the northerners felt, and this undoubtedly led to the hasty decision to unify the two halves of the country as quickly as possible and to move toward complete socialism. The decision was reached in the summer of 1975 at a meeting of the Central Committee held in the resort city of Dalat, in the south, and a few months later, in November, it was officially announced to the southerners at a conference on national reunification in Ho Chi Minh City.

The idea of rapid unification was set forth by Truong Chinh, a leading Politburo member and theoretician, who admitted that the south's stage of revolutionary development lagged far behind the north's but said that this was no reason to wait. He spoke confidently of "the leading role" being played by "Marxism-Leninism—the apex of human thought," and of the creation of "new type socialist men" whose patriotism and "proletarian internationalism," coupled with their love of productive work and their "spirit of socialist cooperation," would make their success a certainty. There were some members of the Party, in both the north and the south, who had doubts about the ability of the inexperienced northern managers and cadres to provide the necessary leadership, and who also doubted the nation's ability to attain the bold industrial and agricultural goals set forth in the first five-year plan of 1976–80. These included the complete collectivization and mechanization of southern agriculture within the five-year period. Beyond the fact that very few northerners had much knowledge of the south, few remembered or would acknowledge that, before the big war with the Americans began in 1965, the north's record for good management in agriculture was extremely poor. Interestingly enough, ten years before that, in the mid-fifties, it had been Truong Chinh who had been responsible for pushing the northern land reform too drastically, which had created wide opposition and had resulted in the purge and death of numbers of people variously estimated at several thousand to scores of thousands. Thereafter, for some time, Truong Chinh was out of favor, but he had doggedly fought his way back to prominence and resumed his role as one of Ho Chi Minh's closest comrades.

Now, once again, in 1975, Truong Chinh was believed to be the principal figure who insisted on full speed ahead, this time in the south. It quickly proved the greatest post-war mistake the northerners made. The effort to force rapid collectivization of agriculture and to destroy all capitalist trade aroused the antipathy and then the passive resistance of the southerners, so long accustomed to doing things their own way—or at least under the guiding hand of the French or the Americans. The Mekong Delta farmers especially, already beleaguered by the border attacks of the Khmer Rouge, and who in 1977–78 faced severe weather problems, including floods, resented the intrusion of the brash northern cadres. They paid little or no attention to what they were told to do—they were used to working no more than a hundred or a hundred and fifty days a year. The overbearing northerners, if they didn't succumb to the lures of leisurely southern life, were resented the harder they tried, in their Marxist terminology, to "break the machine" of the south. Besides the fact that they were heavy-handed and offered unattractive prices for crops, their interpretation of "breaking the machine" meant the introduction of new social and political institutions in the villages and towns with no special concerns for the mores and habits and traditions of southern life, so vastly different from those in the north. Even in most of the villages that had been under Vietcong influence, observers later said, the northern Communists ran into trouble, and this was attributable in large part to the absence of southern Vietcong cadres, who had been decimated during and after the costly Tet offensive, and to the overall depletion of experienced Party members in the south by the end of the war. In Saigon, for example, according to Paul Quinn-Judge, writing in the *Far Eastern Economic Review,* the Party structure in 1975 had been reduced to four hundred members, who were trying to run a city of three and a half million people. Twenty years earlier, at the end of the French war in 1954, the Vietminh had three thousand members and the city was half as big.

Eventually, the lack of southern cadres as a result of the war's attrition forced the north to send down an estimated twenty-five to thirty thousand administrators and experts of one kind or another, particularly police workers. But the newcomers lacked the knowledge or experience to deal with the situation and aroused more suspicion and hostility than support. Despite Truong Chinh's hosannas to Marxism, Le Duc Tho, who outranks him, referred me to an article he, Tho, had written in 1982, which, though it dealt largely with his observations in the north, also applied to the south, where he had traveled frequently. He wrote candidly of mismanagement and corruption during the first five-year period after the war, and of the increase of bad habits, including drinking. While the higher degree of individualism in the north spurred many peasants and kept the cooperatives functioning, the situation in the south, which had become highly urbanized and deeply affected by the American consumer society, was worse, even though on the surface the lives of some people seemed to have improved. In all, however, the war-weary north and the "spoiled" south scarcely complemented each other, and this did not make the overzealous attempt to reconcile their economies and unify the nation any easier. An indication of the failure of the attempt to collectivize agriculture was the collapse of the production teams, the initial stage of collectivization which calls for simple labor sharing by peasant communities. Of more than thirteen thousand such teams set up in the Mekong Delta early in 1979, all but two or three thousand were abandoned within a year. Party criticism blamed the cadres for having used compulsion instead of persuasion with the peasants. Similarly, an effort to eliminate capitalist trade in Ho Chi Minh City in 1978–79 failed when the number of rice merchants actually increased rather than decreased, and private traders in general kept right on doing business. About all the campaign succeeded in doing was to alienate the Chinese community, whose managerial and commercial expertise was sorely needed: by 1979, three-quarters of the Chinese in the city had indicated their desire to leave Vietnam.

(3)

It is against this background of victory in war and initial failures and misjudgments in peace, coupled with Chinese hostility and bad luck, including bad weather, all of which, in Le Duan's words, had created "a truly perilous situation," that we must contemplate the most significant postwar development in Vietnam. This is the economic turnaround that began in 1979–80, but, because of disagreements in the Politburo and the Central Committee and continuing poor management, did not gain real momentum until 1982, and then did so primarily in agriculture. It was not until 1985, in fact, that the new plans and programs took sufficient shape to hazard the prediction that the Vietnamese may finally be moving toward a realistic solution of some of their major problems. This does not mean that the leaders have settled on a course that is either "correct," in terms of Communist or Socialist theory or practice, or easily applicable for the future. Nor does it mean that the economy is functioning well, or even satis-factorily. On the contrary, many imponderables and diffi-culties remain, and the conflict between the pragmatists now in control and the minority of ideologues is one that could still create vast contention. Such a conflict could flare up sectionally or generationally, or with regard to the military as a political force—not perhaps in the compul-sive sense that the Cultural Revolution and its Red Guards tore China apart in bizarre ways two decades ago, but in a manner that could prove significant enough to prompt a change of policy. There are serious questions about what kind of socialism, if any, the individualistic Vietnamese can adapt themselves to, or whether, alternatively, they can evolve into what already, in many ways, looks like a mixed economy—a phrase, incidentally, most of them dislike and abjure; about their ability to get out from under the bleak domination of the Soviet Union, concerning which they have become disillusioned, while the doctrinaire Russians have grown increasingly fretful about them; and about whether, once the Cambodian situation is resolved, they can chart a more independent course and become, along with Laos and Cambodia, a neutral buffer region between China and Japan, to the north, and the increasingly pros-perous Southeast Asian nations, to the south.

A positive resolution of all these questions could point to a rosy future for Vietnam, given its wealth of resources. Many observers, looking on the country as a logical geo-political part of Southeast and South Asia, believe that, notwithstanding the events of the past several decades, Vietnam, once having made peace with China, could in-deed act as a bridge between the Chinese and the South-east Asians, with their large overseas Chinese populations. Where this would leave the deeper conflict between com-munism and democratic capitalism is, of course, not very clear, particularly in the light of the strong military hold that the Russians have over Vietnam; of the recent expression of new interest on the part of the Russians in playing a stronger diplomatic role in Southeast Asia; of the continuing Sino-Russian contest for power and influence; and of the distinction the Communists draw between inter-Party and intergovernmental relations, which retains freedom of maneuver for the Party. All of this makes it more difficult for Vietnam to overcome its long years of isolation and to deal with Asia, let alone the rest of the world, less fearfully and suspiciously, and more realistically and rationally.

When I spoke to Le Duc Tho about some of these questions in relation to domestic problems, he referred at once, almost reflexively, as the Vietnamese are wont to do, to the backwardness of the country and to the fact that in its forty years of revolutionary existence it has been almost constantly at war. "Kissinger used to tell me that we know how to wage war but not peace," he said. "But it's not that we don't know how to deal with peace. Our problem has been lack of time and experience—how, in the short space of a decade, to sort out the objective and subjective conditions, and, particularly, how to handle our shortcomings in economic management. I think we are now finding ways to disentangle this situation. You must remember that Vietnam is an agricultural country, and that we have to find management methods suitable to agricultural development, while facing the consequences of the destruction in the American war of most of the industry we had. And that industry was geared to war production, not to production for peace. Our method of management during the war was bureaucratic, that is, the government directed and supplied everything. You can call it conservative. After liberation, this method was no longer applicable. We have had to find ways of combining unified leadership from the center with extending to the provinces and districts the right to solve their own problems, to become more dynamic by themselves. Unified centralism, as applied in an industrial country, cannot be applied here, where the economy is still agricultural. So we have had to devise new methods of dividing the responsibilities for action, by levels, and we are doing this progressively, step by step, in advancing to socialism. We are using many kinds of economic components suitable to a period of transition. I can tell you that there were periods when we went too quickly. There are always pluses and minuses. As for what you call differences between north and south Vietnam, we do not find this to be a difficulty. We remain one nation; the attempts of the imperialist and aggressive forces to destroy our unity failed. But you are quite right about the cast of mind being different in the north and the south, and we have given great attention to this. We have realized objectively that agricultural reform, for instance, had been going on for a long time in the north, but is only beginning in the south. And that fruit orchards in peasant households are rare in the north, but in the south they are often very big and the income from them is considerable. We have decided not to worry about this, though, and to concern ourselves primarily with rice production. We may never tax these orchards, unless a landlord gets to be too rich. In industry as well as in agriculture, we are now giving a great deal of attention to offering people more incentives to produce. One of the contradictions we are facing is how to maintain a strong defense and build a strong economy simultaneously. We are trying to adjust to this, as well, and we will do so. But like everything else in a period of transition, it will take time."

The new economic reforms that followed the failure to meet any of the important agricultural and industrial targets of the nation's first postwar five-year plan are based on the so-called production contract system, which officially went into effect in 1981. Actually, the idea was tested as early as 1976–77 in the northern province of Vinh Phu, which conducted the first of several grass-roots experiments to stimulate production by drawing up contracts between provincial authorities and peasants. In September 1979, the Central Committee's Sixth Plenum of the Party's Fourth National Congress recommended a number of important changes in economic strategy, including giving more initiative to local planners, removing some of the restrictions on the free or open market, and offering peasants and workers more material incentives. While such reforms already had achieved some spontaneous grass-roots support, the credit for making them a new national policy is generally given to Vo Van Kiet, who was Party secretary in Ho Chi Minh City in the late seventies and is now the country's chief economic planner and a member of the Politburo. At the time of the 1979 Sixth Plenum, Vietnam's food supplies were in perilously poor shape, having dropped about a quarter during the five-year plan period then ending. In 1980, the year before the contract system was formally tested, total grain production had risen to approximately fourteen million tons—not enough to provide for a fast-rising postwar population of between fifty-six and fifty-seven million. Though the government's aim was to maintain the population increase at a rate of 1.7 percent a year, it was growing at between 2.3 and 2.4 percent. To make matters worse, farmers were quitting their land and looking for jobs in the city. The fish catch, meanwhile, had dropped by about 40 percent. (In Vietnam, meat, except for pork and poultry, has never been plentiful.)

The ground was thus ripe for reform by the time the Sixth Plenum met and the way was already prepared for the contract system. Under this system, farmers individually or as a group negotiate with their cooperatives to produce specific amounts of grain, mostly rice, which they agree to sell to the state at fixed prices. The quotas vary and are based on the amount each farmer produces, depending on how much land he has and on the fertility of the soil, which is considerably higher in most parts of the south than in the north. The state is supposed to provide seeds, fertilizers, pesticides, and other essential needs, but because of shortages, especially of fertilizer, these requirements are seldom met in full. Whatever the farmer produces in excess of his quota, he can either keep for his family, sell locally, sell to the state at fixed and profitable prices, or sell on the larger free market for prices that vary, depending on the demand and on competition.

At the outset of the new plan, the state sought to buy most of the surplus grain to supply government workers and especially workers in industry, who also had begun to benefit from the incentive system by being paid on the basis of how much they produced rather than according to the number of hours they worked. The government initially sold this rice for far less than it paid for it. But, particularly in the south, government procurement of rice, though it gradually increased, still lagged in many places because of a continuing shortage in consumer goods the farmers most wanted. As a result, private merchants reemerged as pivotal forces, cornering large amounts of the surplus crops and supplying the farmers with those consumer goods the government was unable to provide. Most farmers in the south, two-thirds of whom were still working individually, having refused to join cooperatives, preferred to deal on their own with the private traders. When the Party's Fifth National Congress met in Hanoi, in March 1982, the new policies received official approbation, but there was still considerable debate between the reformists, led by Kiet, and the Old Guard ideologues typified by Truong Chinh. The debate continued after the congress, and it was not surprising that the "new capitalists" in the south furnished the ideologues with some of their strongest ammunition.

In 1982, the output of grain had risen to 16.25 million

tons, which was somewhat disappointing, but in 1983 it was just under 17 million, and the 1984 total was a record 17.7 million tons, despite some bad weather. Two bad coastal storms in Central Vietnam in the fall of 1985 kept the output about the same. The long-range targets call for increases of a million tons a year, but drought and uneven weather generally cause a shortfall of several hundred thousand tons annually. Professor Tran Phuong, who at the time of my trip was the deputy prime minister for planning and one of the few middle-generation trained economists in the Party hierarchy, told me, "By 1983 we achieved self-sufficiency in food, but only by using the lowest per capita standard—eighteen hundred calories a day. That is still considered barely sufficient. To appreciate our situation, you must place it in historical perspective. In the past thirty-five years, our population has doubled—to almost sixty million—but the amount of cultivated land has not increased very much. Industry has increased only a little since 1975. Since 1979, when China turned against us, our defense burden has grown tremendously. So you can understand that while the achievements of the past few years are encouraging, we are still pursuing prewar goals, and we have a long way to go—I figure five years, until 1990—to rise above the level of bare self-sufficiency. We have also had severe distribution problems, largely because of the breakdown during the war of our transportation facilities. Immediately after the war, we actually had to send the south some of our imported rice—that had never happened before. In good prewar years, the south used to export sizable amounts of rice, but during the war it, too, was importing instead, and importing continued after 1975 in both parts of the country. But the situation is improving and, though the south now sends the north seven hundred thousand tons of rice a year, we're trying, through the contract system and other means, to correct the imbalance and to make the north self-sufficient, so the south can start exporting again."

Tran Phuong, a lively and articulate man who subsequently was dismissed from his job when the new economic and fiscal reforms he initiated ran into trouble, primarily as a result of fresh inflationary pressures, has been a long-time disciple of Vo Van Kiet, who continues to head the State Planning Commission. Kiet, a quiet southerner, prefers to stay in the background and spends much of his time in the provinces, where he feels most at home and which he firmly believes are the true testing grounds of the future. He shuns formal events, such as the Independence Day ceremonies, and apparently has no strong political ambitions. Phuong, for his part, was more visible and more outspoken—he was one of the few people who, when I asked him if Vietnam was not in many respects moving toward the Hungarian model of socialism, did not evade the question. He replied, "You are almost correct." What counts most at the moment, despite Phuong's removal and continuing economic problems, is that Kiet and his group still seem to have the backing of Le Duan and Le Duc Tho, the senior Party leaders. Duan, in particular, in the past two years, has lent his full support to the reformists. As prime minister, Pham Van Dong plays a more passive role, but he, too, is considered to be one of the pragmatists. The opposition ideologues continue to be led by Truong Chinh, who, like Dong, is close to retirement. Another Politburo ideologue, To Huu, and seven other ministers, were peremptorily removed in June 1986, signifying a further trend toward reformism. Perhaps the most formidable of the conservatives is General Van Tien Dung, who has replaced General Vo Nguyen Giap as defense minister and as the leading military man on the Politburo. General Dung has been vocal in stressing the continued need for a strong defense and extolling the soldiers as national heroes who bear the brunt of hard and dangerous work in protecting the country but receive minimal economic benefits for their efforts; he and his disciple General Le Duc Anh, who is running the Cambodian campaign and is also on the Politburo, favor a strong uncompromising line on Cambodia. Pham Hung, the remaining old-timer on the Politburo, is the nation's top security chief. A tough-minded southerner who directed the political campaign in the south during the war, he is considered a hard-liner less for ideological than security reasons; if the prevailing political winds continue to moderate, he might move with them, although he, too, may not survive the continuing changes.

The differences between the ideologues and the pragmatists, which cover the whole spectrum of political and economic matters and include foreign policy, have inevitably had an effect on the growth and discipline of the Communist Party of Vietnam. Created by Ho Chi Minh in 1930 as the Communist Party of Indo-China, the Party has traditionally maintained extremely rigorous standards, and cadres have always been selected and trained with the greatest care. Crises and Party upheavals have occurred periodically, but have been weathered and, for the most part, been kept fairly quiet. The Party's membership today is approximately a million and three-quarters —not large, in a country of sixty million. In recent years, more changes than usual have occurred in the Party's structure and geographical distribution, owing partly to the problems and challenges of the postwar period, including those faced—particularly by younger cadremen—in dealing with corruption and the soft life in the south; and partly to the death of many first generation heroes, and a certain amount of weeding out of older members of the Central Committee, or of individuals who for one reason or another have fallen from favor. In the immediate postwar period, there was a lot of doubt about the loyalty and dedication of the southerners, and the southern leadership was still suffering from the severe wartime losses caused by the American-sponsored Phoenix program of assassination, specifically directed at the Vietcong under-

ground and Party cadres. This doubt and mistrust has by
no means disappeared. Of the former leaders of the wartime Provisional Revolutionary Government in the south,
or of the National Liberation Front which preceded it, the
number who now hold jobs of any significance in the national government is very small, and southern Party membership remains low in proportion to the population.
Nevertheless, about a third of the hundred-and-thirty-odd
members of the current Central Committee are southerners.

Over the past seven or eight years, according to Western
observers who have followed Party matters, about three-
fifths of the new members, who average seventy or eighty
thousand a year, are men with recent army experience—
every man eighteen and over has to serve three years. This
preponderance of military men, which is also reflected in
the turnover of Central Committee members, takes on
special significance in view of the fact that political com-
missars in the army have been abolished. Moreover, the
essentially conservative opinions on economics and politics
which were held by military leaders at the top—particularly General Dung and the new army chief of staff, General Le Trong Tan—carry a great deal of weight, over and
above ideology. Interestingly, women make up less than
20 percent of the Party membership—mainly because
many women drop their Party work after they get married
and have children. Though Vietnam is described in its
constitution as a "dictatorship of the proletariat," workers
make up only about 10 percent of the Party; the country,
still overwhelmingly agricultural, has only about three million industrial workers at most. To complicate the Party
picture further, there is a considerable overlap at the local
and regional level between the people's committees, which
are administrative bodies, and the Party committees,
which transmit policy guidelines from the top. In many
cases, because there are not many tried and trusted mem-

be₁s with enough experience, the same handful of people occupy positions on both committees simultaneously, or switch from one to the other. The lines between the Party and the government are thus blurred, but the Party ends up in the dominant position.

Congresses of the Vietnam Communist Party, which are major policymaking conclaves, are held every few years, usually four or five. Twice a year, plenum meetings of the Central Committee (numbered sequentially during the life of a congress) are summoned to hold debates and decide on the details and implementation of policies set forth by the congresses and by the Politburo. The Politburo meets whenever it chooses to—once or twice a month on the average—and actually runs the country on a regular basis. After the new economic reforms were initially adopted, following the long debate in 1979, there remained a great deal of confusion and uncertainty about both planning and management, and particularly about the lines of authority between the central government and the lower echelons, in the provinces, districts, and major cities. As Hoang Tung explained it to me, "It became apparent that, in our effort to allow more dynamism and initiative at the lower levels while maintaining planning leadership at the center, we had let free market practices get out of hand, and there were many examples of poor management. What the Sixth Plenum of the Fifth Party Congress, in 1984, basically did was examine the experience of the previous four years, analyze what was right and what was wrong, and then correct and refine management practices. Essentially, the new Sixth Plenum consolidated the reforms of the earlier Sixth Plenum [of the Party's Fourth National Congress] of 1979. It did not change the initiative given to local and provincial establishments, but it clarified and specified areas where policy was being misconstrued and misinterpreted by the failure to abide by central guidelines. We also had to decide, for example, what important agricultural and industrial products should be kept off the free market and be controlled by the state. And what other products the state would buy at fair prices but then distribute and sell on the free market. And we had to draw more definite lines for local and provincial groups about fulfilling quotas, both in agriculture and in industry, before they could purchase raw materials for their own use in producing goods to sell domestically or to export."

It was not surprising that the system got out of hand in the early eighties in Ho Chi Minh City, for Saigon's new name had not changed its old ways of operating. Actually, it was Kiet who, as Party secretary in the city in the late seventies, had formulated and initiated the polices that liberalized trade and commerce locally before he became the prime instigator of the central level reforms. By the end of 1982, however, it was apparent that too much freedom and permissiveness had led to widespread chaos, not only in Ho Chi Minh City but in many southern provinces, which had set up their own export-import companies and were trading openly with other nations, most flagrantly with Singapore. In Ho Chi Minh City, according to a former Saigon official who, after a brief period in a reeducation camp after the war, went to work for Kiet, applying Western-acquired knowledge as an economist to the new situation, there were seventeen separate companies, one for each district. There were, in addition, five city-wide companies; an export-import firm called Cholomex, which was backed by the Chinese and had a capitalization of a billion dong; and a similar Vietnamese company with half that much. Starting from zero at the end of the war, an export-import trade of three hundred million dollars a year had been built up in the city.

Following a meeting of the Politburo late in 1982, which was unusual in that it was held in Ho Chi Minh City, a government investigation was conducted and all trading was temporarily suspended. A year later, Le Duan and Kiet attended a Party meeting of the Ho Chi Minh City municipal government. By that time, a single concern called the General Export and Import Company had been established to coordinate procurement, except that the seventeen district companies and Cholomex were permitted to resume supplying their own export commodities, such as shrimp, which went largely to Japan. Freewheeling firms in the provinces also came under the supervision and control of the General Export and Import Company, and the unrestricted competition, which had been accompanied by considerable corruption, was diminished, if not entirely eliminated. Le Duan took much of the edge off the earlier criticism by praising city officials for their aggressive leadership and calling for Ho Chi Minh City to become an "export city." Vietnamese workers in agriculture and industry, he said, should devote a third of their time, or a hundred working days a year, to producing goods for export, and the goods should go to "nationalist, nonaligned, and independent" countries, capitalist as well as socialist. In a subsequent major speech, Le Duan startlingly declared that a worker's main motive, even when carrying out government policy, should be "personal interest," and—in what was a further obvious thrust at the ideologues—he dismissed egalitarianism as "an erroneous tendency alien to Marxism." He quoted Marx as having said: "Once ideology is detached from interest, it will certainly disgrace itself."

By the time the Sixth Plenum of the Fifth National Congress was held in Hanoi in the summer of 1984, it had become apparent that a new reformist path was being laid out. In a long speech, which was published in full, Le Duan, while still maintaining that "priority must be given to developing heavy industry," said: "In the current initial state, agriculture and light industry have the greatest potential for attracting the social work force and [for using land] as well as other natural resources of the country in order to turn out more products to meet the people's subsistence, material, and cultural requirements." He criticized the slow production of consumer goods over recent years and the use of manpower and equipment at only half capacity. Such shortcomings, he added, "have directly stood in the way of agricultural production, created more difficulties for the state to control goods and the market, caused a slow development of exports and imports, and adversely affected the people's life." Presaging what was to come, he emphasized that the state "must strictly manage the circulation of money, stabilize and strengthen the purchasing power of money, and collect part of the surplus money in circulation, especially the large amounts . . . in the hands of dishonest traders, speculators, hoarders, and smugglers." He said that "exercising mastery in the market is currently the most acute problem of our state," and, indicating that there must be firm limits to the free market, added, "The state supply and procurement organizations, through the signing of contracts with producers from the beginning of the crop seasons, must organize the sending of supplies and consumer goods to the countryside to satisfy the demands of production and life promptly." Increasing exports "must truly become a duty of the entire people," Le Duan continued. "Our economic structure must guarantee that each laborer can spend one hundred man days for export activity. . . . We must use millions of people to plant and exploit hundreds of thousands of hectares of rubber, tea, coffee, and other short- and long-term crops." Only by so doing, he said, can Vietnam exchange goods "with nationalist, independent, and nonaligned countries while achieving a breakthrough in the interchange of merchandise with capitalist countries and removing the embargo imposed on us by the imperialists and expansionists." Significantly, he did not mention the Cambodian war.

The subsequent communiqué was preceded by a long and heated debate reflecting the continuing differences between the hard-liners who opposed the liberalization of the economy and those who supported the incentive plans. Ultimately, the communiqué came down on the side of the reformists, particularly upholding a limited free market and a reduced central bureaucracy. It laid special stress on creating "a new mechanism of management" which would "give full play to the collective mastery of the people, the innovative spirit, and all the capabilities of the grass roots in order to reorganize production." In an especially critical and prophetic paragraph, it referred to the "many difficulties and imbalances" in the production of food, energy, and other materials, and condemned the poor management of fiscal and monetary matters. "The free market is still too large," the communiqué added. "Price fluctuation is still too great, and the life of the working people, particularly the workers and public servants and armed forces, still meets with many difficulties. The disparities of the incomes of different sectors of the population in society remain too great." Managers at the grass roots had to be given the right to hire, fire, promote, and train their workers in accordance with the principles of "democratic centralism," the communiqué said, and here it picked up on Le Duan's harsh criticism of the quality of cadres, which he bluntly had said included their loss of "fighting will and revolutionary ardor" and their falling prey to "corruption, seeking private gain, and promoting personal interests." These failures, he added, had resulted in many of them becoming "degenerate and deviant" and to "exploitation, bribery, and bullying of the masses."

There was little doubt after this plenum that the prevailing winds in Vietnam were moderate or reformist, and that, at least for the foreseeable future, the hard-liners were subdued. In my long conversation in the fall of 1984 with Tran Phuong, who used to teach Marxism, he declared, echoing Le Duan, "Marx never said that only one kind of socialism must exist. As the author of scientific socialism, he said that it includes many categories of development. The question in Vietnam is: What proportion do we give to the private economy? I think that in ten years' time, the private sector will still occupy an important position in the national economy. Its existence has a rationale, and it retains its importance. But what is equally important is that it should not occupy a leading position—that we don't allow the capitalists to control big companies." Those who won't accept the concept of a mixed economy thus insist that while their definition of scientific socialism in Marxist terms may appear to embrace aspects of such an economy for the time being, particularly given the background of development in the south, this is basically an expedient and largely semantic formula, with no permanent conceptual validity. As Phuong had put it to me, "It's our intention to have a long coexistence with the capitalists and technocrats in the south, where they are more numerous than in the north. We don't know how much they will develop in ten years' time. But by then their products won't be as good as the state products, even though they may live on as capitalists. In Eastern Europe, their output is often much better than state products, but it won't be that way here."

It is difficult to tell how much of this is wishful thinking, and how much is predicated on Vietnam's bold if belated acceptance of its failures to date and of the need to overhaul the foundations of its economy. It seems evident, however, that the change of course that began in the early eighties was based on hardheaded appraisals, which the Vietnamese can be given credit for reaching with probably less inner turmoil and struggle than either the Russians or the Chinese. And once having moved down the new path, the reformists were determined to push ahead. They undoubtedly benefited from the open support given them by

Le Duan, who in his late seventies began showing clear signs of assuming Ho Chi Minh's mantle of supreme leadership in the Party and the Politburo before he and other members of the Old Guard turn the leadership over to the new generation. In June 1985, with Le Duan again leading the way, the reform process was further accelerated by the Eighth Plenum of the Party's Fifth National Congress, which adopted a series of economic reforms hailed by Party leaders as "a gust of new wind" and "a turning point of decisive significance." In its closing communiqué, this plenum announced an end to the food subsidies long given to state employees as well as an end to "bureaucratic centralism," and declared the adoption of "socialist economic accounting and business" practices to replace the former policies of planning and pricing by administrative edict. Henceforth, salaries would be paid in cash and indexed according to the cost of living, the communiqué said. Prior to the plenum, in April, the dong had been devalued from the highly unrealistic rate of nearly twelve to the dollar to one hundred to one. Now in September, in two important follow-up moves to the abolition of subsidies, the dong was again devalued by 33 percent and new dong were issued, at the rate of one new one for ten old ones. Each person was limited to two thousand new dong, which was equal to one hundred and thirty-three dollars at the new rate, and given a receipt for the balance he or she held. The inflation rate had been running at about 60 percent a year, but for the moment, after the devaluation, the currency seemed to hold relatively stable. Ten days later, a new system of wages was instituted for state employees and for the military which did away with what was described as the "heavy egalitarianism" of the past and established a system based on "pay according to work," taking into consideration both the peculiar difficulties of a job and the skills required to perform it.

One of the principal anticipated benefits of the 1985 reforms was the abolition of the two-tier price system—

state and private. This is something the International Monetary Fund, with which Vietnam has a working relationship, had been urging for years, insisting that the subsidies were draining the government's already meager reserves of funds. As explained to me by one high-ranking official, who asked to remain anonymous, "For over thirty years we failed to pay enough attention to prices because all of our aid was grant aid, both during and after the war. Towns and provinces obtained raw materials at very low prices, and everything, including transport and storage, was calculated at cost or less. The result was the creation of an artificial price climate—and a lot of mismanagement, corruption, and waste. The state-controlled price of rice, for example, was forty Vietnamese cents a kilo, while on the free market a kilo of rice cost forty dong. There was no proper sense of accounting. It was all chaotic, and as the bureaucracy got bigger and bigger, the quality of skilled labor dropped. Too many people were getting a free ride with the subsidies, and then moonlighted to make extra money. Now, under the new system, for the first time, it is hoped that salaries will reflect the price of basic goods on the free market, and they will be reviewed every three months. Productivity and production costs will be the key, along with accountability. We will have to keep track, for example, of how much oil we use, and where and how it is distributed, especially by the military. As for food, the old coupon ration system will be abolished and everything will be handled in cash. The idea is for each worker to be paid enough to feed himself and one child per month—the same holds for a working wife. This will not mean that the free market will be abolished, but the government will try to maintain greater control over the price of goods, especially agricultural commodities and staples such as meats, sugar, dry fish, and flour, by paying the producers reasonable prices. It will thus compete realistically with the free market and salaries will be adjusted accordingly. We will be applying a maxim that Lenin once used—'To avoid being defeated by the free market and free trade, we must know them inside out, and beat them at their own game.' Will the new dong remain stable? That will depend on production and proper distribution, and better management. It will be a real test for the new cadres. If we don't establish better accountability, the system will fail and the rate of inflation will again get out of hand."

The government announcements of the new system, while hailing its "great revolutionary success," were cautionary. "The adjustment of prices, wages, and money in accordance with the spirit of the Central Committee's eighth plenum resolution as well as the new management system are not magic wands that can immediately improve our national economy and our people's daily life," *Nhan Dan* warned late in September 1985. "These measures are not designed to solve all the problems of our people in the initial stage of the transitional period toward socialism. . . . Implementation of this resolution requires firm capability and vast experience which we are lacking. . . ." Subsequently, in November, *Nhan Dan* spoke of the gap between "the political line and practical action," and added that it "could take years" for the economic reforms to be effectively completed.

As it turned out, *Nhan Dan's* warnings were well taken. By the spring of 1986, the reforms of the eighth plenum were in serious trouble. The rate of inflation had again soared, this time by 500 percent. The abolition of subsidies on such staples as rice and pork and the compensatory wage raises given to state workers had been well received, but many of the basic goods were simply not there to be bought. Pork and rice prices tripled between September 1985 and March 1986. Electricity rates for homes nearly doubled, while bus fares increased tenfold. In January, the government was forced to reintroduce rationing on eight basic commodities, at least temporarily. The currency reforms proved particularly disastrous, primarily because they were initiated without sufficient preparation. Despite the devaluations, the black market for the dong had soared to 260 to the dollar, nearly ten times what it was just after the devaluation of the previous September. Shortages of energy were as bad or worse than before; industry in the north was operating at only 20 percent capacity and at 40 percent in the south. Moonlighting was as prevalent as ever, and despite the effort to crack down on forms of private enterprise regarded as wasteful or unproductive, the number of small traders in Ho Chi Minh City was said to have increased by more than a third since the war's end in 1975. While the reforms had been generally well received, and were still widely approved in principle, the timing of the structural, monetary, and pricing aspects had not been well coordinated. For this, the blame was cast on Tran Phuong, the deputy prime minister. He was accused of having ordered the devaluation and exchange of old dong for new at the ten to one rate without consulting members of the Politburo, though it seems hard to imagine he would have taken such drastic steps on his own. Vo Van Kiet, his mentor, was reported to have opposed the devaluations on the grounds that they should have been accompanied by other changes in monetary policy, which were now likely to be made and would possibly include an overall wage and price freeze. In any event, Tran Phuong became the scapegoat. The national assembly demanded his resignation, along with those of the director of the state bank and the head of the price commission, and Prime Minister Pham Van Dong personally apologized to the assembly. As the ministerial dismissals of the eight ministers, including To Huu, in June 1986, indicated, however, the reformists did not suffer a serious political setback.*

---

* Le Duan's death and the continuing monetary crisis are not expected to halt the basic drive toward economic reforms. But the impending appointment of new leaders by the Sixth Party Congress may delay the process.

Western diplomats, who had initially hailed the reforms and had wondered why the Vietnamese had taken so long to act, ascribed their limited success and the continuing problems to more bad management and lack of overall planning. "The Vietnamese are simply inexperienced in these matters," one of them said, "and they're forced to proceed by trial and error. They will undoubtedly make more mistakes before they find the answers." There was some speculation that they had taken their cue from the Russians rather than from the Chinese, despite the fact that, on the surface, the new reforms seemed to resemble those already introduced by Peking. When Le Duan visited Moscow at the end of June 1985, the new Gorbachev leadership had begun to introduce its own series of economic reforms, including adjustments in prices and profits to stimulate the economy. Both Le Duan and Gorbachev, for example, used the phrase "economic levers" and there were similarities in the two men's subtle use of nuances to hide past failures of policy. Although Le Duan obtained a new five-year contract for concessional credits and rescheduling of Vietnam's ruble debt, his reception, compared with that on his past visits, was rather cool. There were other—political rather than economic—reasons for this. Gorbachev made it clear that he wanted Vietnam to endorse his efforts to reach some degree of new accommodation, if not normalization, with the Chinese. There was obvious irony here. While the Vietnamese wished, more than anything else, to establish their own better relations with China, they had all along been frightened by the prospect of a rapprochement between the two big Communist powers. Under the circumstances, Le Duan had no choice but to go along with Soviet wishes. The joint declaration at the end of the meeting declared that "the normalization of the relations of the Soviet Union and the Socialist Republic of Vietnam with the People's Republic of China" contributes to the "aims of

strengthening peace in Asia and international security."
While Moscow gave no indication of cutting down its support of the Vietnamese military campaign in Cambodia—
in fact, military and economic aid to Vietnam overall for
the period 1986–89 was doubled to an estimated 1.6 billion dollars a year—it was apparent that the Sino-Soviet
discussions held first priority.

Much as the Vietnamese would like to break out of the
isolation in which they have found themselves since their
invasion of Cambodia and to reestablish relations with
both China and the Western world, led by the United
States, they are still not making much headway. As a consequence, their overdependence on Soviet aid is a cross
they must continue to bear. Vietnam pays off part of its
heavy debt to the Russians by charging them little or nothing for the military facilities at the Danang air base and at
the former American naval and air base at Cam Ranh Bay
farther south. In the past year the Soviets have noticeably
increased their presence at Cam Ranh Bay, which has become their major forward base outside mainland Russia,
capable of monitoring all shipping between the Indian
and Pacific Oceans and virtually all American military activity in the South China Sea. A squadron of MIG-23s is
now stationed at the base, supplementing TU-16 Badger
bombers and TU-95 long-range Bear reconnaissance
planes with an operational range of almost four thousand
miles. As many as thirty naval vessels at one time, including half a dozen submarines, now move in and out of the
expansive harbor, which has five drydocks and underground fuel tanks. Four or five hundred Soviet personnel,
mostly weapons and electronics specialists, are regularly
seen coming ashore. Given their long history of stubborn
independence and especially their thousand-year struggle
to oust the Chinese, the Vietnamese could at some point
prove the exception to the rule that it is all but impossible
to edge the Russians out of a country where Moscow has

established a military presence; but there are certainly no signs of this happening yet. In fact, adding to Hanoi's worries was the statement in April 1985 by Deng Xiaoping that Peking would not object to Moscow's continuing presence in Cam Ranh Bay if the Russians could persuade the Vietnamese to remove their troops from Cambodia.

Over the past year or so, to make things more difficult, the Vietnamese and the Russians have grown increasingly edgy with each other, and it has become apparent that the relationship sometimes borders on mutual dislike. Beyond obvious cultural and behavioral differences and tensions, relations have become touchier on a day-to-day functional basis the longer they go on and become enmeshed in bureaucratic red tape and project delays. On an official level, this is seldom discussed publicly, but the average Vietnamese, being an individualist, is not afraid to express his opinions and enjoys exchanging stories about the Russians. One American friend of mine, who holds an important job in Washington and has known the Vietnamese well for many years, recently visited Hanoi and traveled there via Fukien, in south China. En route, the car passed over a bridge built by the Russians, the construction of which had taken far longer than expected, due partly to faulty planning and pilferage. "You better hurry on over, this thing might collapse," my friend suggested. Both his interpreter and the driver couldn't stop laughing. A number of East Europeans I met in Hanoi also enjoyed repeating stories about the Russians and their inability to adapt to life in Hanoi. "The Russians who come here live completely separate lives," one East German commented to me. "They make no effort to get to know the country and the people. They don't seem to care. They might as well be on another planet." I was also told that it was not unusual for the windows of Soviet cars to be mysteriously smashed on isolated streets. The surprisingly cool reception Gorbachev gave Le Duan in June 1985 was a more serious sign of deteriorating relations between the Russians and the Vietnamese. Despite increasing their aid and rescheduling Vietnam's debts, the Soviets expressed their impatience, as the East Europeans have also done, over Vietnam's failure to live up to its Comecon trade agreements and ship commissioned supplies of fruits and vegetables, among other things, to Europe. Gorbachev's stress on the importance of improved Sino-Soviet relations was obviously more than a ploy to frighten the Vietnamese. As for his urging Hanoi to come to terms with Peking, Le Duan's assurances that the Vietnamese were doing their best evoked a contemptuous response from Peking spokesmen, who said that Vietnam's comments were only "empty talk" since the Vietnamese had shown no signs of making significant troop withdrawals from Cambodia.

The Soviet Union's principal contribution to the Vietnamese economy has been in heavy industrialization, but many of these programs are often way behind schedule— and, besides, what the country needs most right now is improvements in light industry to produce consumer goods. The annual industrial growth is between 10 and 15 percent but construction of new factories has progressed slowly because of the continued shortage of raw materials and energy. Although there are four new cement factories producing more than a million tons a year, there is not yet nearly enough—the new five-year goal calls for a fourfold increase, half of which is coming from two new plants being built by the Russians and the French. Both for apatite and cement production, as well as for many other industries, oil is needed, for which the Vietnamese are now totally dependent on the Russians; offshore oil deposits have been explored for many years, going back to the final years of the war when American companies were involved in the search, and some promising wells were found. But further exploration and development have not taken place because the Russians lack the technology to go deep enough below the ocean floor.

Along with the shortage of oil, there is a dire need for

electric power. Plans are under way to increase the current output many times over, but this will take five to ten years. A huge hydroelectric power plant being built by the Russians at Hoa Binh, southwest of Hanoi on the Da River, is scheduled for completion in the early 1990s, and this in itself will provide a twofold increase—its ultimate capacity will be 8.8 billion kilowatt-hours annually. The first two of eight generators won't be in operation until 1987, however, and no one really knows if the whole project will be completed on time or whether the Russians will run out of patience and money. Two other plants, with a combined capacity of 700,000 kilowatt-hours a year, are also planned —one of them in the south—but these will come later. And even when Hoa Binh is finished, it cannot function without vast reconstruction of the country's run-down electricity-distribution grid, which dates back to French days, and the Russians insist that Vietnam will have to bear part of this cost. The Vietnamese hope that they will eventually be able to obtain aid for this reconstruction from the West, including the United States, which is still regarded as having an obligation to "heal the wounds of war," though the phrase is heard less often nowadays. Still another undeveloped energy source is coal; the country has large deposits, but only five or six million tons a year are being produced, and the goal is fifty million tons, including some for export. Electric power and coal are particularly necessary for the development of the chemical industry, and for the production of aluminum—there are large bauxite deposits in Vietnam—and for steel production; there is plentiful iron ore, too, but during the current five-year plan production fell way behind modest targets. Though the earlier overemphasis on heavy industry as an immediate priority has now been dropped, balanced industrialization, as Le Duan and others have recently emphasized, is considered essential. So far, the country's experience with foreign-built factories has not been good.

Russian and East European–bloc equipment is invariably outmoded. Sweden has donated close to a quarter billion dollars to help construct a modern pulp-and-paper mill, which, after ten years, is currently running at only a quarter of its projected annual capacity of fifty-five thousand tons, chiefly because the Vietnamese miscalculated their forestry reserves and chose to put the factory in a remote, isolated area north of Hanoi. There are some three hundred factories in and around Hanoi today, including fifty large ones, employing more than a thousand workers each, that are run by the state. They produce some machines and machine tools and engineering equipment, and, among other goods, textiles, chemicals, tires, porcelain, glassware, building materials, a wide variety of handicrafts, and processed foods. Pham Sy Lien, the first vice-president of Hanoi's executive committee, told me, "Our biggest achievement of the past thirty years is that, especially since the war, this has become an industrialized instead of a consumers' city." To a visitor, however, the city still seems pretty much of a quiet capital with more of a rustic than an industrial air.

If the Vietnamese could afford it, they would import enough raw materials and spare parts to run their light industries at 70 percent capacity instead of the current 50 percent or less, and this would not only provide more of the consumer goods they need so badly but would also enable them to produce more goods for export. Exports, mainly seafood, handicrafts, and footwear, have been growing over the past few years, according to the International Monetary Fund, but are still more than 50 percent below target. In 1984, the value of the nation's exports was about seven hundred and fifty million dollars. Only about two hundred million dollars of the total was earned from convertible or hard-currency areas. Vietnam rescheduled part of its debts to hard-currency countries— Japan, Libya, and Iraq among them—and had to use two hundred million to pay for debt servicing of other out-standing dollar obligations. Its total debt—principal and interest—to hard-currency nations comes to about two billion dollars, and it owes the Socialist bloc the equivalent of four billion in soft currencies. Balance of payments thus continues to be a major problem, which makes it harder to obtain much-needed imports, including petroleum products for industry and fertilizer for agricultural production. Foreign exchange reserves at the end of 1984 stood at a paltry sixteen million dollars—enough for a fortnight's basic purchases. The 1984 budget deficit was about 15 percent, but the government hopes that the abolition of subsidies and the new incentive schemes in industry and agriculture will improve productivity, stimulate spending, and eventually eliminate any deficit. Tax collections have improved somewhat in the last two or three years. Farmers are taxed at an average of 8 percent of their annual rice production—less fertile paddy land is assessed at 4 percent, and other crops are not taxed at all. In industry, small entrepreneurs and workshops operating cooperatively or privately are taxed at 10 or 15 percent of income; but such larger establishments as undesirable restaurants, few of which remain open, pay as much as 70 percent. There are no personal income taxes, in part because wages have been so low, but now that they have been raised this may change, though with so much moonlighting in the country it will still be impossible to determine who makes what. In the past two years, a new program to raise funds from the sale of Fatherland Construction bonds has had a moderate success, and a government-run lottery has done better—like the Chinese, the Vietnamese are born gamblers.

However the Vietnamese basic economy develops over the next few years, the country's best hope over that span is to build up its agro-industrial base. The major product and biggest potential earner of export income is rubber.

In prewar years, in South Vietnam, where most of the rubber plantations are situated, a hundred and forty thousand hectares (346,000 acres) were devoted to rubber. Nearly all of these plantations were destroyed by bombing or defoliation, or by being allowed to become run-down, but the level of land in use is now back to one hundred thousand hectares; the five-year goal is to double that, and the long-range goal is to reach eight hundred thousand or a million hectares by the year 2000, and to extend the plantations back into central Vietnam and perhaps to a few areas in the north, too. In many of the so-called New Economic Zones, to which a million and a half people have been relocated, plantations have been developed on what used to be nonarable land, often in remote and unprepossessing regions. Food processing, including both canning and freezing, is another industry that can be developed for export income. Large tea and coffee plantations that were destroyed in the war by defoliation are slowly being restored, and jute and cassava are other potential exports.

It remains to be seen if new salary and incentive schemes and a moderate program of industrial development will provide the stimuli for Vietnam to make significant economic progress by 1990. The decisions at the top in the Politburo are being made and remade and the formulas prescribed, but one skeptical Western diplomat who knows the country well told me, "The Vietnamese have improved their lines of command, and they're trying to manage things better, but it's still all cast in terms of Confucian exhortation. In this sense, they're as orthodox as ever. What you have is the old Soviet Union framework—the Dnepropetrovsk dam idea, reflected in big projects like the one at Hoa Binh—imposed upon a society that remains overwhelmingly peasant and backward. It's odd how an innate sense of pragmatism, or peasant common sense, can overcome ideology in some respects, as with agricultural reforms, and yet how the Vietnamese can stay firmly cast in the old mold at the same time. There are certain things they are reluctant or refuse to get involved with. Family planning is one. They pay lip service to it, but they haven't mounted a real campaign, a determined effort, to come to grips with the problem, even though they're being given help by the United Nations. The leadership here hasn't done what the Chinese have done, despite the Confucian tradition in China being, if anything, stronger; the Vietnamese haven't provided the discipline for family planning, which means direct interference at the family level to have one or two children instead of three or four or five, and to impose penalties if need be. This remains a very serious matter, which increasing agricultural production can't cope with over the long run. It could keep the Vietnamese on the knife's edge economically."

For the Vietnamese, advocacy of birth control has a certain irony about it. Ho Chi Minh, who was never married, loved children—he referred to all Vietnamese as "my children," and they, of course, revered him as Uncle Ho. Whenever he met with a group of young men or women, he would give them two admonitions: "Don't smoke, and don't stay single." The Ho myth lives on, as strong as ever, though whether it will continue through future generations is hard to tell. Certainly the few remaining Vietnamese leaders of his generation, like Pham Van Dong, and their immediate potential successors in the Central Committee, are making every effort to carry on the myth, which is such a vital part of the Vietnamese past, of the heavy mixture of lore and legend and revolutionary adventure that underlies the nation's emotional and political history and has inspired and motivated its citizens for four decades.

The impact of Ho is felt and seen everywhere in Hanoi, but most strongly at his tomb, a huge, columned structure on one side of a spacious and beautifully landscaped

square fronting the national Parliament and Party headquarters. The tomb is a striking black-and-gray granite
building—the stone came from quarries all over the country—and it was not completed until August 1975, six years
after Ho's death. Fifteen thousand persons visit it each
week. I went there late one Sunday morning, when long
lines, including many schoolchildren, stretched around
the block, waiting to pass slowly up the granite steps, past
the engraved quotation from Ho which one sees everywhere—"Nothing is more precious than independence
and freedom"—then up a short flight of stairs and around
a small chamber where, constantly guarded by four armed
soldiers at attention, Ho's small embalmed body lies on a
raised platform. His arms are folded across his stomach,
and his expression is grave and peaceful. His famous
wispy goatee looks wispier than ever below his broad brow.
The crowds—and the children especially—are somber
and obviously awed at the sight. Once outside again, the
young ones resume their chatter and play.

As I walked out of the tomb into the hot, glaring sunlight, I thought of the irony of Vietnam's birth-control
problems and reflected that Ho would have appreciated it.
Unfortunately, I never met him, but I have spoken with
many scholars and others who knew him, including some
of his closest Vietnamese associates, and I have read a
good deal about his life. Being a highly practical and often
calculating and devious man as well as a sentimental one,
he would, I believe, have tempered his love for children
with an awareness of the serious problem of Vietnam's too
rapidly growing population. If he were still alive today, or
even if he had lived through the years just after the war,
he would have been the first to go out into the countryside
and talk to the peasants about birth control, and what to
do about it; he would have done this graphically, and, as
he did with so many things, dramatized the issue with
whimsical humor. Although he passed through several

stages of orthodox Bolshevik and Communist ideology, in France, in the Soviet Union, and in other Southeast Asian nations, as well as in Vietnam when he was the chief Comintern agent in the area in the thirties, he always encouraged new ideas and anticipated new situations. For that reason, he would probably have also sought the liberal economic reforms that are now being introduced. My guess is that he would have done this sooner rather than later, too, and that he would have done his utmost to avoid or ameliorate some of the other postwar problems that have beset Vietnam, including the cleavages that still exist between the north and the south. He would, for example, have done what his comrades would never allow him to do during the war for reasons of security and because of his fragility (though he kept exercising regularly to get himself into shape): visit the south and travel the country from what he used to describe, so fervidly, as its southernmost tip, on the Gulf of Thailand, to its farthest northern reaches, in the mountains overlooking China.

CHAPTER THREE

The Proud Center

(1)

If Saigon had seemed to me still Saigon, however ideologically ambivalent and idiosyncratic Ho Chi Minh City now is—and if Hanoi is still defining its new character as the capital of a not yet united nation—revisiting towns like Danang, Hué, Dongha, Quangtri, and Conthien jogged mixed memories of a different sort. These are places where some of the fiercest military as well as political battles of the war occurred, and where some important turning points were reached. Many of the towns and surrounding areas are among those left most devastated and barren by the long years of fighting, the legacy of which is still very real: unexploded bombs imbedded in the ground and booby traps set off accidentally have killed thousands of Vietnamese since 1975, and it may be another decade or more before they are all cleared away and the fields are cultivated again. The rusted wreckage of American planes, tanks, and trucks and other detritus of countless battles and air raids are still everywhere visible. Herbicide spraying has left vast parts of the countryside denuded of trees and vegetation, although along the once beautiful but gutted coast, palm and coconut trees have started to grow back. Some of the cities and towns look much the same, but others are altogether new and have been relocated. The houses, as in Quangtri, which was

117

totally leveled, have red tile roofs and modern conve-
niences, including plumbing and electricity, they never
had before. Hué, on the other hand, large parts of which
were destroyed during the Tet offensive of 1968, is as
beautiful and distinctively its old self as ever, though lack
of funds has held back reconstruction of some buildings,
including much of the old Citadel. Overall I was struck—
as I had been before and during the war—by how attitudes and behavior still varied between this central part of
Vietnam, revolutionary and proud in its own right, and
both the north and the south. Ten years later, this sense
of independence and determination to remain distinctive
and do things its own way was still true; though ostensibly
part of one nation, and paying heed to the flow of national
directives charting new courses and establishing new
goals, the central region remains uniquely assertive.

Hué, with a population of three hundred and fifty thousand—twice what it was in 1975—has become the thriving
capital of Binh Tri Thien province, which is a consolidation of three former provinces. Officials here have high
hopes that Binh Tri Thien, with nearly two million people
in all and two million hectares of arable land, with one of
the country's longest coastlines, and with ample ports, will
become a principal export center in the next few years. It
has a wealth of products under some degree of cultivation,
including rubber, sugarcane, peanuts, tobacco, coffee, and
pepper, and these, along with shrimp and other seafood,
are its principal trade items. It also has a potential for
industrial development, particularly in textiles, porcelain
and earthenware, forest products, and some steel and machinery. "If we can exploit all that we have, we can become
one of the richest provinces in Vietnam," Nguyen Van
Luong, who is both chairman of the provincial people's
committee and deputy secretary of the Party committee,
told me, over a delicious local lunch atop the Huong Giang
Hotel, on the banks of the Perfume River, where I had

stayed several times in the past. Luong, a slight man in his early fifties, with graying hair and clear dark eyes that sparkle and join with a ready smile to express enthusiasm, was the underground leader of Quangtri province during the war. Now he is constantly on the go trying to run his much larger province; today he was in the midst of rushing around conferring with local officials about a brewing tropical storm, which fortunately veered to the north at the last moment, but he had taken time off to entertain me at lunch, partly because he was eager to obtain American aid for his development projects.

"Our province was one of those that suffered most during the war," he said. "Our rice crops were burned, and six hundred thousand people were herded into refugee camps that were like concentration camps. In 1975, they came back, many of them balancing poles with two baskets, a child in each. They had no houses and very little clothing or food. It was extremely difficult at first, and the mines everywhere made things worse. Today, we are no longer so poor, and both the peasants in the countryside and the workers in the city are well off compared with their situation then. We wish to forget the war. Please tell the American people that we have a high regard for those who understand and support us and we would welcome joint ventures on the basis of mutual interest." Luong gazed at the sky above the river, which looked gray and menacing. Sampans scuttled like water bugs for the safety of the shore. "We must always worry about the weather," he said. "In 1983, the storms and floods were the worst in fifty years, and we lost much of our grain production. This year, if the storms are not too bad we should approach half a million tons of paddy—that is, rice and subsidiary crops. Life for the farmers has become more stable. The grain bought by the government is only fifteen percent of their crop—we sell that to the workers at low prices—and the farmers end up with a good surplus for the free market. We are not yet self-sufficient in rice, however, and the government gives us a hundred thousand tons or so a year, from the Mekong Delta. We believe that collectivization is necessary, but the form and speed at which it takes place depend on current conditions. We do not force it, among either peasants or merchants. We let the people choose the way to follow, and for the present that's more important than whether a business is collective or not."

During the war, aside from being the center of Buddhist religious and political action and, with a famous university, a hub of intellectual and radical student life, Hué was primarily a service city, furnishing food and other necessities for the South Vietnamese troops in the First Corps area. Today, it is a handicrafts center and is turning to the production of textiles. "By 1985," Luong told me, "we will have fifty thousand spindles and make eighty million meters of cloth a year." During a walk through the large Dong Ba market, across the river from the hotel, I had noticed many stalls selling cloth and clothes, in addition to the usual wide variety of foods and consumer items. Now I remarked to Luong that it all seemed pretty much the same as before. "The old ladies may appear to run their shops on the same basis," Luong replied, "but, actually, many of them are now grouped into merchandise organizations. We encourage that, so they can help each other out, but it's all voluntary." Hué is also a tourist center, as it always has been, and though I had seen the emperors' tombs on the outskirts numerous times—there are seven large ones clustered in one area and another six that are smaller and scattered around the outskirts of the city—my hosts insisted on conducting me through some of them again. Among those we visited was the tomb of Emperor Tu Duc, who reigned in the middle of the nineteenth century and, though isolated from his people, wrote a four-part autobiography that began with his childhood and ended with his describing his lonely and sick old age, when be blamed himself for letting the French capture the country and having no son to continue the dynasty. It was raining when we arrived at the various buildings of the compound, but even so there were several groups of visitors, including some road construction workers from the northern province of Nghe An, Ho Chi Minh's birthplace, who had been rewarded for their good work by a trip to Hué. During the French and American wars the tombs were used as hideouts and storage areas by the guerrillas, and many of the court buildings were partially destroyed by shellfire. I walked into one of the smaller buildings where the principal and virtually only piece of furniture was a huge wooden bed. Four youths in their late twenties were watching the rain from a window. They said they were maintenance workers who had only recently been discharged from the army and were receiving two hundred dong a month plus food. One of them had a guitar and they were singing Vietnamese love songs softly. "We would like to go back to the university," the boy with the guitar said, "but we have to work to help our families."

After our tour of the tombs we walked around the buildings of the old imperial palace, back along the banks of the Perfume River, and through the battered Citadel. The Vietnamese in Hué remain inordinately proud and respectful of their imperial and cultural history, which is ironic in that, when the emperors were alive, ordinary citizens were never allowed anywhere near the palace and tombs. After another hour of wandering around these historic sites, I finally persuaded my guards to let me walk through the other end of the Citadel, which had been turned into rubble during the fierce month-long Tet offensive, when the Communists captured the area and held it for three weeks before the South Vietnamese government, with the help of the Americans, could recover it. I wanted to see how much of it had been rebuilt and what the city's commercial life there was like.

The place was as busy as ever and, like the market, seemed unchanged, with rows of small shops and artisans engaged in what appeared to be mostly private enterprise. We spoke with a seventy-three-year-old mason who worked and lived in a small hut, which, he said, he had rebuilt in 1968 after seeking refuge for three weeks in a pagoda to the south. "Many of my friends and neighbors were killed," he told me. "I work by myself, mostly for people in the neighborhood. Some masons have joined the co-op, but I'm too old anyway, so no one bothers me. I manage to make enough to live on." A few doors away, a slightly younger man, who repaired bicycles, was also working alone, though he said that his twenty-year-old son, a tailor, sometimes helped him out. On the busiest street, Mai Thuc Luan, customers flowed in and out of the shops on both sides; it was hard to tell, though, how many were doing any buying. There was an abundance of tailor shops and it seemed doubtful that they could all survive. I stopped at one in which four employees shared the work and income with the young director, and he maintained that business was "pretty good." A new suit, including the material, cost five hundred and fifty dong, he said—which was about fifty dollars at the then official rate, and less than three dollars at the black market rate—but a pair of jeans made from material smuggled in from Bangkok cost nearly three times as much. "They're the fad nowadays," the young man said. "We sell quite a few." He added that his taxes came to between 20 and 30 percent of the shop's income. I later had a talk with Nguyen Minh Ky, the permanent chief of the provincial secretariat, during which he explained, "We allow tailors to remain independent if they want to, but even those that do are assigned a certain amount of work by the government. We supply them with materials. There are some forms of business, like welding, which have to be organized cooperatively because what welders do complements what others do. Some of the fine arts are also being collectivized, where there are different skills using a variety of raw materials—wood, metals, cloth, lacquer, and so on—that have to be apportioned." I asked Ky if he thought the country was developing a mixed economy, and, like most others I had put this question to, he avoided a direct answer but agreed that "we are slowly working out our own system," adding, "Here in this province we are midway between the north and the south. Our policies represent the north's point of view, as set forth in the Party plenums, but we have our own interpretations of how these policies should be applied, and the government in Hanoi permits us to do things our own way. We have our own traditions here in Hué, including our purity of language, our soft tones, and we are preserving those too."

(2)

From Hué we drove north, stopping first at Dongha, in Cam Lo district, which had been the scene of almost constant fighting and bombing. Dongha, at the junction of Route 1 and Route 9, which runs for about fifty miles across the narrowest part of Vietnam, from the Laotian border to the sea, is the hub of commercial activity involving Laos and Vietnam. The stalls and shops lining both roads for several hundred yards were full of goods, and the air was saturated with dust from the bicycle and foot traffic, and the occasional cars and trucks. Youngsters wearing Western hats and shirts with slogans like "Law Man" dashed up to stare at us. The town was surrounded by uncultivated fields—a sign of still unexploded bombs. A cart came along pulled by an elderly man and a young woman, with a young boy perched on top guarding a new threshing machine, which the old man said he had just bought from his brother for a thousand dong. He was on his way home to his half hectare of rice land along the Ben Hai River, which used to divide North and South Vietnam near the seventeenth parallel. The young girl was his daughter, and she had been a guerrilla in the region during the war; the boy was her nephew. "The bombs were like a steady rain," the old man said. "Many were killed, and those who survived lived underground or were evacuated. Now life is much better." He was very happy about his threshing machine, which he said would cut his work time in half.

A few miles farther north, near the village of Docmieu, the roadside for several hundred yards was piled high with scrap metal from blown-up tanks, armed personnel carriers, and a few shot-down planes and helicopters. Much of this scrap is now being collected and shipped south by rail for melting down and recycling in construction. A sign in English said that this was the site of "the electronic eyes wall of McNamara [the former secretary of defense]. It was destroyed by our forces March 30, 1972." The sign went on to explain that the "wall," which had consisted of radar stations that were supposed to send out signals from several elevations to detect infiltration of troops, was planned originally to extend all the way across to Laos, but only a small portion was completed "before the area was liberated." As we moved slowly along the road toward the river, we passed crowds of women heading home from the Dongha market with baskets on poles laden with vegetables and other goods. The fields here were mostly planted with new rice or had been turned into grazing land. On the south side of the river, a department store was just closing for the long midday break. We walked over the bridge, past a large overhead sign that said "Long Live the Communist Party of Vietnam." Wrecks of amphibious boats still lay in the river. The bridge was built in 1973, but stumps of supports of an old one bombed by the South Vietnamese in 1967 were still standing alongside in the shallow river. Phuong told me that this was the spot where the Provisional Revolutionary Government of South Vietnam had had a forward headquarters and that foreign ambassadors had come here to present their credentials to Madame Nguyen Thi Binh, the PRG foreign minister. Phuong said he had brought George Marchais, the head of the French Communist Party, down to the site from Hanoi, and that among other visitors had been Fidel Castro. The North Vietnamese used to operate a floating theater in the river for propaganda purposes, Phuong added. Less than a mile north of the river, we drove through the new town of Hoxa, the administrative capital of Ben Hai district, which was close to where the town of Conthien had been, another of the war's most devastated and fought-over spots. Hoxa, with new red-brick and red-tiled shops and houses and various administrative headquarters, was the cleanest and neatest place I saw in Vietnam and was an obvious showcase. About the only sign of old-style village rural life was a group of buffalo boys cooling their huge animals and themselves in a large fish pond.

On the way back to Hué I asked to see Quangtri, a few miles to the east, and we swung over there by a side road. The old city, on the banks of the Thach Ham River, was being partially built up, but the new one was being built a mile or so to the south. During the war, Quangtri, which changed hands several times, was the most destroyed city I saw. Refugees by the thousands used to stream back and forth, depending on the tide of battle, seeking temporary safety in Hué or Danang, or on the coast. I remember visiting there in the summer of 1972, soon after the Americans and South Vietnamese had recaptured it after a costly battle that, according to a sign posted along the river, cost "the enemy 28,000 troops killed; including well-known units of the Saigon puppets, paratroopers, marines, commandos, and infantry destroyed or decimated; one hundred and twenty planes, two groups of U. S. puppet tanks and great quantities of war material." The entire town had been reduced to rubble, and much of this remained piled in empty spaces. What I recalled most vividly was that not a single house had been left standing and a lone wall, about eighteen feet high, bore, in huge red scrawl, an obscenity about Jane Fonda. It all seemed like a long time ago, and I suddenly realized that it was.

I had this feeling again the next morning when, back in Hué, I visited the Tu Dam pagoda, one of the country's principal Buddhist shrines, standing in a garden of gnarled trees and wild flowers not far from the center of the city. I had met here several times with Tri Quang and other priests during the height of the Buddhist struggle in the mid-sixties, when Hué rather than Saigon was the center of the antigovernment rebellion. Thich Thien Sieu, who had been the ranking priest back then, was still in charge, I learned, but was unavailable. Instead, after a short wait, I was introduced to thirty-six-year-old Thich Chanh Nghiep, a high priest despite his youth, and the principal provincial secretary of the Unified Vietnamese Buddhist Church, which the Communists established in 1981. It quickly became apparent that Chanh Nghiep belonged to the new breed of bonzes; he had come to terms early on with the regime and, in effect, had become a spokesman for it. "In the old puppet society, our position was one of opposition," he said. "At the outset, we didn't know what the attitude of the new government was, but by the time the Unified Church was created we understood each other better. Now we are stabilized. We have our own charter, and are free to practice our rituals and beliefs. We are established in all districts and villages. People come to us now if they are real believers in Buddhism as a religion. We retain a political role, because the church is closely connected with the nation and both are passing through a historic stage. In the past, we supported the struggle for independence and freedom. Now we can contribute to rebuilding and restoration. There are five hundred and fifty priests and nuns in this province, and a hundred pagodas, and they all have close relations with the people. Problems arise in a few places, where some people don't yet understand the new regulations, such as the limits of political discussion. Our task is to explain these when necessary."

It was difficult to tell whether Chanh Nghiep, who had a schoolmasterish and somewhat smug air about him, was typical of the new priests, but it was significant, I thought, that he, like the government officials I had asked, refused to say much about Tri Quang or other members of the earlier Buddhist leadership who had played such an important part in the sixties and seventies. "Tri Quang is involved in the translation of prayers and no longer has a public role," Chanh Nghiep said. "He is a sedentary man nowadays and doesn't go out much. In the old days he went out whenever there were problems."

From different sources, I subsequently received news of two of the other old-time priests: Thich Thien Minh, who had been more of an active operator than Tri Quang and had played his own ambitious political game, had died in prison in Phan Thiet province, on the coast, after the war; and Thich Minh Chau, who had belonged to a Saigon pagoda whose priests frequently opposed the South Vietnamese government, is now secretary general of the Unified Vietnamese Buddhist Church. Most of the other former Buddhist leaders had fled the country, and of those who had remained behind some had gone underground and been arrested for dissident activity. Of the total of fifteen thousand priests and nuns in 1975, about two-thirds had left the Buddhist movement voluntarily, or been persuaded to leave, and a good many of these, according to what I was able to piece together from informants in Vietnam and refugees in the United States, are now working in opposition to the government in some way

—especially in the south, but to some extent in central Vietnam too. Of some five thousand church people who are still active Buddhists, however, the majority, like Chanh Nghiep, have made their compromises. In discussing religious matters with a number of Western diplomats, I found far more interest in the Catholics, whose position is more complicated and anomalous nowadays. "The Buddhists will survive more readily because they're a more homogeneous group," one of these men said. "They adapt to change more readily and they're no longer as politically motivated as they were. Like all Vietnamese, they know how to survive."

The Catholics have had a longer official history in Vietnam, going back three hundred years; they came to the country as missionaries, even before the French colonists. Politically as well as religiously, they were always active, either behind the scenes, under the French, or openly under Diem, who was a Catholic himself. After 1954, when the country was partitioned following the French defeat, nearly a million Vietnamese fled the north, and the majority of these were Catholics, many of whom assumed leadership roles in professional fields in the south and held top political jobs under Diem. Though they were less dominant after the overthrow of Diem, in 1963, their influence remained considerable until the defeat in 1975 of the government of Nguyen Van Thieu, who was a Catholic convert. The Communists have since cleverly followed a double course. They have permitted the three and a half million Catholics in the country leeway in carrying out formal liturgical ceremonies and rites (confession, however, is discouraged), but have circumscribed any social action, particularly on the part of the Jesuits. Most important, they have limited the replacement of parish priests, now numbering about eighteen hundred, to vacancies that arise upon priests' deaths—an arrangement that does not take into account the country's high birthrate, of nearly

2.5 percent. The number of bishops, about forty, has remained the same, but their activities are carefully watched, and they meet only once every two years at an official conference. Two are under house arrest. The sole cardinal, Trinh Van Canh, who is in poor health, plays a very cautious role, and is a virtual prisoner or recluse in his house in Hanoi. He seldom appears in church and has been allowed to visit the Vatican only once. He has only one servant and hardly ever receives any visitors, Vietnamese or foreign. A priest who is with him much of the time is generally regarded by Westerners as a government spy. Letters and messages Canh receives from other priests are undoubtedly scrutinized before he reads them. His policy is one of discretion and what was described to me as "divine survival," and to the degree that Catholics are free to go to services, which are always well attended and have been characterized by Western Catholics as "joyous occasions," this policy has paid off.

My requests to see the two rebel Catholic bishops, one in Hanoi and the other in Hué, were quickly refused. Of the two, Nguyen Kim Dien, in Hué, has been the most outspoken and confrontational. He was subjected to prolonged questioning in 1984 and suffered a heart attack; after hospitalization, he has remained under strict house arrest. His opposition to the government continues: he objects strenuously to the strictures under which the Church operates—particularly the monitoring of sermons and the failure to allow more than two or three priests a year to be ordained, though some Westerners say others may be ordained secretly; surprisingly, the government is somewhat less strict about nuns, accepting a few more each year and allowing them to work fairly freely in hospitals and orphanages, especially in the south.

The rebel bishop in Hanoi is Nguyen Van Thuan. He is Ngo Dinh Diem's first cousin and was bishop of Nhatrang, in the south, during the war. In 1975, the French papal representative, as one of his final acts before leaving the country, appointed Thuan coadjutor with Archbishop Nguyen Van Binh in Ho Chi Minh City. Soon thereafter, however, as a well-known and outspoken anti-Communist, Thuan was arrested and brought to Hanoi, where he has chosen to remain despite attempts by his brother and sister to persuade him to emigrate to Australia, where they now live.

Archbishop Binh, who presides over the two-thirds of the Catholic population living in the south, has played a cooperative role since 1975. He reportedly said to a departing American at the time, "Tell them in Rome I won't betray the faith or the Church of the Pope. However, I will be pliable where it is possible, and collaborate with the government as long as it asks nothing of me which is contrary to my faith." He voluntarily underwent one week of "reeducation through labor." Binh did not issue a strong protest in June 1983 when thirteen priests and laymen, many of them Jesuits, were brought to trial in Ho Chi Minh City for publishing what were alleged to be counter-revolutionary statements in a Catholic journal called *Religion Incarnate*. The thirteen had been arrested in 1980 and 1981 and held for trial over many months. One man received a life sentence, six received sentences of from three to fifteen years (including the senior Jesuit in the country, who received a twelve-year sentence), two were put on probation, and four were set free. The Vatican took critical notice of the trial but, like Binh, it has adopted a discreet policy toward Vietnam and so far has avoided what has happened in China—an open schism. In the fall of 1983, however, a few months after the trial, the government set up a Committee for the Solidarity of Patriotic Vietnamese Catholics, to succeed an earlier Liaison Committee established in 1955. A number of so-called progressive priests have joined the new committee, but the bishops have ignored it, though they have carefully avoided any public condemnation of it.

Some things, it appears, don't change, no matter who runs a country. Just as Hué has retained its charm, Danang, a two-hour drive to the south along the coast and through the scenic Hai Van Pass, remains as shabby and unprepossessing as it always has been. Where Hué has doubled in size, Danang's population is down by a half, to three hundred and fifty thousand; most of the swollen population, which worked for the Americans in one capacity or another—next to Saigon, Danang had the largest concentration of Americans in Vietnam—has returned to the countryside. All through the war, Danang had a reputation for being anti-American, and I sensed a strong aura of this in the two days I spent there, during which, in contrast to the welcome and help extended to me in Hué, I received virtually no cooperation from the local officials. I was not even permitted to walk, escorted, through the former press camp, which is now a shrimp cannery, the secrecy of which, though not the smell, eluded me. (The smell of foreign exchange, however, as a result of direct sales to Japan and Hong Kong, I later found out, appeals to provincial officials.) I did visit the Cham Museum, across the road, and was happy to see that it had been refurbished with its former stone relics of eleventh-century civilization, which had been stored in nearby mountain caves during the war. The adjacent waterfront, which I spent some time exploring in the afternoon and evening, was far quieter than Ho Chi Minh City's, and the run-down atmosphere was palpable in the empty shops and the looks of boredom on the faces of the shopkeepers and the people lounging about—especially the young men who, as everywhere else, sat idly gossiping in coffee shops. The city, I was told, has the highest rate of unemployment in Vietnam.

At the foot of Marble Mountain, on the outskirts of town, which during the war was the scene of constant guerrilla skirmishes and is now a tourist center featuring stone carvers and a rest center with a beach nearby for factory workers, I ran into a group of army veterans, including a gaunt young man in his mid-thirties on crutches who told me he had been wounded at Chulai, not far to the south. He told me he lived on a small pension. "There is no work here," he said, tonelessly. "There is a lot of unemployment in Danang, things are not good here." When I confirmed, in response to his question, that I was an American, he asked me how much money I made. Before I could reply, he pointed to a teenage boy watching us who was obviously a black Amerasian. The youngster told me he didn't know where his Vietnamese mother was, let alone his American father, but that, like most of the other Amerasian children in Vietnam, he hoped to go to America "soon." The crippled veteran and his friends listened to this conversation with apparent disdain. "There are a lot like him around here," the veteran said, waving his crutch at me. I walked a hundred yards to the beautiful white beach the marines used to use, when there was a lull in the fighting. A man and three boys, who were his son and two nephews, he said, were skimming pebbles over the quiet surf. When I asked him how things were going, he said "difficult." After a careful look around to make sure no one was listening, he told me he was a mechanic and that his wife was a schoolteacher, but that to make ends meet he moonlighted repairing autos on the side. When I told him I was American, he smiled and, after a moment, with a wave of his hand at the scenery, said, "Things have changed here, haven't they?"

I was up at dawn both mornings in Danang, partly because my room at the dismal hotel was infested by ants. Looking out my window, I watched the city come to life and particularly enjoyed the contest—apparently a daily one—between an old woman and a girl who didn't look more than twelve, to see which could set up her vendor's stall first at the choice corner across the steet. They both were selling the same narrow selection of cigarettes and lottery tickets. Each won once, and the loser established herself on her chair ten yards away. During the times I watched, neither sold anything.

(3)

Back in Hanoi, I realized that I had seen very few Chinese during my long trips around the country. Except in Ho Chi Minh City—specifically in Cholon, where there are still perhaps half a million Hoa, as the Vietnamese call them—and in Hanoi and Haiphong, where there are less than half as many, the Chinese population is visibly diminished compared to what it was before the Sino-Vietnamese confrontation of 1978–79. The departure or flight, by one means or another, of an estimated half million Chinese occurred in several phases, or waves. In 1975, in the months before the end of the war and during the period that followed, tens of thousands fled South Vietnam, first with the help of the Americans and then by paying exit bribes to Communist officials and buying their way out in small boats. This exodus continued, somewhat more slowly, until the second half of 1978. Then, after the regime cracked down on capitalist traders and issued new currency to curb inflation and black market money, the next wave left the south. Although this campaign was not directed solely at the Hoa, most of the affected merchants and artisans were Chinese, and subsequently their skills and services were sorely missed. Some months afterward, the government let many of the remaining Hoa leave semi-legally by boat for Hong Kong, Singapore, and Taiwan upon payment of what amounted to a combined tax and bribe. The departure of the Chinese from the north, including many artisans and industrial workers, began in the spring of 1978 and was initially encouraged by the Peking government, which accused Hanoi of persecuting the Hoa minority. There is some evidence that the Vietnamese, preparing to invade Cambodia, did force the Hoa out, in the hope of avoiding any pretext for a Peking counterattack. Other evidence, however, indicates the Vietnamese tried to persuade the Hoa to stay. By the time Peking canceled its aid program and closed its border with Vietnam, in July of that year, about two-thirds of some quarter million Hoa who fled to China from the north had already left. The rest went across the border after the seventeen-day war in February and March 1979, when Hanoi informed them that their only alternative was to go to resettlement areas in the far reaches of the country.

The expulsion or flight of the Hoa certainly contributed to the breakdown of relations with China, which has now become the overriding concern of the Vietnamese, if not as much so of the Chinese. Even when they ultimately do come to some sort of terms with each other, the relationship will never again be as close as it was in the early days of their respective revolutions, from 1924, when Ho Chi Minh arrived in Canton from Moscow and many of his original cadres received training from the Chinese, until the end of the French war in 1954. As already noted, despite the alliance between the two nations being described as "close as lips and teeth," the sporadic friction in the sixties and seventies that led to the break in 1978 and the brief war early in 1979 heralded fundamental differences that were bound to be difficult to overcome. They derived, and still derive, in large part from the suspicions and objectives both countries share. Perhaps even more than the Chinese and the Russians—which is saying a lot —the Vietnamese are obsessed with the idea of their own security and protection of their own borders. For that reason, among others, they still have every intention of dominating all of the former Indo-China area embracing both Laos and Cambodia—and this is the main reason they have been willing to go on fighting in Cambodia for so long at the expense of sacrificing the goodwill and economic support of the Western world and Japan. And, in the final reckoning, as the Chinese are fully aware, China still holds the key to that situation, as it has from the start.

During the war with the Americans, the Vietnamese rode high with confidence and emerged as revolutionary heroes of the world. But things have changed since then. When I saw Prime Minister Pham Van Dong in Hanoi in 1984, he told me of his visit to Peking in 1972, when he spoke with Mao Zedong and Mao warned him, "We Chinese don't have a broom long enough to wipe away Chiang Kai-shek in Taiwan, and you cannot wipe away [Nguyen Van] Thieu either." Dong replied, "We think we do have a broom long enough." Dong was proved right, but Mao's admonition was an omen of what was to come. A resolution of the Taiwan problem has not yet been reached, though sooner or later, in their own way, the Chinese will solve that problem. In the case of the more obdurate and less patient Vietnamese, however, they may discover that they do not have a broom long enough to eliminate the Khmer Rouge in Cambodia, short of making the compromises they have only lately begun to edge toward.

Foreign policy in Communist countries is invariably a reflection of domestic policy, and this is clearly true in Vietnam today. The ascendancy of the pragmatists in propounding and introducing the new liberal economic reforms, including incentives to encourage production, new wage scales, and a clearer redefining of what constitutes the free market, has subdued (though by no means silenced) the hard-line ideologues in the area of foreign policy too. The minorities in the Politburo and on the Party's Central Committee, who see the reforms as opening the country to the dangers of capitalism, are also hesitant to open Vietnam to Western influence at the expense of continuing close ties to the Soviet Union and the Eastern European bloc. If it is true that the pragmatists have won the fight, it seems unlikely that there will be a swing back to conservatism and away from reform when the current Old Guard is replaced by younger leaders. The stage for this important change, in all likelihood, will be set at the Party's Sixth National Congress, which is supposed to take place some time late in 1986 or early in 1987.

The new approach to foreign policy has been reflected in the conduct and statements over the past year or so of the top Vietnamese leaders, including Party secretary Le Duan and Le Duc Tho. In my unusually long and frank talk with Tho in the fall of 1984, he dealt both directly and obliquely with these broad policy matters. About the Chinese he was tolerant and almost forgiving. "We are not surprised about the betrayal of Marxism-Leninism by the Chinese rulers," he said. "The path followed by the Communist Party is never smooth. Even in Vietnam, this has happened. We experienced periods of victory, setback, and then progress again. These things are normal. I am confident that the genuine Chinese Communists will not allow China to continue the present line forever. In the future, they will bring China back to the right course." Tho was careful, as Le Duan has been, in expressing criticism of the Soviet Union, but he said, "We are different from the Soviet Union, which is an industrial country, while we have to find methods of management suitable to an agricultural nation. Severe criticism has been leveled against us because of our supposed conservatism. During the war the assistance given by the Soviet Union and the Eastern bloc was mostly to fight the war and solve questions of the people's living. Our method of management then was bureaucratic, but now we are advancing to socialism by moving away from bureaucratic centralism and using many economic components suitable to a period of transition."

The cautious way in which the Vietnamese are handling these domestic and foreign policy matters reflects a continuing ambivalence and underlines the fact that, like it or not, the country is still heavily dependent on the Soviet

Union for military and economic assistance. Some seven thousand Russians, mostly technicians, are still in Vietnam, along with about fifteen hundred Eastern Europeans. Pham Binh, the head of a think tank called the Institute for International Relations, attached to the Foreign Ministry, and with whom I also spoke at length, clearly espoused the old Party line, coupling harsh criticism of China with an almost idolatrous defense of the Soviet Union. "Our relationship of friendship and solidarity with the Soviet Union is our paramount concern," he said. "There is no other country in the world that could do what the Soviet Union has done—give us a billion dollars' worth of aid a year for twenty years, and build nearly two hundred factories for us. Good economic relations with other countries are no obstacle as far as the Russians are concerned, but we resent any effort to use such aid as a tool to separate us from the Soviet Union." The Vietnamese have been making some efforts lately to broaden their foreign contacts, not only with Indonesia and other ASEAN countries but with India, which has always been considered a friend. In the fall of 1984, Le Duan made his first diplomatic visit to a non-Communist nation when he visited India, and in 1985 General Van Tien Dung, the defense minister, who is considered a hard-liner, visited both India and Indonesia.

After the Politburo's decision at the end of 1984 to change tactics and make conciliatory approaches toward both Washington and Peking, Le Duan, in a speech marking the fifty-fifth anniversary of the founding of the Vietnamese Communist Party, in Hanoi in February 1985, followed this up by declaring he was "firmly convinced that friendship between China and Vietnam will have to be restored. This cannot be otherwise." A week or so later, in mid-February, Le Duc Tho visited France to attend a congress of the French Communist Party—something he had never done before—and in his speech there, beyond avoiding any attacks on China or use of the usual pejorative term "hegemonists" to describe China, said, "The time has come for all parties concerned to sit down together to seek a peaceful solution to the problems concerning the three Indochinese countries." There were reports later, though they were unconfirmed, that Tho had met secretly with the Chinese in Paris. Furthermore, Foreign Minister Thach, who has been given increasing leeway to make diplomatic moves on his own, although the Politburo still makes the final decisions, recently wrote a highly conciliatory letter to Wu Xueqian, the Chinese foreign minister, thanking China for all its help to Vietnam in the past and suggesting "secret talks in order to restore our old friendship." The Chinese did not respond officially, apparently doubting Vietnam's sincerity and deciding to wait for a more positive sign of Vietnamese willingness to compromise on Cambodia. However, Hu Yaobang, the Chinese Communist Party general secretary, did say in a subsequent speech that China favored better relations with Vietnam and that a commitment by the Vietnamese in principle to get out of Cambodia would be favorably received. And at the fortieth anniversary of Vietnam's independence, in September 1985, the Chinese sent a congratulatory message which expressed hopes for normalization on the part of the Chinese "government" as well as "the Chinese people." In November, the Vietnamese attended an international trade fair in Peking, for the first time. As a member of the Vietnamese delegation to the United Nations in New York commented to me a few weeks later, "We have begun at least to reach the state of what you Americans called Ping-Pong diplomacy."

(4)

The road from Hanoi north to Langson and the Chinese border twists and winds and eventually climbs for a total of a hundred miles through some of the most starkly beautiful parts of the country. History unrolls along the way; the residue of violence that depicts the four decades of Vietnam's embattled revolutionary existence; the faded brick hilltop remnants of old French forts and bunkers built seventy-five or a hundred years ago; the bombed and broken bridges and still unrepaired factories destroyed in the war against the Americans; and then Langson itself, a sleepy, vulnerable town which the Chinese battered badly in their brief and inconclusive attack in 1979. The road is drenched in the dust of swarms of carts and trucks and bouncing bicycles loaded with fruits and vegetables, the carcasses of skinny cattle and fat pigs, and chickens and ducks, dead or alive, tied together with ropes or staring and bobbing foolishly in wicker and wire cages. The new green rice rising high after the recent rains stands ready to be harvested, and farther along the way, on the higher slopes, there are fields of maize and soybeans and manioc. Women by the roadside peddle baskets of pineapples, coconuts, and, mostly, lush breadfruit; we bargain for and finally buy five breadfruit for a hundred and sixty dong, which is less than a dollar at the black market rate. No one in Vietnam lives by the rules, whether farmer or city dweller, and, despite the constant talk about poverty and underdevelopment, the people, including the children and the elderly, look healthy. Food is obviously no longer a problem, but, as in all underdeveloped nations, and some developed ones, too, distribution is. We only had to look at the dilapidated trains—ancient French, Chinese, and Russian rolling stock—that chugged alongside us at twenty miles an hour, if they chugged at all. A Belgian woman I know who works for a consortium that markets locomotives has been trying for three years to sell a few to the Vietnamese. "They want them, they need them, but I keep being sent from office to office," she told

me. "No one can make a decision. That's the story of
Vietnam."

In Langson, at the headquarters of the Ha Tuyen Provincial People's Committee, Nguyen Phi Long, the secretary, who is a plump man in his mid-fifties, invites me to
join him at a long table set with tea and cookies as I get
the usual briefing. Long reveals that he is ethnically a Kinh
—as are the overwhelming majority of the Vietnamese—
and he tells me that minority ethnic groups in the north
include the Nung, the Tai, the San Chi, the Dao, the
Muong, the Cao Lan, and the Hoa. "We consider them all
Vietnamese," he said.

"Even the Hoa?" I ask.

"Yes, those that are still left," Long replies, with a smile.
"The minorities have lived together for thousands of
years. They are good fighters. They have fought against
the Chinese for centuries. In almost every century there
was at least one famous battle." He starts listing them for
me, and I listen, sipping the hot tea. The Vietnamese love
to tell stories about the war—any war. Long's voice drones
on. "In the thirteenth century we defeated Kublai Khan,"
he is saying. Then, after a while: "This was one of Ho's
earliest revolutionary headquarters. During the battle of
Dienbienphu it was a storage area." He passes over the
American war, perhaps because there was little bombing
this far north, but he recounts the details of the Chinese
invasion six years ago. "They came through Friendship
Pass, just up the road," he said. "There were six columns
attacking and one column struck for Langson. But they
only occupied the city for two days, from March third until
March fifth. By the eleventh we had driven them out of
the province. But they did a lot of damage." He takes a
piece of paper out of his pocket and reads a list to me:
thirty schools, five district hospitals, fifty-seven bridges
and water tunnels, and twenty-seven industrial establishments. As for the present, Long says, "The Chinese have

stationed three kinds of troops along the border—regular, local, and guerrilla—and they still shell us regularly. They are building new roads now. The tension will continue. I consider these activities closely related to the Chinese Communist action in Cambodia and support of Pol Pot forces there. They are trying to weaken our economy, and they will attack us again if the opportunity arises. We must carry out the twin tasks—production and defense."

It has started to rain, and by the time my interpreter and I reach the entrance to Friendship Pass, which is the historic invasion route from China, it is pouring hard. We walk the final few hundred yards near the border and then run for a small guard post, where a single twenty-one-year-old soldier is on duty. He, too, is Kinh, he tells us, and his home is only a kilometer or so away. He is assigned here for two months. Though the shelling has diminished lately, the Chinese have increased their loud-speaker propaganda messages from twice a day to even sometimes one or two at night. "They keep talking about Le Duan as a tyrant and about our being aggressors," he said. "But a moment later they suggest we barter goods—they want to give us blankets and cloth for our flashlights and medicinal products."

I can barely make out a Chinese radio station at the top of the highest hill on the other side of the border. It does not look like much of a threat, and it all remains very peaceful, if wet. Standing there in the mist with the soldier and my guide at the bottom of the long ridge of mountains, I feel like a small figure barely visible against the huge majesty of nature in a Sung-dynasty landscape. And I think, as I so often did during the war, that Vietnam would be a breathtakingly beautiful country for the rest of the world to get to know, if only it could find the way to enduring peace.

CHAPTER FOUR

The War Through Vietnamese Eyes

(1)

Much has been written about the Vietnam war during the past decade by historians and military analysts, as well as by novelists, poets, and playwrights. More is bound to appear as additional information becomes available and as perspectives continue to be revised and modified. This has been the case with most wars, from both a literary and historical standpoint, and it is likely to be all the more true of Vietnam because of the long and acrimonious debate the war provoked and the many conflicting emotions it aroused. The fact that it is the only war the United States has ever lost—though how and why and to what degree *we* lost it, over and above the pain and damage we caused, is part of the ongoing discussion and debate—will in itself keep the pot boiling. A certain amount of revisionist opinion has already been expressed, by military officers among others, some of whom have been critical of what we didn't do, or did badly, while others have blamed us for doing too much. Writers of fiction have begun to adopt broader, and in some instances less angry or strident, points of view, and it seems likely that many more novels and short stories will be written about the Vietnam "experience"—a widely used word that, in itself, denotes a broad spectrum of shifting emotions and reactions.

Considerable official data have been released by American sources, but a lot more remain classified or have not yet been fully interpreted. Motives and motivations are being reappraised by participants and nonparticipants encompassing a variety of academic disciplines, and biographers are resorting to personal accounts of heroes and anti-heroes to make judgments about the war. Its impact on America's role in the world will continue to be argued by political and social scientists for years to come, and there may be no final or definitive answers.

To make all this more complicated and intriguing, we still have only part of the picture before us—the American part. What about the Vietnamese? As I discovered during my six weeks' visit to Vietnam, they have only begun to pull the pieces of the war's history together; they have been so preoccupied with pulling the country itself together while prosecuting a new war in Cambodia that the process of recording and evaluating the American war, let alone the French war that preceded it, is likely to take many more years. As one army historian in Hanoi commented to me, "We've been too busy fighting for forty years to have time for much else. But we are trying to set down as much as we can, including the history of all the battalions that were engaged in battle. The task is not made easier by the fact that we lost so many lives—more than one million—and that we don't actually know where many of our former soldiers are now."

Even when the Vietnamese do record as much of their war history as possible, it will take additional time to translate and analyze the results, and to correlate all the material and compare it with American sources. However, some important works have already appeared in English, notably a number of personal memoirs, both fiction and nonfiction, and two seminal histories of the final campaign that culminated in the fall of Saigon on April 29–30, 1975. These are *Our Great Spring Victory*, by General Van Tien Dung, who led the climactic battle for "the liberation of

South Vietnam" and who is now minister of defense and a Politburo member, and a more controversial and interesting work translated by the Foreign Broadcast Information Service entitled *Vietnam: History of the Bulwark B-2 Theatre. Volume 5: Concluding the 30-Years War* by Lieutenant General Tran Van Tra, who was a deputy commander during the final campaign. Ten thousand copies of General Tra's account were printed in Vietnamese and put on sale in Hanoi and elsewhere early in 1983 and were then suddenly withdrawn from circulation, without any announcement. He had chosen to write the last of five projected volumes first, he said in his Preface, because "it is appropriate to the requirements of so many people, especially the men of B-2," which is the "code-name of the land and people in the southernmost part of the homeland during the anti-U.S. war period," including the Mekong Delta, Saigon, and part of the jungle and mountain area north of the capital. The B-2 front accounted for about half the land and two-thirds of the people in South Vietnam. Although no reason was given for the withdrawal of the book—and none of the other four volumes has yet appeared—the unofficial explanation I heard was that it was too "self-serving," "too oriented to the concerns of the south," and contained too many "questionable" conclusions. General Tra, though an early member of the Laodong (Workers') Party and of the North Vietnamese Army, is a southerner who grew up partly in Saigon. Since the book appeared, he has been living in seclusion north of the city and has not been allowed to receive any foreign visitors.

The final drive to capture Saigon, which became known as the Ho Chi Minh Campaign, was a remarkable and unusual example of how the North Vietnamese high command, guided by the Politburo, was able to make quick, flexible readjustments in its strategy and tactics during the first four months of 1975 in order to seize the capital and end the war a year earlier than had originally been planned. This was the result of the unexpectedly rapid collapse of South Vietnamese forces, beginning with the loss, for the first time in the war, of an entire province, Phuoc Long, northwest of Saigon on the Cambodian border, which took place late in December of 1974 and early in January of 1975. Phuoc Long set the stage for the capture, two months later, on March 10, of the key city of Banmethuot in the Central Highlands, which the Vietnamese call the Tay Nguyen. Thereafter, in panic and flight, the South Vietnamese gave up the rest of the highlands, including the cities of Pleiku and Kontum, in a desperate and futile effort to bolster their forces in the northern tier of the country, along the coast from Quangtri province and city and the cities of Hué and Danang, all of which fell to the Communists in the last part of March. Pushing swiftly southward along coastal Route 1, they then took one province after another so rapidly that, as General Dung quoted one of his Front Command cadres as saying, "I can't draw maps fast enough to keep up with our troops."

Not even the most pessimistic Americans, following the withdrawal of American forces from Vietnam in 1973, had predicted that the South Vietnamese would collapse so precipitately. Nor, as both Generals Dung and Tra make clear in their detailed accounts of the last six months of the war and the decisions that were made, did the North Vietnamese expect such a debacle. Even after the fall of Banmethuot and the surrender without any further major fighting of the rest of the highlands, several high level discussions and debates were conducted in Hanoi over whether to press ahead more quickly "if the opportune moment presents itself," or to stick to the original plan and move slowly, attacking the Mekong Delta and key provinces in other areas around Saigon before mounting the final assault in the dry season of 1976. But on

March 25, when pandemonium on the South Vietnamese side set in at Danang and troops fought each other to escape aboard helicopters and transport planes—and even before the rest of the coastal plain had begun to collapse—the Politburo decided to go for broke and take Saigon before the onset of the monsoon season in May. Early in April, southern forces put up one last valiant defense at the town of Xuanloc in Long Khanh province, just northeast of Saigon. After a fierce eleven-day battle, Xuanloc fell on April 20, and nine days later, after troops were carefully positioned all around the city, North Vietnamese tanks were at Saigon's gates. From the hotel roofs, we could see them coming down the Bien Hoa highway on the night of April 28–29, their lights and those of troop-carrying trucks brazenly shining.

Though the South Vietnamese fought bravely to protect some of the bridges leading into the city, and a few other key points, everyone knew it was over, and by the morning of the twenty-ninth, most government leaders, including President Nguyen Van Thieu, had fled the country. It was Thieu, who had once been a division commander, who personally ordered the ill-conceived retreat from the highlands that led to such quick disaster. He still blames the United States for having let him down by failing to replenish South Vietnam's arms and ammunition losses of the previous months, as the Americans had pledged to do when they signed the 1973 peace agreement with the North Vietnamese, and in effect forced the South Vietnamese to go along with it. The proclaimed cease-fire never worked, and a fresh round of skirmishing began at once, soon followed by renewed serious fighting. In the first few months after the cease-fire, and in the weeks prior to it, the United States did give the South Vietnamese ample assistance, replacing equipment losses on a one-for-one basis as promised and even adding substantially more; but thereafter the amount dropped off sharply and, at the end, Congress refused any further emergency aid, military or economic. In my own view, having been in Vietnam much of the time after the Paris 1973 agreement and been there when Saigon was about to fall, additional American aid after the capture of Banmethuot would have made little or no difference. The will to fight and the ability to withstand the North Vietnamese final onslaught simply did not exist.

Throughout the long war, and in the war against the French climaxed by their stunning victory at Dienbienphu in May 1954, the North Vietnamese had won a reputation for their meticulous long-term planning—in their words, for "preparing the battlefield"—before launching an attack. More often than not, they set their plans down in documents, many of which, including some false ones containing "disinformation," were captured by the Americans and the South Vietnamese. Nevertheless, the Communists invariably managed to retain the element of surprise, in their major battles as well as in the hundreds of small-scale attacks and counterattacks that overall cost their foreign enemies—both the Americans and the French—some of the wars' heaviest casualties. Neither the French nor the Americans, let alone the South Vietnamese—who lacked the determination and revolutionary convictions and the prescience of their northern compatriots—ever sufficiently realized that preparing the battlefield was a twofold process—political as well as military. The Vietnamese term for political struggle is *dau tranh chinh tri,* and throughout the war it involved the use of hundreds and ultimately thousands of agit-prop and administrative cadres who constantly worked in South Vietnam's twenty-five hundred villages to undermine Saigon's tenuous control of the countryside. Indeed, so careful and cautious were the Communists that they seldom committed their forces to *dau tranh vu trang,* or armed struggle, until the political ground had been fully prepared. A number of experienced American observers believe that this combined political and military caution caused the Communists to make their biggest mistake of the war early in 1965, just before the first American troops landed in Danang, when they were on the verge of cutting South Vietnam in two in the highlands and thereby gaining victory, ten years earlier.

Despite the fact that the Vietnamese history of the recent war is not yet written, I had the opportunity, when I was in Hanoi, of interviewing a number of military experts and historians and obtaining their preliminary opinions and judgments about the conflict against the Americans and South Vietnamese, and how they compared it to the war against the French and France's supporting colonial troops, including Senegalese, Moroccans, Foreign Legionnaires, and others, as well as South Vietnamese. Among those I spoke with at length were Brigadier General Hoang Phuong, the chief army historian, and retired Major General Dinh Duc Thien, who is Le Duc Tho's brother and who was in charge of logistics during the French war; from 1965 until the capture of Saigon, he was again chief of the General Logistics Department and directed the major expansion of the famous Ho Chi Minh Trail, supervising the transport of men and material—including oil flowing through two specially constructed pipelines—down the length of the trail from the rear areas of the north to the farflung battlefields of the south. I had naturally heard of and written a good deal about the trail during many years in South Vietnam, but it was not until I spoke with Generals Phuong and Thien and others, and obtained as much written material about the trail as I could, that I realized what a truly vital role it played in the North Vietnamese victory. All those I spoke with agreed that it was the single most important factor in the war's success, and the more I learned about it the more impressed I was by the remarkable performance, the amazing ingenuity, and the unbelievable feats of endurance of the thousands of Vietnamese, women as well as men, who took part in its construction and operation.

(2)

On Ho Chi Minh's birthday, May 19, 1959, a few days after the North Vietnamese Politburo had met and agreed to support the new armed struggle in the south, Major General Nguyen Van Vinh, a standing member of the Central Military Committee, telephoned Brigadier General Vo Bam and asked him to come immediately to the committee's office in Hanoi. As General Bam recently recalled, Vinh told him to start organizing "a special military communications line to send supplies to the revolution in the south and to create conditions for its development." Vinh pledged Bam to "absolute secrecy"—he told him not to take notes and henceforth to commit to memory all orders and communications. Vinh further said that "the special trail" was to be used for "cadres, combatants, arms, and medical supplies" and that, for a start, Bam would be assigned five hundred men who were "southern comrades regrouped in the north" after the Geneva Conference of 1954, when Vietnam was divided at the seventeenth parallel. All the men chosen to work on the trail would be regroupees, Vinh added, and weapons would be confined to those seized from the French. Neither of the last two stipulations proved to be permanent, but they demonstrate the narrow and somewhat skeptical basis on which the trail was initially conceived to give limited assistance to the southern revolutionaries, who were expected to be mainly self-supporting.

That same afternoon, according to General Bam's account, he met with a man named Tran Luong, who had been one of his political officers during the war against the French in central Vietnam and had now been chosen as one of a small group of leaders assigned to building up the South Vietnam Armed Liberation Forces. Luong told him that by the end of 1959 a hundred military cadres up to the rank of lieutenant colonel had to be sent south, along with seven thousand weapons, in order to organize seven hundred self-defense platoons that would serve as the nucleus of the new southern army. Bam next visited several other South Vietnamese veterans of the French war who had come north and told them of the plans. When he said he intended to hand over supplies at a point north of the Ben Hai River at the seventeenth parallel, they demurred. "That means you're giving the south nothing," one of them said. "We have no porters, no scouts, no liaison men, no rice. We can rely only on people. How can we take weapons from here to the south? The most difficult part of the trip is the crossing of Highway 9, which is patrolled by the enemy day and night." This key road, which I had visited a fortnight before my conversations in Hanoi, runs westward from the port of Cuaviet on the China Sea through Dongha and Khesanh to lower Laos. It was both an economic lifeline and a defense line dividing the two Vietnams, and in both wars it had been the scene of major fighting. When he had heard the southerners' complaints, General Bam obtained General Vinh's agreement to set up three secret way stations south of Highway 9 to serve as logistic transfer points.

After selecting a main storehouse on the outskirts of Hanoi to stock arms and other supplies, General Bam and a small group of his scouts went on a three-day trek through the jungle and mountains of Quang Binh and Vinh Linh provinces in North Vietnam, following the trails of lumbermen and of local Van Kieu tribesmen. They chose a spot in the Khe Ho forest not far north of the Ben Hai as a starting point for the original battalion of Group 559, as the secret unit was named (signifying

May 1959). In June, the first of the battalion's twelve platoons crossed the Ben Hai, and in August word came from
the south that the first small shipments of arms and medical supplies, totaling about six hundred pounds, had been
safely received. Shortly afterward, General Bam made his
initial inspection trip of the new trail. It took him four
days to reach Highway 9 along the newly plotted paths,
and each day he and his scouts were conducted by a different native guide, sometimes an old man with a crossbow
slung over his shoulder and a chignon of poisoned bam-
boo arrows on his head, or a young boy in a loincloth, or
occasionally a young Van Kieu girl wearing a brightly col-
ored skirt and blouse. When they reached the highway, at
a point between two enemy posts so close that they could
hear voices and laughter, the guide of the day, a middle-
aged Van Kieu, laid a plastic sheet across the road, and
the last member of the group to cross rolled it up and
carried it with him. Later, a culvert under the roadbed was
discovered and this became a safer way of crossing. The
culvert emerged near the north bank of the Thach Ham
river in South Vietnam, where a hidden sampan lay ready
to transfer goods to the next relay post on the southern
bank. As General Bam subsequently wrote, "Only here in
the south could we have an idea of the difficulties and
hardships our porters had to endure." At the outset new
trails had to be hacked out of the heavy jungle while the
porters struggled to carry loads of ammunition and guns
averaging a hundred or more pounds per man. "Most of
the southern porters wore a pair of shorts, a patched-up
shirt, and a leaf-hat, and had with them a ball of rice and
some salt." Bam added, "They walked day after day,
month after month, scrupulously obeying the instruction,
'No footprint, no cooking smoke, no sound of conversation.' In the dry season we would gather dead leaves into
something like the lair of a wild boar in which to sleep.
The greatest hardships came with the rainy season. Often,

in order to sleep at all at night, we had to drape plastic sheets over our heads and sit with our backs leaning against a tree."

The Truong Son chain of mountains below the seventeenth parallel has peaks that vary from eighteen hundred to three thousand feet in height. Running northwest to southeast, the chain consists of an eastern and a western range, with the eastern being generally steeper; after some towering peaks near the Laos-Vietnam border, the western range slopes down toward the Laotian plains. More than two hundred rivers cut deep ravines and valleys through both ranges, which the French called the Annamite chain, and, during the rainy season of sudden tropical storms, flash floods send water cascading toward the Vietnamese coast and cause vast damage to peasants cultivating their fields. In the dry season, the "Lao wind" from the southwest sweeps through valleys and foothills causing a prolonged dryness that withers all vegetation. Dense tropical forests below the twenty-four-hundred-foot level cover the mountains and cut off the sun's rays, while higher up evergreens laden with moss from the tropical rains create a constant vapor and a dense humidity. The forests abound in wild animals, including elephants, tigers, panthers, and wild boars, as well as large numbers of deer and smaller creatures, and, at lower levels, countless varieties of birds.

The Ho Chi Minh Trail initially followed the eastern range. For many months after it was staked out, the South Vietnamese and their newly arrived American advisers knew nothing of the transport columns that were slowly bringing material south. But the friendly Van Kieu tribesmen observed everything, though they kept out of sight so as not to cause the porters concern. The transport groups often wondered why the paths they traversed were so deserted, though occasionally they would find clusters of ripe bananas and other fruit mysteriously hung on branches along the sides of the paths. At first the porters were afraid to eat them, but then Vietminh underground cadres in the Truong Son villages explained that the tribesmen were offering gifts and that, out of courtesy, let alone hunger, the porters should accept them. Early in 1960, however, when the South Vietnamese set up more military outposts in the mountain areas and dispatched Protestant missionaries to the highland hamlets in an effort to win over the ethnic minorities, suspicions about what the North Vietnamese were up to began to grow. The discovery of a bundle of rifles inadvertently left behind one night alongside Highway 9, near a coffee plantation, led to a South Vietnamese troop sweep through the area and interrupted the flow of material for several weeks. This also prompted General Bam to report to Party Secretary Le Duan personally about progress on the trail, and when Duan heard about its being discovered he asked Bam to "try and find another route which would attract less enemy attention."

After mulling the problem over, Bam suggested that the only workable alternative would be to use the western side of the Truong Son range. To do so, however, would require diplomatic arrangements with Laos. Bam reconnoitered the area to make sure it was feasible, and then returned to Hanoi in January 1961 to discuss it with Tran Luong, who had given him his original instructions to open a trail to the south. Luong told him he had already spoken with Lao Party leaders, who had agreed to let the Vietnamese use their territory in return for help in transporting supplies south to prosecute their own revolution against right-wing Lao forces. Under the terms of the Zurich agreement of 1961, a tripartite coalition was to be set up in Laos to include forces of the royal government, revolutionary elements led by Prince Souphanouvong, and right-wingers led by Phoumi Nosavan. The Lao Communists wanted the Vietnamese to wipe out right-wing positions along Highway 9 and open a fifty-kilometer corridor to facilitate the dispatch of troops and material south. According to a subsequent agreement on Laos, in 1962, which the United States helped arrange, North Vietnam pledged to respect Laotian neutrality, but Hanoi never abided by its terms. Instead, the Vietnamese Communists quickly gained control of a whole stretch of eastern Laos from the town of Tchepone southward to Muongphin. This seizure and consolidation of territory thus created the conditions for the success of both the Lao and Vietnamese revolutions and formed a solid base for the establishment of what became a major part of the Ho Chi Minh Trail.

As this new trail in western Vietnam and eastern Laos was built up, the problem of feeding thousands of porters and troops moving southward at the rate of twelve to twenty miles a day became more difficult. In these early years, transit time from the north to the south was about six months, including periodic "rest days" to recuperate from the arduous jungle treks and from attacks of malaria, which affected about half the people who traveled the trail. Initially, approximately one hundred way stations a day's march apart were established along the route, and the porters would shuttle rice and weapons from one station to another in shifts, often making two round trips in twenty-four hours. The going was slow and painful, even with the help of trucks north of the seventeenth parallel to bring material to the starting point at the Lao-Vietnamese border. In the early sixties, the North Vietnamese General Staff decided for a time to use cargo planes to carry goods as far as Tchepone, where a large storage depot was set up in a valley of the Lum Bum plain in the Lao province of Savannakhet. Rice and ammunition were dropped there by parachute. Although the use of planes had to be abandoned when the Americans began bombing the Ho Chi Minh Trail regularly, in May 1965, the Lum Dum depot remained a major storage point for the truck traffic, which by that time had begun to move along the extended route of the trail. Actually, the supply route can be said to have begun at the China border or the port of Haiphong and reached all the way down to the outskirts of Saigon, a distance of more than a thousand miles; but, more strictly, the trail began at the two main mountain passes between Vietnam and Laos, Mu Gia and Ban Karai, and ended in the three South Vietnamese mountain provinces of Pleiku, Kontum, and Darlac; a further link, via Cambodia, reached deeper south to the key border province of Tay Ninh, northwest of Saigon.

The widening and expansion of the trail was a slow but steady procedure. As it was broadened and hard-packed with mud and clay, bicycles were introduced, mostly ordinary Czechoslovak-made ones converted to carrying as much ammunition, food, and medicines as possible. Similar bikes had been used at Dienbienphu in 1954. The average vehicle carried a load of two hundred and fifty to three hundred pounds, but the record on the Ho Chi Minh Trail was established by a man named Nguyen Dieu, who managed to load more than nine hundred pounds on his "steel horse," which was about two hundred pounds more than the Dienbienphu record. The history and function of the trail underwent their most important changes in 1965, when motorized transport was introduced. This coincided with the return to active duty of Major General Thien, who since the end of the French war had been in charge of industry for the army. A tall man for a Vietnamese, who resembles his more famous brother, Le Duc Tho, Thien, when I spoke with him in Hanoi, began by emphasizing the importance of the lessons learned at Dienbienphu. "If we had had our routes of approach to the battlefield built in advance of 1954," he said, "the campaign would not have been so protracted. As it was, we had to build hundreds of kilometers of roads from scratch, in difficult country, and our approaches were not just from Hanoi but from the whole northern area. Something else we learned at Dienbienphu was the use of camouflage on a large scale. History can always serve your needs and your goals, and in building the Ho Chi Minh Trail we learned how to apply those valuable lessons of the past to the present as well as to the future. In 1965, the trail, of course, was already in existence, but to meet the requirements of the battlefield by changing to truck transport, and then to build alternate routes and side roads because of the heavy American bombing and U.S. technology of detection, required new methods and responses on our part that went far beyond the experience of Dienbienphu."

Thien pointed out that, in the war against the Americans, the North Vietnamese rear was the vital element, which was not a factor in the French war, when there was no rear as such. By rear, he added, he meant both "the national rear, including the political and economic system and everyone working toward the single goal of victory," and the specific "military rear" of supply, which the army ran. "There were three things to keep in mind," Thien said. "The importance of transportation in the rear zone, the Ho Chi Minh Trail in the middle, and the various routes to the front in the south." The basic middle section zigzagged and crisscrossed along a rectangular mountain corridor that covered about seven hundred miles. But within the corridor the parallel routes ranging from passable roadways to almost impassable tracks, and including about ten rivers or navigable streams that became an integral part of the trail system, totaled another thirty-five hundred miles. One American helicopter pilot commented about this complex pattern, "The Ho Chi Minh Trail is no Pennsylvania Turnpike. It's more like a plate of spaghetti."

As this vast network grew, and as the North Vietnamese

gradually took over the burden of the war after the Tet offensive of 1968, which cost the Vietcong such heavy casualties, the operation of the trail required many more men and supplies than it had at the outset. Regular army engineering battalions with modern road-building and other equipment took charge, and a whole panoply of twelve major storage depots, underground offices, bunkers, infirmaries, classrooms, and living quarters was built. According to General Thien, about thirty thousand men worked and served on the trail at the height of its activity, not including those in the rear and front areas. American estimates were higher—fifty thousand by the end of the war, mostly porters, plus another fifty thousand engineering and maintenance workers, and twelve thousand North Vietnamese antiaircraft artillerymen defending the trail complex against air attacks. Thien estimated that in the decade between 1965 and 1975, half a million fighting soldiers passed up and down the trail, in addition to those working on it. From a total of eighteen hundred persons who used the trail in 1959, when the eastern branch was opened, the infiltration rate rose to five thousand soldiers a year in the sixties, and then went up sharply in the seventies when, as General Dung wrote, "a river of revolutionary forces" moved down. Tonnage along the trail increased from a paltry hundred tons a week in 1963 to more than ten thousand weekly in 1970. Based on aerial surveys, the Americans estimated that in the period between 1969 and 1973 an average of two to three thousand trucks a day were on the trail, but on one exceptional day in December 1970, a survey showed that fifteen thousand trucks were moving along the whole length of the corridor and subsidiary roads. Much of the tonnage that came down was necessarily consumed by those working on the trail; the Americans figured that ten tons of supplies had to be moved to deliver one ton to its ultimate destination on a battlefront.

Between 1965 and 1975, General Thien told me, American aircraft dropped nearly four million tons of bombs on the trail. The Americans admit to only half that tonnage, which they say was a quarter of the total of bombs dropped during the entire Vietnam war, and they estimate that they destroyed between 15 and 20 percent of the cargo transported on the trail. No area during the war was exposed to greater steady bombardment. The United States constantly sent waves of high-flying B-52 bombers from Guam and from Thailand over the trail's length, and used every variety of plane down to helicopter gunships that swept low over the treetops firing rockets from pods. In turn, the Vietnamese employed about a thousand antiaircraft weapons emplaced in a hundred and fifty gun batteries, including 37 mm and 100 mm guns, and surface-to-air missiles. They claim to have shot down 2,450 planes in more than a hundred thousand attacks. The North Vietnamese used a variety of camouflage tactics to throw the Americans off track, such as false truck convoys with fake headlights, and fake bridges and supply dumps. As the war went on, camouflage techniques played an increasingly important function. This was notably the case when the Americans began using A-130 surveillance planes specially equipped with heat and light sensors and noise detectors, along with rockets and 40 mm cannon. Flying at relatively low levels at night, the A-130s, which the North Vietnamese nicknamed Thugs, caused heavy damage to trucks traveling in the dark, when the sensitive equipment installed in the planes could easily detect the flow of traffic and a few buttons were pressed to release the sophisticated destructive armament. But during the day, truck drivers reported, the A-130s appeared to be far less dangerous because their light sensors didn't respond to ordinary daylight and because they had to fly considerably higher to avoid being shot down by antiaircraft fire. "We then decided to return to daylight trucking," General

Thien said, "but this created fresh problems, mostly how to avoid being seen on the roads. The answer was a whole new form of camouflage." Along some parts of the trail, natural canopies of forest provided a safe cover for traffic. But there were many open spaces and river crossings where daytime travel was hazardous. Trucks had to be specially and heavily camouflaged, and many sections of roads were partially covered by transplanting trees with broad branches along the sides and by stringing across creeping vines and hanging baskets of plants. By 1973, after several thousand miles of freshly canopied roads had been built, trucks were able to move by day as well as night along the entire route of the trail. The traffic flow was uninterrupted and was heavier than ever. Then, when the Americans withdrew from the war, the bombing virtually ceased.

At the outset of the war, the Americans used conventional methods of detecting the trail traffic, mostly local tribesmen perched on mountaintops to keep watch of all movements. Long-range infiltration teams from Vietnam were later sent in to gather data and radio them to various headquarters in Thailand to help guide bomber pilots. As the war progressed, sophisticated technology took over and a variety of new devices were employed to cut down traffic. These included sensors dropped from the air that dug into the ground with only their plantlike antenna exposed, or that hung in trees; they were so sensitive that they could pick up voices and the sound of truck engines hundreds of yards away. Other smaller sensors called buttons were dropped into areas of deep vegetation and sent out short bursts of radio signals when they were stepped on or touched; planes overhead then computerized the signals and relayed the information to pilots. Infrared photography helped detect tunnels and caves used for storage or as hiding places, while a specially designed camera called Starlight, capable of picking up and magnifying a small light on the ground from the air, helped steer planes to targets. None of these devices, as the Americans later admitted, led to any major reduction of traffic along the trail. General Thien told me, "Sensors, time bombs, cluster bombs, magnetic mines—they all looked like great dangers at first, but we always found ways to detect them and render them useless. For example, by moving a man with a long wire ahead of a line of trucks or porters we were able to set off a whole series of hidden mines. We learned how to tell a sensor drop from a bomb drop—the sensors were long-bodied and came down more slowly, while the bombs were round and dropped quickly. A plane laying sensors made a different kind of dive than a bomber, so we knew when to take cover and when it was safe. We also figured out how to handle cluster bombs, which consisted of a mother bomb linked to smaller clusters by eight wires: all we had to do was throw grenades at them, or just drag a heavy tree branch across the wires from a safe distance. We called this *bom vuong no,* or 'bomb tangle explode.' We had a lot of admiration for the Americans' technology, but in the long run it proved futile because we could foil it. You can cope with even the most sophisticated inventions if you know how. Once we found answers, we had to teach the people what to do, including the tribal and local population along the trail, and this in itself required a tremendous human effort which the civilian government, not the army, directed."

Thien, who was in charge of all trail transportation, found this a more difficult part of his job than dealing with bombs and the technology of surveillance. During the rainy season, when the roads were often impassable, the task of supplying trail workers with food and adequate medical care was especially difficult. In fact, Thien said, "the climate and overall problems of the environment were the greatest obstacles we faced." The seasons varied over different sections of the Truong Son chain, and this meant that there were only three months or so a year when the weather was generally dry all over. "Rivers were a great help to us but also a hindrance because of the heavy floods they caused in the rainy season," Thien continued, "so we had to be as flexible as possible, always adjusting our logistics to the weather, which varied from year to year as well as from season to season." One of the key rivers is the Sekong, which flows through several provinces of Laos before it empties into the Mekong in Cambodia. At the outset, porters used sampans capable of carrying as much as a ton of supplies, but later, as the waterway systems were further developed, motorboats and ferries with capacities that ranged from five to thirty tons were employed. Dangerous rapids on the Sekong required careful navigating, and supplies had to be wrapped in plastic bags or sealed containers for floating downstream. Crocodiles in the Sekong were another hazard, and some of the workers on the river became expert crocodile hunters. In time, engineers were able to convert a number of rivers into virtual "roads," parts of which, in certain months of the year, could be used by trucks as well as by shallow-draft boats. Heavy shrubbery along the shores provided natural cover and protection from bombs.

"Running the Unified Logistics Command wasn't just a matter of operating the transport service," Thien added. "I had to deal with the engineer corps, with communications, with the medical service, and with those who ran the two oil pipelines all the way from the north to Loc Ninh, near the end of the trail, and eventually further south to Ha Tien near the Gulf of Thailand. We could never have kept all our traffic moving without the pipelines—they were essential. All of this, as well as a large body of troops working on the trail, came under my command, and at the same time, during the last two or three years, I was minister of transport and went back and forth between Hanoi and various parts of the trail. Communications were vital, and we created a network of wireless and telephone lines that stretched from Hanoi to Loc Ninh and then out to various headquarters in the field. This required laying hundreds of miles of wires so the high command in Hanoi and in the south could reach any unit they wished in a matter of minutes. After our victory at Xuanloc, we faced a tremendous engineering task of repairing roads and bridges damaged or destroyed by the government troops in retreat. Fortunately, we were able to utilize the wealth of American materials the government abandoned, such as pontoons for bridges. After 1972, in fact, long before Xuonloc, we rebuilt the whole original trail along the eastern Truong Son range, where now we were able to put in solid steel and concrete bridges and metal-surfaced roads that could accommodate heavy vehicles, such as artillery pieces, armored cars, and ground-to-air missile carriers. In the last two years of the war, after the Americans were gone, we actually reduced the total trail network of roads by scrapping secondary routes and improving the main arteries of both the west and east Truong Son, and some of the transverse roads linking them. Our lifeline thus changed completely, and the volume of goods transported to the different fronts was vastly increased. In 1974, it was twenty-two times as great as in 1966, the first year of motorized transport. And a trip down the trail that used to take six months was accomplished in ten days."

(3)

All Vietnamese, as I discovered during my visit to the country, are inordinately proud of the Ho Chi Minh Trail and have begun to visit the parts of it that have been reopened and will eventually be developed into a tourist attraction, for foreigners as well as the Vietnamese themselves. In his book about the B-2 front and the war's final campaign, General Tra described a trip he made from the south to the north late in 1974. "We once again set out on the route that follows the nation's mighty Truong Son range, along Route 559, the Ho Chi Minh Trail," he wrote. "But this time we traveled much faster and with less hardship, for we went the entire distance by motorboat or automobile. The route passed through eastern Kampuchea [Cambodia], crossed southern Laos via Route 9 past Camlo and Dongha, passed through the former Zone 4, and went on to Hanoi. The 'Ho Chi Minh Trail' was no longer a trail but was a system of motor roads with many north-south and east-west branches which were supplemented by rivers, chiefly the Mekong, the Sekong, etc. and which had been further embellished by communications lines stretched taut by the wind and by POL [petroleum, oil, and lubricants] pipelines that crossed streams and climbed mountains. Here and there POL stations, machine shops, truck parks, and headquarters were operating busily. On one hill after another there were cleverly camouflaged gun emplacements and antiaircraft proudly and imposingly pointing skyward. That was a far cry from May 1959—the birthday of the trail—to the early sixties, a period during which I was in charge and assigned comrade Vo Bam and a number of other 'old reliables' the task of gropingly tracing out the route."

General Dung, in *Our Great Spring Victory,* is equally laudatory. "The state and our people poured a great amount of strength and material into this project," he wrote. "Thousands of motorized vehicles of all kinds, tens of thousands of soldiers, workers, engineers, Vanguard Youths, and volunteer workers overcame innumerable hardships and suffering caused by the climate and the weather and by enemy bombs and shells—flattened mountains and passes, turning them to gravel to build the road, constructed culverts and bridges—a proud exploit in the western part of our land. It was indeed our 'eight meter wide road,' permitting large trucks and heavy combat vehicles of all kinds to drive quickly in both directions in all four seasons. Day and night they enthusiastically carried hundreds of thousands of tons of supplies of every description down to the stockpiles for the various battlefields, to ensure the success of our large-scale attacks. . . . It was a picture to be proud of. In that region of towering mountains in the western sector of our Fatherland were more than twenty thousand kilometers of strategic roads running north to south, with campaign roads running west to east—strong ropes inching gradually, day by day, around the neck, arms, and legs of a demon, awaiting the order to jerk tight and bring the creature's life to an end."

Even those Vietnamese who have broken with the Hanoi regime have only praise for the accomplishments of the men and women who built the trail. Truong Nhu Tang was one of the founders of the National Liberation Front and the minister of justice in the Provisional Revolutionary Government. In 1978 he fled the country by small boat after concluding that the Politburo had never intended to allow the southern leaders of the NLF and the PRG any independent voice in running the government once the war was over. Four years earlier, he had made the trip from the south to the north, shortly before he was sent to Europe as a PRG ambassador, a convenient way of getting him out of the way. In his book *Vietcong Memoir*, published in the United States in 1985, he wrote: "Threading through the jungles and mountains of eastern Cambodia and Laos, the network of all-weather roads we were traveling would not have been recognized by the hardy souls who had pioneered the route. . . . In the suffocating humidity they had climbed and hacked their way through the thick foliage of the mountain jungles, struggling for survival in one of the world's most hostile environments. Malaria, dysentery, and vicious jungle fungus infections were the lot of everyone who came down the trail in those days, carrying with them only the most rudimentary of medicines, and nothing at all to counteract the venomous snakes or the clouds of mosquitoes. . . . Only half of them survived it, and those who did said that afterward death held no fears for them. One of these early travelers wrote in his diary:

> 'We march all day bent under the weight of our packs. In the heat and humidity we are forced to stop often for rest and to get our breath back. In the evening, utterly exhausted, we hang our hammocks and mosquito nets from the trees, and sleep under the stars. At times we have to search far from the trail for a waterfall or spring where we can drink and fill our canteens. There are tigers and leopards in the jungle, and we knew about attacks on stragglers and people who have become separated. We climb mountain faces of over a thousand meters, pulling our headbands down over our eyes to filter the sun's rays. From the summit a spectacle of splendor and magnificence offers itself to us. It is like a countryside of fairytales. Those who get sick we leave at the next way-post. The group continues to march. We must have faith in our struggle, in our leaders and in our country to endure these tests of suffering and pain, when we can no longer distinguish the line between life and death.' "

Tang, like the others who traveled the modern trail, spoke with awe of the "barracks, armories, storage and shop facilities, farms, dispensaries, guest houses, fueling stations, everything imaginable for defense, repair, and transportation" along the way, and of "the veritable army of workers [that] included youth groups, contingents of Montagnards (tribal people), and peasant volunteers. Some had lived on the road for eight or ten years without seeing their homes. Some of the Volunteer Youth had arrived as teenagers and were now in their early thirties. The magnitude of their task was apparent everywhere one looked. Huge bomb craters pocked the roadside for much of its length and many bombs had obviously scored near or direct hits. Yet the artery had not only never been closed; it had kept expanding and developing. . . . We drove along this marvel of construction at a constant speed of about thirty miles a kilometer, amidst a continual flow of traffic not much different from what I would later experience heading into an American city during rush hour. At one point we passed a slow-moving convoy carrying American jet planes (their wings detached) toward the North. Each night an eerie and beautiful spectacle would emerge before our eyes, an endless stream of flickering headlights tracing curved patterns against the blackened wilderness, as far in both directions as the eye could see."

The Vietnamese who built and operated the trail took special pride in having successfully defended it against the mightiest war machine in the world. "Here was a case of ingenuity and determination defeating superior strength and power," General Thien said, at the end of our day-long conversation. "The United States was infinitely superior to us in every way—in population, balance of forces, science and technology, firepower, and air power. You spent billions of dollars to build up your logistics systems and to fight a modern war based on high levels of technology. In comparison, our economy was akin to the Middle Ages. But despite the great admiration I had for the United States, you were weak in one thing—in your ability to analyze and estimate the unknown elements of the war. You didn't even know how to use the intelligence you collected, the documents you captured, and so on. You were never able to respond to our strategy and tactics and particularly to our flexibility, to our surprise movements. Our national will and spirit of determination, of course, were what made the big difference. If it weren't for that, I could not explain how and why we were able to win. The difference also lay in the fact that Vietnam was not a patriotic war for you, or a war of survival, as it was for us. Unlike the Vietnamese, the Americans never felt threatened, and you were unable to understand the basic nature and character of the Vietnamese, what we were like. Perhaps some of this was due to the fact that America is a multinational country, whereas Vietnam is one nation, fighting for unification as well as survival. As Vietnamese, many of us have fought for thirty years against the French and then against the Americans. Under your rotation system, you Americans, with some exceptions, fought in Vietnam for one year. How could a soldier discover and respond to the unknown elements of the war in so short a time?"

General Thien made the further point that, aside from not taking sufficient account of the unknown factors, the Americans failed to place the war in context historically, and especially to the earlier French-Vietnamese war. "You should have considered more carefully the human and spiritual strength of the Vietnamese, how we had previously defeated a bigger and stronger nation, or for that matter how we had waged war against the Chinese over the centuries. If we compare France and America, I can't say which war was more difficult for us. We were empty-handed at the start against the French, we began with virtually nothing, with a handful of Japanese, French, American, and Chinese guns, and yet we won out. That was most important. We built a lot of our own arsenal and then captured many more weapons as we went along. Later we were able to use our experience of fighting the French in the war against the Americans and the South Vietnamese, and by then our means were far more ample." (Thien made no specific mention here of the amount of Soviet and Chinese assistance the Vietnamese received.)

I asked him what difference it would have made if the United States had bombed North Vietnam more heavily, effectively cut the Ho Chi Minh Trail at the top near Laos, and attacked the Cambodian sanctuaries sooner. "You must see the difference between bombing an industrial country and an agricultural country," he replied. "If you hit an industrial conglomeration hard, it would upset the whole economy. But even if you had destroyed Hanoi, bombed it flat, we would still have gone into the country-side, and if you had carpetbombed us there the peasants would still have struggled on. An industrial country can-not defeat an agricultural nation by bombing. And while industrial nations cannot return to agricultural conditions when bombed, agricultural nations can, even when badly hurt. You bombed most of the industry we had, but it made no real difference." (Thien, at this juncture, again made no reference to Soviet aid replenishing industrial losses. Nor did he speculate about the possible effects all-out American bombing of the north might have had in 1965, or at subsequent crucial moments prior to the heavy bombing during the Christmas period of 1972. These at-tacks, far exceeding anything seen before, are generally credited with forcing the North Vietnamese back to the conference table at Paris, where they then gained their principal objective of American withdrawal from the war, leaving one hundred fifty thousand North Vietnamese troops in the south and paving the way for ultimate victory two years later. However, these omissions do not necessar-ily contradict Thien's basic premise about the unlikelihood of all-out bombing forcing an agricultural nation to its knees.)

"As to your attacking the sanctuaries in Cambodia sooner than you did," Thien concluded, "in effect, you actually achieved your military aims by having already es-tablished and supported the Lon Nol regime. In any event, you would never have sent enough troops, a million men or more, to Vietnam and Cambodia, which is what you would have required to defend all of Indo-China. Moreover, we were far too active militarily in Cambodia all along, and you could not have forced us out. If you had carpetbombed the entire area, you would surely have risked a war of annihilation by bringing in the Russians and the Chinese, and you were not prepared to do that either. So, you chose instead to fight a limited war and a war of escalation. There is no such thing as a limited war! And escalation tends to be endless, and leads to weariness and eventually to giving up. Once more, this is where the importance of the Ho Chi Minh Trail lay. We had to build it in a relatively limited time, against conditions of vast destruction, including defoliation, which often had a bad effect on the health of our soldiers and our forests. But, fortunately, it did not seriously affect the traffic on the trail. Once we had created the whole system of roads and alternate routes and had learned how to defend them, no amount of bombing—neither napalm or chemical sprays —could stop us. As I have already said, our chief obstacles were malaria and other illnesses, heat, fatigue, exhaustion, and tension. This is why organizing our medical transportation units on the trail, and supplying enough food, were so vital. And all that was part of the flexibility I have stressed, and of adjusting to changing conditions and demands."

(4)

Brigadier General Hoang Phuong, the military historian and head of Vietnam's military academy, with whom I had two long talks, is a veteran of both long wars, against the French and the Americans. In the French war, he was in charge of artillery at Dienbienphu in the spring of 1954, directing the unique and historic hauling of eighty-five large guns, including twenty-eight 105 mm and twenty-four 75 mm artillery pieces, up the steep mountains overlooking the Dienbienphu valley, a feat the French had figured would be impossible. "We had to use heavy ropes to pull rocks and blocks of wood to hold the heavy guns in place as we dragged them up the ravines," General Phuong recalled, "and we had to camouflage all the work as we went along so we would be able to retain the element of surprise. Even when we got the guns emplaced, we had to keep moving them about for protection and retargeting, and this required building new paths up and down the steepest jungle hills. There were many examples of heroism. The rope broke once and a soldier named To Vinh Dien threw himself in front of a large gun to keep it from rolling down the mountain. We had four divisions of infantry and a division of artillerymen and engineers—about fifty thousand men in all—and we all knew that we were facing the fiercest battle of our lives. But we were confident that we'd succeed, especially with the guns we had. General [Henri] Navarre, the French commander, made the big mistake of underestimating our strength and capabilities and overestimating his own. He figured that his superiority in firepower and air power would win, but he was too subjective in his analysis. This was a major mistake the French and Americans both made. The French were always too passive, and they were never able to solve the contradiction between mobility and a fixed strategy."

After the Geneva Conference of 1954 and until 1959, General Phuong said, the North Vietnamese leaders and the people as a whole had little confidence that the terms of the agreement would be heeded and that a nationwide plebiscite, originally scheduled for 1956, would ever be held. Had it been, there is little doubt that Ho Chi Minh, by this time a nationally popular figure, would have won. After the return of the French forces to the south in late

1954, the guerrillas of the Vietminh had resumed their underground activity and a new period of alternating repression and terror began. In the immediate years after Geneva, according to General Phuong, Hanoi's leaders, still hoping that a diplomatic solution might be attained, tried "to restrain" the Vietminh from starting a full-scale armed rebellion. "By 1959, however, the situation in the south had become explosive," Phuong said. It came to a head with the first popular uprising in Tra Bong, a mountainous region in the province of Quang Ngai, in the northern part of South Vietnam. "The direct cause was the government's exploitation of the local people, including several ethnic groups. One section of the people, armed only with swords and knives, managed to seize sixteen communes of the district, and the revolt quickly spread through the province. Some of the puppet soldiers then joined, with their rifles. This was in the fall of 1959, and you can say that this marked the start of the 'second Indo-China war.' By 1960, the new fervor and reaction had spread elsewhere, to Ben Tre in the Mekong Delta, for example. Although there were growing instances of armed rebellion, the struggle was mostly political at this juncture, but we in the north began to filter small quantities of arms south, mostly rifles. We can also now say that the movement in the south, from the outset, was under the direction of the Laodong Party, which organized the Committee for the South, or COSVN, headed by Pham Hung."

General Phuong continued: "By the end of 1960, the so-called special war had begun, based on an increasing number of American advisers and the buildup of puppet forces with American weapons. Both the French and American wars had many common points. Both were unjust wars in the eyes of the Vietnamese people, and, as time went on, of the American people as well. Strategically, both were falsely based on the premise of rapid fighting, rapid victory, though different means of mobilizing the population were used. Another thing in common was the overemphasis on subjectivity: the United States failed to benefit from the mistakes the French made and followed the same military principles, predicated on the belief that the disposition of superior firepower and air power would win the war. The Americans, in particular, were bewitched by the preponderance of firepower and air mobility. They succeeded in creating a better puppet force than the French had, chiefly because the French fought an old-style colonial war, while the Americans used their combined economic and military aid to improve the puppet army and administration. But this strategy failed because most of the Vietnamese in the south realized, from the beginning, that the government and army were corrupt, that the Diem regime practiced religious persecution, and that the war being waged was as unjust as the French war had been. The fact that we had a large rear in the north made a great difference. Moreover, the Democratic Republic of Vietnam had by now been established. It had diplomatic status, which brought us international support."

Phuong cited two major battles during the special war period which he said were crucial. The first was the twelve-hour fight that took place at Apbac, a small hamlet near Mytho in the Mekong Delta, on January 2, 1963. "This was the first time that our liberation forces defeated an assault by amphibious personnel carriers (APCs) and helicopters," he said. "A company of our main force guerrillas, a local forces company, and a district group of additional local guerrillas repulsed five attacks by more than two thousand government troops supported by twenty American helicopters, eight fighter planes, a dozen reconnaisance planes, thirteen APCS, and some heavy artillery." Phuong claimed that the South Vietnamese, who were accompanied by an American adviser, suffered 450 casualties and that eight helicopters were shot down. "After Apbac we knew that we could contend with armor and mobile tactics," he added, "and the enemy realized it would be hard to win this war. Our confidence was greatly roused." The second vital battle he cited took place in Binh Gia province southeast of Saigon over a three-month period from early December 1964 until early March 1965. The National Liberation Forces of the south, now secretly supported by northern cadres and weapons, used their main force elements up to regimental size for the first time —so-called crack Vietcong troops. According to Phuong's figures, the South Vietnamese suffered more than seventeen hundred killed and wounded and the Americans fifty-two casualties. "After Binh Gia," Phuong said, "the enemy realized he might lose the war."

The Binh Gia battle occurred half a year after the famous Tonkin Gulf incident of July 30, 1964, which resulted in Congress's passing the Tonkin Gulf Resolution, giving President Johnson virtually a free hand in prosecuting the war. According to General Phuong, who has recently made a special study of the incident for his military archives, there should no longer be any doubt that the incident began when two American destroyers, the *Maddox* and the *Turner Joy*, entered North Vietnamese waters and shelled two small islands off the coast believed to have radar installations on them. (In Saigon at the time, I was privately told that the radar stations were initially attacked with gunfire by two smaller American patrol boats manned by South Vietnamese sailors and marines, but that the two destroyers were in Vietnamese waters and had subsequently shelled the islands and possibly the mainland coast. On August 4 and 5, United States carrier-based planes attacked and destroyed two dozen North Vietnamese patrol boats and supporting facilities, including an oil depot, along a hundred-mile stretch of the North Vietnamese coast. There was further evidence afterward indicating that the American destroyers and patrol craft had actually goaded the North Vietnamese into attacking them. This was done, it was said, in part to shore up the government of General Nguyen Khanh, then the leader of South Vietnam, who had strong United States support but was facing fresh opposition and a new coup threat, and in part to obtain support for the Tonkin Gulf Resolution in Washington.)

By March 1965, when the first American marines landed at Danang, with the restricted objective, initially, of protecting the perimeter around the airfield base, the liberation forces were increasing their attacks throughout South Vietnam, General Phuong said. "By this time the United States realized that its policy of conducting a special war had failed. Early in April, Prime Minister Pham Van Dong made public our four points as a basis for negotiations, but the United States ignored them instead of accepting a chance to end the war. Johnson quickly escalated the number of troops in South Vietnam and broadened their mission, permitting them to join in the fighting. We responded by sending two North Vietnamese divisions south, and the war grew much fiercer. The Americans now called it a limited war, accepting the concept of their participation on a limited scale but expecting the South Vietnamese still to do most of the fighting. We had no experience in fighting the Americans, but we had been told they were strong and tough, fought gallantly, and had never before been defeated. Many discussions were held about how to deal with this matter, especially how to contend with the Americans' heavy firepower and air strength. Eventually we reached an important decision— to engage them at first hand and to find out the answers. Our motto became, 'Grasp the Belt of the GI and Fight Him.' This motto had a practical as well as theoretical meaning: if you get close to the enemy, engage him in hand-to-hand fighting. You can then avoid air and artillery attacks, at which he is superior, and which are so destructive. How, then, could we achieve this? First, we had to cover long distances and at the same time not let the enemy know where we were. We had to learn how the enemy lives and behaves, to understand him as thoroughly as possible, his methods of fighting, and so on. And while we had no helicopters, we had to be more mobile than the Americans; we had to continue our guerrilla tactics and strategy."

The first testing of the new motto, General Phuong told me, took place in the battle for Van Tuong, a district in Quang Nam province, in the northern tier of the country, in mid-August 1965. "We followed the tactic of initiating an attack, fighting the enemy closely, and then withdrawing. Hurt him as much as possible but don't hold the ground. The more famous battle of testing ourselves against the GI was at Pleime, in the highlands, where we fought the Americans for more than a month, mostly in the Iadrang valley, from mid-October until the third week of November 1965. This was one of the most important battles of the war. Here, again, our motto was to attack an enemy strongpoint, destroy as much of his force as possible, but then withdraw, don't try to hold the land, but come back later. As a result, the American 1st Cavalry (airborne) Division suffered its first defeat, and we learned many things. First, we found out we could inflict heavy losses on the enemy's troops which, despite his helicopters, he could not always replace. We learned how to preserve our own forces by knowing when to withdraw. We found out that, in battle, the GIs had many strong points, including their superior equipment and their ability to resupply their troops, but over the long run they also had many weaknesses. Mostly, the Americans were not prepared for this kind of close fighting. Their tactics were too conventional. They were unable to mobilize their firepower the way they wanted because the battlefield was too fluid.

Their organization was not appropriate to the terrain of Vietnam. Furthermore, the cavalry division was *too* big, it had too many helicopters that used up far too much gasoline. Moreover, its air mobility, including the guns the helicopters carried, was no match for our ground mobility, and we were able to shoot back at the helicopters and hit them with a variety of guns. And while the aircav division had its choppers, it had no APCs, or less than other divisions had, so when its gasoline reserves ran out or the planes were hit and grounded, the GIs were forced to walk out of the jungle. We killed many and wounded many others, and a lot of the wounded died when the helicopters no longer could rescue them."

The Americans, it should be said here, while admitting that the battle for Iadrang valley was extremely difficult and costly, also claim it as a victory. Colonel Harry G. Summers, a Vietnam veteran who is now on the faculty of the U.S. War College and is the author of *On Strategy: A Critical Analysis of the Vietnam War,* begins his book by citing a conversation he had in Hanoi in April 1975, a few days before the end of the war, with one of the North Vietnamese negotiators, also a colonel. Summers said to him, "The North Vietnamese never defeated us on the battlefield." After pondering the remark a moment, according to Summers, the Vietnamese colonel replied, "That may be so, but it is also irrelevant." Summers' analysis, although it deals only with American strategy, offers many reasons why the United States lost the war, despite its superiority in logistics and, he maintains, in tactics too. Among other things, he argues that "What was missing was the link that should have been provided by the military strategists— 'how' to take the systems analyst's *means* and use them to attain the political scientist's *ends*." This is simply another way of saying that the United States never understood that the Vietnam war was primarily a political conflict, or that it at least was a two-ply war, with both military and political aspects and characteristics that could not be considered apart. This, of course, was what the North Vietnamese theory of *dau tranh,* or struggle movement, so ably, if sometimes fuzzily, propounded. Most of the Americans I knew in Vietnam, certainly most of the military officers and most of the senior diplomats—some of the younger ones proved exceptions—were confounded by the war's politics, and tended to belittle and scoff at them. Or they allowed their anti-Communist convictions to guide their thinking so strongly that their traditionalist Western views of a democratic society and government had little patience for nationalist solutions or revolutionary concepts that were Asian oriented, and that might have provided feasible non-Communist alternatives. Unfortunately, as far as the Vietnamese were concerned, this left out in the cold many decent elements whose voices were ignored, including some who came to sympathize with or join the National Liberation Front or other front movements that emerged as the war progressed. A number of such Vietnamese are now also writing books, expressing their disillusion with the Communists they supported, sometimes with their eyes open and sometimes closed, or simply explaining their predicament of having all along been caught in the middle.

In a separate analysis of the battle of Iadrang, in an article that appeared in *American Heritage* in March 1984, Summers elaborates on his argument that the Americans won that battle, as they won all the other major battles in Vietnam. He traces the start of Iadrang to the decision made by the Politburo a year before—to commit North Vietnamese forces to fighting in the south. The military high command chose the Special Forces camp at Pleime in the highlands as the object of the first assault. The objective, which the Vietcong had come so close to achieving on their own just prior to the American entry into the war a few months earlier, was to cut South Vietnam in two. Summers admits that the North Vietnamese got off to a good start, at Pleime, but says that the 1st Cavalry Division, by switching from the tactical defensive to the tactical offensive and reenforcing its troops, then met the North Vietnamese head on in their chief staging area of the Iadrang valley. He gives a play-by-play account of the bitter jungle fighting that ensued, which reached a climax during two days in mid-November when the Americans suffered seventy-nine killed and one hundred and twenty-four wounded, "while the enemy left six hundred and thirty-four bodies on the battlefield—a disparity that was to carry forward throughout the entire war. . . ." In admitting that "the final balance" of the war, nevertheless, was a victory for the North Vietnamese, Summers cites their wise selection of Banmethuot, just a few miles south of the Iadrang valley, as the launching point for their climactic campaign of conquest and the capture of Saigon. With the Americans gone, and above all the United States firepower, he says, the North Vietnamese Army at Banmethuot repeated the tactics it had used at Iadrang and, this time, quickly achieved its aim of capturing the highlands and dividing the south in two.

While the Americans won at Iadrang, Summers says, they failed to realize that "the whole nature of the war had changed" and that it had become more conventional than unconventional. Thereafter, the Vietcong acted as "picadors" in a bullfight, seeking to wear the bull down, while the North Vietnamese Army was the "matador, waiting in the wings until it was time for the killing blow." In Summers' estimation, the Americans made a great mistake in concentrating after Iadrang on pacification schemes and other "nation-building programs" instead of "turning attention to North Vietnam . . . and applying military power to block infiltration into the south." Summers concludes: "Terrible as it may be to say, it might have been better in the long run if we had lost the first battle [at Iadrang], as we lost the first major battle of the Second World War," in the Sbeitla Valley in North Africa in February 1943, where "at the Faid and Kasserine passes, American forces were outgunned, outranged, and outfought, and we suffered a disastrous defeat," but learned a valuable lesson—how to devise better strategies and tactics to avoid further defeats. "The sad truth is that in Vietnam our mind was never concentrated on how to win the war," Summers says. "Our initial victory had lulled us into the delusion that no matter what we did, we couldn't lose." This was a fatal error Clausewitz had warned about, of "taking the first step without considering the last."

Other American experts on the war, notably Douglas Pike, author of an early (1966) seminal volume entitled *Vietcong: The Organization and Techniques of the National Liberation Front of South Vietnam,* and of a recent (1986) book, *PAVN—People's Army of Vietnam,* elaborates on some of these same themes in a paper he delivered in January 1983 at a symposium on the war held at the Wilson Center in Washington, D.C. Discussing the significance of *dau tranh,* which for the Vietnamese represents a "summons to consecration, the call to heroic duty, the trumpet of the apocalypse," whose "psychological subliminal elements are a compound of hate, grievance, ambition and determination of revenge," Pike emphasizes that the two elements of the strategy are a "seamless web." He adds: "Neither struggle arm alone can deliver victory. Only in combination, with the marriage of violence to politics, can the strategy succeed." He makes the point that the South Vietnamese and the Americans and the other smaller allied forces, but the Americans in particular, successfully dealt with armed *dau tranh.* The United States "won every significant battle fought, a record virtually unparalleled in the history of warfare. But the South Vietnamese government and the United States were not able to deal successfully with the second arm, political *dau tranh,* and therein lay the seeds of defeat."

Pike maintains that while the North Vietnamese had a

"monolithic view" of the struggle based on "implacable determination and moral superiority . . . there were within from the start vast doctrinal differences which rent the high command and the civilian leadership at the Politburo level." The debate, he says, based largely on his reading of hundreds of North Vietnamese documents in translation and on interviews with Communist prisoners, was mainly concerned with the timing and balance of the two arms of the *dau tranh* strategy. This mainly came down to quarrels over important subissues such as allocation of resources and the amount of external support required. However, personalities became deeply involved in the debate. General Vo Nguyen Giap, the hero of the war against the French whose role in the American war was gradually taken over by General Van Tien Dung, was the leading "professional" general, while Truong Chinh was the Party man who represented the "political" generals and laid more stress throughout both wars, but especially the American war, on political *dau tranh* than armed *dau tranh*. Pike argues that there were three shifts in emphasis between the two men from 1965, when political *dau tranh* was more important, until the end, in 1975, when armed *dau tranh* prevailed. The National Liberation Front at the outset practiced more political than armed *dau tranh* and then went through a period when its armed strength increased and it fought more battles. But the North Vietnamese all along had certain doubts about the NLF and the southern leaders, and kept them "on a short leash." As more and more military material came down the Ho Chi Minh Trail, and more North Vietnamese troops, the northern forces took over the war, and after the heavy losses suffered by the Vietcong at Tet 1968, the latter were of relatively little importance.

Pike also emphasizes American air power and its effect on the *dau tranh* strategy. Initially, he says, North Vietnam looked upon the air attacks "with enormous dismay and apprehension." While the Americans regarded them as "selective and incremental, designed to 'choke off' the supply route to the south," Hanoi's perception was that "the Americans were engaged in an all-out air assault, punitive but tolerable." Hanoi's theory was badly shattered by the Christmas 1972 all-out bombing attack which prompted its return to the bargaining table in Paris. Pike suggests, as others have, that if such a bombing assault had taken place as early as 1965, "the Vietnam war as we know it might have been over within a matter of months, even weeks." The North Vietnamese, including those I spoke with during my recent trip, while admitting that the 1972 air bombardment was both unexpected and severe, were adamant in maintaining that the worst that would have happened would have been the complete removal of the high command and the Politburo back to the jungle, from where the war would have been prosecuted with equal determination.

In Pike's analysis, the war was divided by Hanoi theorists into four periods: the Revolutionary Guerrilla War period, from May 1959 until February 1965 (when the United States decided to intervene with ground troops and air power); the Regular Force Strategy, or "big unit" warfare period, from February 1965 until June 1968, culminating in the Tet offensive; the Neo-Revolutionary War period, from July 1968 until April 1972 (when the North Vietnamese launched their major Easter offensive in the spring); and the Negotiated Settlement Period, or what Hanoi described as the "Talk-Fight" period, from the late summer of 1972, when it became apparent that the big Easter offensive was failing, until the end of the war in April 1975. These four periods more or less correspond to the back-and-forth shifts between political and armed *dau tranh*. The American intervention obviously was what prompted the first move toward an armed strategy. Initially, Hanoi's assessment of the American intervention

was that it came too late, and, in fact, the National Liberation Front agit-prop cadres in the south coined the slogan,
"The greater the American intervention, the greater the
American defeat." This was the point when the liberation
troops in the south seemed on the brink of victory and
then, oddly, pulled back, in the highlands. "The reason
for this remains something of a mystery even to this day,"
Pike says. When I asked General Phuong about this in
Hanoi, I received no firm answer beyond the implication
that the southern liberation forces were not fully prepared
to prosecute a final victory drive and that the American
move had to be dealt with as a new factor by the high
command. Pike still believes that "by all logic, the liberation forces should have destroyed the remaining South
Vietnamese armed units before American prowess could
make itself felt."

However, instead of beating the Americans to the
punch and applying his ongoing strategy to end the war
before they got in place, General Giap decided to revamp
the strategy and meet the new threat of American military
power head on, as he sets forth in his major book, *Big
Victory, Great Task.* To offset the advantages of American
firepower, mobility through use of helicopters, and tactical
air power, Giap sent as many troops and as much heavy
weaponry as possible down the Ho trail. Simultaneously,
he built up North Vietnam's air defenses. On the ground,
he devised a new set of "fighting methods," which he
called "coordinated fighting methods" and "independent
fighting methods." The first denoted set-piece battles, of
medium or large scale, and fought on difficult terrain in
remote areas. Iadrang was an example of this. Independent fighting methods signified dozens of small-sized military attacks launched over a wide area, at which the
Communists were particularly adept. Together, the two
created what Giap termed a "continuous comprehensive
offensive." The 1968 Tet offensive was preceded in the

winter-spring campaign of 1967–68 by a number of set-piece battles, which Pike and others maintain the Communists lost. The Tet battles, in turn, represented a set of simultaneous smaller fights throughout South Vietnam which exemplified the independent fighting methods, during which the Vietcong lost eighty-five thousand troops. "Ironically—since it tended to prove Giap wrong and his critic, Truong Chinh, correct—the campaign was remarkably successful in political *dau tranh* terms," Pike says. "It brought down the president of the United States." The men I spoke with in Hanoi, while denying that Tet was a military defeat, admitted that it was primarily a political victory and in effect corroborated Pike's conclusion that they did not understand President Johnson's actions. In any event, it became clear to Giap as well as to his critics in the Politburo that his strategy to date had either failed or succeeded for the wrong reasons.

The "neo-revolutionary warfare" period that followed laid the stress on political *dau tranh* but did not abandon big unit warfare. As Pike suggests, it was "a casting about for strategy and tactics with a more political character as a substitute for mindlessly slugging it out toe to toe with the Americans." In essence, this meant that, for the time being at least, Truong Chinh and his supporters in the Politburo, who had severely questioned the efficacy of Giap's strategy and tactics, "now had their turn at bat." The war had obviously become much more intense and required a new approach that would provide "some better mix of armed and political *dau tranh*." One manifestation of this was the development of sapper teams, or specially equipped commando units, which, in the remaining years of the war, caused great damage to the South Vietnamese and to the Americans, as long as they remained in Vietnam. As Pike says, "These sapper units were equipped with the best weapons the bloc country research and development laboratories could supply. These included weapons with great killing power, new kinds of explosives and sophisticated communications systems." Giap and his armed *dau tranh* believers regarded their introduction as launching a holding operation, coinciding with the start of peace talks in Paris, that would give him the chance to reorganize and reequip his main force units for another full-scale military attack. In buying time, the main advantage the North Vietnamese obtained was the erosion of American patience with the war, while "North Vietnam, because of its political system and leaders, was better able to hide its feelings."

The fourth and final period of war, the "talk-fight" period, was a time of great uncertainty for advocates of both political and armed *dau tranh*. In Pike's estimation, the period was also marked by severe factional struggles in the Politburo, during which the issue of strategy in the south was paramount. Although General Phuong and the others I spoke with in Hanoi would not admit this (which would have been highly out of character under any circumstances), I had the feeling that one reason it is taking them a long time to write the history of the war is the continuation of factional struggles, which have been aggravated by different perceptions of the war in Cambodia—whether to seek a political solution there or, as General Dung proposes, to achieve a military victory on the ground. (Significantly, with regard to the Cambodian war, Giap is said to have warned against the army's getting bogged down there, adding that it would take a lot of time and effort.)

In any event, it seems true that, by 1972, Giap and the high command persuaded the Politburo that the neo-revolutionary war strategy was not good enough and that a new and better form of armed *dau tranh* had to be devised. This meant obtaining more and improved sophisticated weapons, including tanks, long-range artillery, and missiles from the Soviet Union, as well as additional help from the Chinese. Opposing Giap were others in the Politburo, now including Premier Pham Van Dong, who wanted to pursue a negotiatory track and who maintained that a resumption of large-scale, big-unit fighting was too costly. The result, Pike says, was a compromise that was adopted at the Party's twentieth plenum, in February 1972. This authorized a major new military campaign, code-named Nguyen Hue. Giap regarded this as a small-scale conventional war not unlike the Korean war, and it involved a maximum effort in men, weapons, and logistics. By midsummer of 1972, all of North Vietnam's fourteen divisions were engaged in combat outside the country for the first time. The Nguyen Hue campaign was primarily fought on three fronts, along the demilitarized zone, in the highlands around Kontum, and in Binh Long province just north of Saigon. The fighting was extremely violent, and, in Pike's terms, at times resembled the panzer-style warfare of the Second World War: "fast moving, hard-hitting, deliberately traumatic." (The description is one that, after watching part of the battle of Kontum between Vietnamese tanks and American planes from the vantage point of a helicopter above the battlefield, I can readily agree with.)

While the North Vietnamese initially achieved considerable success in this 1972 Easter offensive, they were unable to sustain their attacks. Giap probably overestimated the ability of the army to conduct a high-technology war and sustain its momentum, while he underestimated the determination and ability of the South Vietnamese to resist on the ground and the Americans' military response in the air. Moreover, his expectations of full-scale Russian and Chinese support were unfulfilled, and, in fact, such support was sometimes lukewarm. The political *dau tranh* campaign waged in Paris by Le Duc Tho, on the other hand, was highly successful, combining serious political diplomatic talks with both Washington and Moscow with coalition overtures in South Vietnam and an international stress on the theme of peace. What the North Vietnamese now sought, as described in Pike's paper, was "the American-managed disestablishment of the government of South Vietnam." What the North Vietnamese effectively negotiated, in time, was a favorable political arrangement in South Vietnam for themselves, including the right to keep 150,000 troops there, in return for orderly withdrawal by the Americans. Whatever success or failure the plan for Vietnamization had, it remains doubtful that the United States would have been able to disengage itself without such a scheme. For one thing, the Americans were able to convince Hanoi of their continued determination to help the south, and the south also believed this, to a greater or lesser degree. With the election of President Nixon, however, Hanoi changed its focus somewhat and set out to negotiate an American withdrawal "at the best possible price." This altered stance was the result of a new balance in the factional struggle within the Politburo, Pike believes. The result was an agreement to separate the military and political aspects of the negotiations, and "to drop the requirement that the political future of South Vietnam be settled before a cease-fire could be reached." The Paris agreements of January and March 1973 achieved this aim. This meant that the war would continue "but once again as essentially an indigenous Vietnamese affair."

A new period of political *dau tranh* began, symbolized by the so-called battle of the flags during which the South Vietnamese government sought to install and sustain its presence in as many places as possible, while North Vietnam protected its areas. Additional areas were "contested." Meanwhile, both the South Vietnamese and North Vietnamese rebuilt and strengthened their main forces, but the South Vietnamese found this increasingly difficult to do when the United States slackened off in its military aid shipments. With the onset of Watergate, Hanoi realized that it would soon be able to attack the South Vietnamese with impunity, and the high command began to prepare for a full-scale return to armed *dau tranh* by 1976. When it became apparent that the limited military operations culminating in the capture of Banmethuot had triggered the dissolution of the South Vietnamese army, the timetable was speeded up. But in spite of the success of the new campaign to take Saigon, Pike, as well as other American experts, still maintain that "in the end the North Vietnamese army did not win, the army of South Vietnam lost." What was not settled was the doctrinal issue between political and armed *dau tranh*. Believers in each, as Pike says, claimed and still claim vindication, and Hanoi's official version of what took place at the end of the war has switched back and forth and remains unclear.

Pike concludes his important paper by declaring: "Hanoi historians today tend to finesse the issue, seeking to put victory in broader context than only strategy. The outcome of the war, they say, was a victory for the Party, for the ruling Politburo and for the imperishable Marxist thought. Indeed it was a victory for the organizational prowess of the Party, especially for the mobilizational and motivational skills of that unique institution, the Party cadre. And certainly it was something of a victory for the little band of North Vietnamese leaders, General Vo Nguyen Giap, chief doctrinaire Truong Chinh, and, in ways difficult to measure, Ho Chi Minh. It was not, however, much of a victory for Marxist thinking, for there is little in the strategy that can be traced that far west—to Mao and China perhaps, but not to Marx, Lenin or Soviet ideological doctrine."

In my conversations with North Vietnamese military analysts, I found less of an inclination than might have been expected to break the war down into sharply defined periods or phases. They may yet do so in the definitive accounts they claim to be preparing, but, in any event, there appears little doubt that there remain sharp differences of opinion about what happened during the war and why, especially during the latter half and at its climax, when the South Vietnamese collapsed. For the moment, their analyses tend to be somewhat oversimplified, though General Tra's account of the final campaign—to which I shall come shortly—is something of an exception. In any case, in my long conversation with General Phuong, for example, he acknowledged that if the North Vietnamese "victory" at Iadrang was "a big turning point," the Americans remained "confident and arrogant." In successive dry season offensives over the next two years, he said, which included some of the biggest and bloodiest battles of the war, the United States had two main objectives—to conduct search and destroy campaigns, and to extend the concept and scope of pacification. Phuong did not elaborate on or analyze these battles in any detail, but he made a point of emphasizing, as General Thien had done, that whatever the American successes or failures, the United States was unable to stop the heavy flow of traffic down the Ho Chi Minh Trail. "Large supplies of weapons for our divisions in the south and new troop units and replacements kept flowing southward," Phuong said. During the 1967–68 dry season, it was the American intention to launch another large-scale offensive, or counteroffensive. "The United States failed, however, to guess the main direction of our attack, which you thought would come in the north, in South Vietnam's I Corps. You made the mistake of believing we had lost at Khesanh, along Route 9, when, in fact, we had withdrawn and were planning for the general offensive throughout the country, to take place at Tet, in February. Again, you didn't understand our combination of military and political strategy." When I asked General Phuong about the results of the Tet battles, he replied: "We did suffer heavy casualties. Our bases in the rural areas were weakened as a consequence, in some cases, of your successful pacification efforts and, in other cases, as a result of counteroffensives by the Americans and South Vietnamese." He would not admit, though, that the Communists suffered an overall military defeat at Tet, though he agreed that the Vietcong was badly hurt as a fighting force and that the North Vietnamese thereafter took over the main burden of the war.

Phuong laid the stress on the political defeat the Americans suffered during the Tet battles, which led to Johnson's decision not to run again and "forced an end to the war of escalation, which had proved a failure." Thereafter, he pointed out, the strategy of "de-Americanization and Vietnamization under President Nixon was a passive strategy with many contradictions. You had been unable to defeat the North Vietnamese forces or the liberation forces of the south, so how could the South Vietnamese puppets do this? Morale on our side, on the other hand, had improved as we gained more experience and confidence." He cited the battle code-named Lam Son 119 in 1971, when, with American air support, the South Vietnamese sought to strike across Route 9 toward Laos and cut the Ho Chi Minh Trail at its head, but were set back with heavy losses. "This was a major defeat of Vietnamization," General Phuong said. "We were on the spot and prepared, and we didn't even have to move our troops around. After this, there were few major battles though some hard fighting took place in the provinces of Quang Tri, Quang Nam, and Quang Ngai, in the northern tier; and in a number of other places." He did not discuss the American invasion of Cambodia or its aftermath, or what happened after 1973, when the United States completed the withdrawal of its forces from Vietnam following the renewal of the Paris peace talks and the Christmas bombing of the north. Despite the ferocity of the B-52 attacks during that final bombing, General Phuong said that North Vietnamese antiaircraft or missiles shot down thirty-six B-52's or more than half of the sixty-four they shot down throughout the war.

Like most top Vietnamese officers and officials I spoke with, General Phuong was reluctant to discuss the case of General Tran Van Tra, whose highly readable book on the B-2 front in the south and the campaign to capture Saigon was withdrawn from circulation a few months after it was published in 1982. The book deserves careful reading not only because of its dramatic narrative style and wealth of detail and description, but because it reveals much of the thinking and motivation of the leaders in the Politburo and the military high command who made the key decisions about the war. Subjectively as well as objectively, Tra analyzes and occasionally obliquely criticizes some of these decisions. He makes clear, for example, that there was by no means unanimity of opinion in all cases in the higher military and political ranks over strategy and tactics, and he deals in discursive fashion with these issues, repeating conversations in which he took part and rendering judgments on the outcome. In dealing with certain matters, Tra is often amazingly frank, and it is easy to see why the book offended his cohorts, leading both to its withdrawal from public sale and to his withdrawal from public life. He is reported to be writing some of the earlier history of the war he had originally projected in five volumes (of which the story of the B-2 front was to be the last rather than the first), but I was unable to find out if this was true.

One of the frankest passages in the book discusses the Tet offensive of 1968, which Tra describes as "a unique event in the history of war." After summarizing the events of the many Tet battles, and emphasizing, as had General Phuong, that they brought to an end the American policy of waging a limited war, Tra says:

> However, during Tet of 1968 we did not correctly evaluate the specific balance of forces between ourselves and the enemy, did not fully realize that the

enemy still had considerable capabilities and that our
capabilities were limited, and set requirements that
were beyond our actual strength. In other words, we
did not base ourselves on scientific calculation or a
careful weighing of all factors, but in part on an illusion
based on our subjective desires. For that reason, although that decision was wise, ingenious and timely,
and although its implementation was well organized
and bold, there was excellent coordination on all battle
fields, everyone acted very bravely, sacrificed their
lives, and there was created a significant turning point
in Vietnam and Indo-China, we suffered large losses
with regard to manpower and material, especially
cadres at the various echelons, which clearly weakened
us. Afterwards, we were not only unable to retain the
gains we had made but had to overcome a myriad of
difficulties in 1969 and 1970 so that the revolution
could stand firm in the storm. Although it is true that
the revolutionary path is never a primrose path that
always goes upward, and there can never be a victory
without sacrifice, in the case of Tet 1968, if we had
weighed and considered things meticulously, taken
into consideration the balance of forces of the two
sides, and set forth correct requirements, our victory
would have been even greater, less blood would have
been spilled by the cadres, enlisted men and people,
and the future development of the revolution would
certainly have been far different.

This is a far more open and revealing account of what
happened at Tet than has been rendered by any other
high-ranking Vietnamese, and Tra is equally frank,
though sometimes cryptic, in dealing with various aspects
of the war. (One wonders, for instance, just what he meant
by the last sentence in his Tet passage. Is he implying that,
if the Vietcong had not been so decimated, it would have
played a stronger role in the subsequent conduct of the
war, and afterward?) It is not difficult to see why Tra

ruffled some feathers. In describing the confused situation in the south after the Paris agreement, when the "battle of the flags" took place despite the cease-fire and there were hundreds of government-claimed, Communist-claimed, and "contested" areas, Tra again writes frankly of confronting "many difficulties" and "weaknesses." "Our armed forces were in disarray and had to be urgently supplemented and consolidated. Our local troops and guerrillas were still too few and there were still many deficiencies in our proselyting work among the enemy." He then recounts some of the discussions and debates that went on in Party and military ranks over such issues as whether the contested areas should be temporarily abandoned, and offers arguments both pro and con. Eventually, because it was decided that it would cost too much to recapture these places if they were given up, it was decided not to abandon them and to respond with force to the government's "landgrabbing," which was the effort by Thieu to get his agents and troops out into as many neutral places as possible; as things turned out, this led to the already weary South Vietnamese spreading themselves far too thinly around the country, which later helped bring on their rapid collapse. In discussing these and other matters that blended strategy and tactics with diplomacy, Tra is at his best. He lays it all out, the joyous penultimate meetings in the jungle, the debates and arguments over logistics and the movement of troops, the meticulous final planning. He spares no one's feelings. Nor does he tread lightly in depicting the Americans and other foreign nationals he dealt with as the head of the Vietnamese negotiating delegation in Saigon in 1973, and again in 1975.

The book is all the more graphic for the manner in which Tra describes the actions and opinions of the Americans and South Vietnamese in retreat, and as they then faced defeat at the last moment. Here he is often contemptuous of his opponents, including the last American ambassador in Vietnam, Graham Martin. He draws heavily on a number of United States sources that were already in print by the time he wrote his account, some of which were highly critical themselves of the decisions that were taken, or not taken, and of the men, particularly Martin, who made them. If the book ends on an elegiac note, with the capture of Saigon, and if Tra is always careful to hedge his subtle and caustic comments and to give credit to his superiors for making the wise and "correct" determinations when there were serious differences, he also gives due, and perhaps undue, credit to himself. During the long discussions that were held late in 1974 and early in 1975, for example, in Hanoi and at forward headquarters in South Vietnam, he claims to have been chiefly instrumental in the decision taken to attack Banmethuot, in March 1975, which was surely one of the war's most crucial. Given Tra's high rank and position, there is little doubt that he took part in many such key deliberations; but one also has the feeling that he was something of a maverick and outsider, and that as a naturally loqacious southerner he was regarded by his sterner and less outspoken northern peers with some degree of wariness and skepticism.

In talking to other veterans of the French and American wars in Hanoi, I was surprised to discover that most of them had more respect and admiration for the manner in which the French fought than the Americans. Retired Major General Tran Cong Man, who is now the editor of the army newspaper, told me, "The French colonialists were more dangerous than the Americans, although the scale of the war with the United States was much greater. We tried to isolate the French, to neutralize the United States, and we put great efforts into this but without success. You gave so much support to the French that after Dienbienphu we expected we would have to fight you." Bui Tin, now the editor of *Nhan Dan*, the major daily paper, fought against the French in central Vietnam, then in the far north, and was a battalion commander at Dien-bienphu. In the American war he served on the general staff as an analyst but was frequently in the field as a jour-nalist as well, and traveled up and down the Ho Chi Minh Trail five times. As a colonel as well as an editor and writer, he was in Saigon at the end and helped accept the surrender from General Duong Van Minh, who had briefly become president of South Vietnam.

"The French understood Vietnam and the Vietnamese far better than the Americans," Tin said, over lunch one day at my hotel. "They had troops from Africa who could withstand the climate and who had served in the colonial army for years. The average American had no such expe-rience. The French selection of recruits, both Vietnamese and tribal people, was also better because they had more knowledge of the local folk, such as the Tai, the Muong, and the Nung, though the Americans did a better job of training the Vietnamese. The French were also more prac-tical in their strategy. General officers like Navarre, Cogny, and de Lattre de Tassigny were superior to senior American officers. The chief fault of the Americans is what I call 'weaponism'—you believed more in your weap-ons than you believed in yourselves. You never really came to grips with the war, you were not that involved. That was evident on the battlefield, where you showed no flexi-bility. You would shell and bomb the same area with the same patterns day after day, at the same hours. There was seldom any element of surprise in your strategy and tac-tics. And for every weapon you used we found a way to counteract it. We respected your helicopters—I myself was captured by them twice in Quang Ngai province—but after two years or so we found ways to counteract them too. Neither the French nor the Americans were prepared to fight a long war, even though both of you thought the wars were long. In sheer fighting ability, the French were better soldiers because they had more experience and they stayed here longer. The Americans only stayed a year. For us it was life or death."

One of the most perceptive comments I heard came from Nguyen Dinh Thi, the novelist, poet, and play-wright, whom I met a number of times in Hanoi. "In personal terms, the French learned very little from their colonial experience in Vietnam," he said. "Afterward, they blotted out the war. I don't think the Americans learned very much either. As for us, I would have to say that, having myself fought for eight years with the Vietminh, starting in 1945 with only a knapsack and a long stick, not even a rifle, we were always close to the earth, to the sky, to storms and natural calamities. That made a big difference. We fought on known terrain, we got our firewood from the jungle, our protection, and even our food. The human sentiment of the struggle was deeper and more real and more comradely than in the war with the Americans. There was a brotherhood composed of all of us. The American war was more distant and remote. There was no brotherhood then, or not as much. The war was disembodied. It was like a ball of fire, like your napalm. It made us fight harder for survival, yes, but we also lost part of our identity. Perhaps we are still trying to recover it."

CHAPTER FIVE

Cambodia in Captivity

(1)

Twenty years ago, during one of the first of many half-hour flights I made from Saigon to Phnom Penh, I reflected upon the odd sensation of leaving the acrid atmosphere and constant tension of the war in Vietnam to be set down so quickly amid the fragrant serenity of the Cambodian capital. Actually, the sensation was somewhat misleading. Though Phnom Penh itself, with its exquisite charm, showed few visible signs of it, Cambodia was already caught in the war's gathering vortex that would soon engulf the whole nation. The North Vietnamese and the Vietcong had regularly begun to use the heavy jungle of the largely unpopulated border areas that divided the two countries to forage for food and to hide from American and South Vietnamese ground and air attacks. Smuggling of Chinese arms, rice, and medicines from the southern port of Sihanoukville, on the Gulf of Thailand, to the Vietnamese Communist troops in the sanctuaries had begun to be supplemented by supplies moved down from North Vietnam along the Ho Chi Minh Trail. Prince Norodom Sihanouk, the politically agile and unpredictable Cambodian chief of state, who took special pride in having built the port bearing his name, was fully aware of these activities but was unable to do much about them; he professed to follow a course of neutrality between Com-

munist China, North Vietnam, and the National Liberation Front of South Vietnam, on the one hand, and the
Western nations and their anti-Communist Asian allies on
the other. Privately, however, what Sihanouk feared more
than anything else was an ultimate Vietnamese takeover
of his small country. He had devoted most of his adult life
and renounced his throne to lead his people, albeit more
imperiously than democratically, in what amounted to a
one-man crusade to preserve what was left of the once
great Khmer nation. Between the ninth and the thirteenth
centuries, the Khmer ruled much of Southeast Asia, including what is now Vietnam and Cambodia, and their
kingdom, with its capital set amid the historic temples of
Angkor Wat, had a population of ten million. But then
the Thais and the Vietnamese, who are yellow-skinned
mainland people—the Khmer are darker skinned and are
racially related to the island Polynesians—sought compet-
itively to destroy the Khmer. One or both would have
succeeded had it not been for the French, who arrived in
Cambodia in 1863 and thereby became its temporary saviors as well as its colonial rulers—and coincidentally
planted the seeds for the two major Indo-China wars of
the twentieth century.

Today, more than two decades after Sihanouk began his
climactic struggle against the Vietnamese Communists,
who had already defeated the French in the first of those
two wars and would soon defeat the Americans in the
second, Vietnamese troops appear to have confirmed his
worst fears. "Eaters of the Khmer soil," he used to call
them, even as he sought to mollify and cajole them or play
them off against the Chinese or the Americans, with both
of whom he carried on love-hate relationships. Sihanouk's
relations with nations were not unlike his earlier widely
rumored relations with women: he flirted with them and
sometimes loved them, dropped them and scorned them,
forgave and befriended them anew, and ultimately put

them in his private pantheon, where he could ruminate or muse about them at will according to his momentary whim and what he regarded as their present or potential usefulness. Despite his elaborate machinations and largely because of his numerous mistakes and misjudgments, the Vietnamese have occupied Cambodia for the past seven years, after invading it in December 1978, ironically in the declared role of saviors, to rid the nation of the tyranny of another avowedly Marxist faction, the Khmer Rouge, led by the enigmatic despot who calls himself Pol Pot. During three and a half years of Pol Pot's draconian rule, at least a million Cambodians died—an estimated one-third by deliberate execution and the rest as a result of disease or starvation. Some estimates place the total dead at two million or more. The present Cambodian rulers claim their population to be more than seven million, about a million more than it was before the war, but in the absence of any new census figures, such estimates are unverifiable. Most educated guesses, including Sihanouk's own, place the total at between five and six million.

The original Vietnamese invasion force, at the end of 1978, of ten or twelve divisions grew into an occupation force of about a hundred and eighty thousand soldiers. Despite their claims of withdrawing some elements in the past three years, the Vietnamese still probably have a hundred and fifty thousand troops in the country, or perhaps a few less, as they slowly train a new Khmer army, a process they admit will not be completed until 1990. Even then, should the Vietnamese remove the bulk of their army, they would undoubtedly seek to keep thirty or forty thousand troops in Cambodia indefinitely for reasons of "regional security," as they have done in Laos since the end of the war there in the mid-seventies. Opposing the Vietnamese and their thirty thousand or so Khmer recruits is a motley opposition of some fifty or sixty thousand, more than half of which is composed of Khmer

Rouge soldiers still loyal to Pol Pot. The rest support either Sihanouk or Son Sann, a former Cambodian prime minister and economic and fiscal expert under Sihanouk. Over the past several years, this oddly mixed force has fought sporadic battles against the Vietnamese and their Khmer surrogates in isolated areas inside Cambodia and along the borders with Thailand.

By late 1984, more than two hundred thousand Cambodian refugees from the Pol Pot period and from the current regime were uncomfortably commingled in a score of camps on the Cambodian side of the border or across the way in Thailand, under the protection, not always welcomed by the civilian inmates, of the antigovernment troops. Following a series of coordinated attacks by the Vietnamese that continued throughout the dry season ending in the spring of 1985—the most intensive in the six and a half year occupation of the country—all the opposition camps in Cambodia were overrun and destroyed and the civilian inhabitants forced to flee into Thailand, where they set up new relocation centers and added to the Thais' already swollen refugee population. Unlike the earlier refugees, most of these newcomers were not eligible for resettlement in the United States, which has taken about half the total of a million and a half refugees from the Indo-China wars, or acceptable elsewhere. As for the antigovernment troops of Pol Pot, Son Sann, and Sihanouk, they re-formed as best they could into smaller guerrilla groups in the mountainous regions of southeastern and northern Cambodia or in the pockets inside the country. Though they had suffered a severe setback, their determination to continue fighting until the Vietnamese left Cambodia was by no means subdued, and they were still receiving steady supplies of weapons and other necessities from China and additional aid from Thailand, as well as the right of sanctuary. On a number of occasions, Vietnamese troops crossed over into Thailand, where brief firefights or artillery duels took place with Thai troops, and these skirmishes heightened the general border tension.

The fighting in Cambodia continued throughout 1985, mostly in the central and northwest parts of the country. The loss of border bases made it more difficult for the opposition forces to obtain supplies from their two main outside sources, but they managed to receive enough to sustain themselves. As the year progressed, there were signs on both sides, for the first time, of a willingness to seek a political settlement, though it seemed likely that, at the very least, several more rounds of fighting would take place. Nevertheless, both Sihanouk, as president of the opposition coalition, and the Vietnamese, as well as the regime in Phnom Penh they had put in place, began talking about a "reconciliation government" as an alternative to continuing the war indefinitely.

In October 1985, I had a long conversation with Sihanouk in New York, where he was attending the fortieth anniversary meeting of the United Nations General Assembly. He told me, "I have proposed the formation of a national reconciliation government that would include the various Cambodian factions representing both their own national interests and those of their patrons and allies." He proceeded to enumerate these: the former royalists, represented by Sihanouk himself, who also claims to speak for the nonaligned nations; the Son Sann contingent, which can be described as representing both capitalists and so-called democrats as well as Western interests, including those of the United States; the Khmer Rouge, who speak for themselves and for China and who would probably be represented by Khieu Samphan, vice-president of the coalition led by Sihanouk; and, finally, the government in Phnom Penh, the so-called People's Republic of Kampuchea, headed by Heng Samrin.

"The main problem, of course," Sihanouk said, "is getting the various sponsors, including the major powers, to agree to attend a big conference that would follow a smaller preliminary one of the Cambodian parties. The Vietnamese, for example, and the Russians don't accept the Khmer Rouge as such, let alone Pol Pot as an individual. And the Chinese and Thais don't accept Heng Samrin. On the other hand, the different Cambodian groups are ready to talk to one another. I am ready to talk without preconditions. We must give ourselves a chance. We can talk anywhere, in Paris, Geneva, at the UN, in Stockholm, Vienna, or other places—the locale is unimportant, the meeting is what counts. Afterward, there would be an international conference which all interested countries, such as the Southeast Asians and India, as well as the major powers would attend. I would like to see the United States help get these talks started. The Chinese and Thais are still more interested in having the war continue, in relying on us, the coalition forces, to bleed the Vietnamese."

Nevertheless, the Vietnamese position on the Cambodian question, as I discerned it during this same session of the United Nations, had continued to soften during the year that followed my visit to Vietnam, in August and September 1984. At that time, in speaking with Le Duc Tho, the number two man in the Politburo, and Nguyen Co Thach, the foreign minister, I detected a beginning interest in reaching a compromise on the Cambodian question. Now, at the UN a year later, in discussions with members of the Hanoi delegation, I found them more willing, if not eager, to reach a political solution prior to 1990. As one member of the delegation (who did not want to be identified) told me, "Vietnam prefers to obtain a political solution because we can then withdraw from Cambodia even more quickly and solve the situation sooner, not only there but also in Southeast Asia. We can then concentrate on our own economic development. A peace in Cambodia recognized by other nations would be much more preferable than a military solution. The conditions for a political solution are ripening. There is now agreement on the broad principles." The avowedly "softer" Vietnamese position, which has evolved over the past year or so, is based on Vietnam's pledge to withdraw its troops as scheduled by 1990, but not, under any circumstances, to permit the return of "the genocidal Pol Pot regime." Like Sihanouk, the Vietnamese propose "national reconciliation" among the various Khmer parties, but they adamantly exclude "the Pol Pot clique as a military or political entity." Both the Vietnamese and Sihanouk seek international guarantees of agreements reached.

An agreement of any kind on Cambodia will require a great deal of forbearance and patience by all sides, and a sincere desire to establish a truly neutral new nation that would serve genuine interests of peace in the region. Unfortunately, as Sihanouk is the first to acknowledge, such a resolution is still a long way off, and may prove unattainable. "I fear the future," he said to me, somewhat forlornly. "I am not a defeatist but I am realistic. There must be free elections, the right to choose our own political system through self-determination, and our own economic system. So far, I see no signs of this happening. And I am worried about many other things, including demographic changes. Soon we will have a whole new generation of young people in Cambodia, and this will pose a danger to us. Time remains in favor of the Vietnamese." Sihanouk pointed out to me a section in his speech, which he had delivered a few days before to the General Assembly, and in which he had said, "The fact remains that being unable to impose its fait accompli in Cambodia by force of arms, Vietnam tries to achieve it through diplomatic maneuvers, the cynicism and effrontery of which consist in arrogating to itself the right to speak and act as master, in the name of so-called 'Indo-China.'" Sihanouk put the speech down, paused a moment, and then added, "Neither the Soviet Union nor China will want to give up its strategic position in Southeast Asia. And the Vietnamese will not surrender their position in Cambodia simply for the shadow of a compromise. How can they expel the delicious cake of Cambodia from their throat and stomach for something less substantial and consistent? The Khmer Rouge, for their part, can fight until most of the country is in ashes, but it's wishful thinking to hope that they can ruin or exhaust the Vietnamese. In the long run, the Vietnamese are uncompromising. They will surely not give up what they have for something fanciful."

(2)

A year before my conversations with Sihanouk and the Vietnamese in New York, in the early fall of 1984 and shortly before that year's big Vietnamese dry season offensive had begun, I returned to Cambodia for a short visit for the first time in eleven years. More saddened than shocked, I found a nation so ravaged and destroyed by the traumatic events of the past decade that it had to summon all its remnant energies and carefully muster what little foreign aid it was able to obtain simply to survive. Phnom Penh, which had been virtually emptied by the Khmer Rouge when they captured it in 1975 and ordered all but a handful of the population of half a million out into the countryside, was back to its former size; but most of the residents were new countryfolk who were strangers to the city, and they seemed lost and out of place on its drab and dusty streets. Compared to Saigon and other busy Vietnamese cities and towns, Phnom Penh had always moved at a quieter pace, which had been part of its charm; but now it seemed lackluster, if not torpid, and terribly dirty. Despite the paucity of vehicles other than bicycles and a few motorbikes, clouds of dust and debris swirled in the sunlight and created a steady yellowish-brown haze, as if the city, fittingly, were covered with a shroud. The old stucco homes and offices with their subtle pastel tones and shades seemed duller, the plaster cracked and pocked by shrapnel and bullet holes. Overall, the city seemed to have lost its color, zest, and character, as if it had been struck by some peculiar blight from which it had been unable to recover. Hordes of flies and fleas and other insects added to this impression. Yet some sections were as lively as before, particularly the markets—markets are amazing survivors—which were full of goods smuggled in from Thailand and Singapore, including radios, recorders, cassettes, expensive watches and cameras, jeans and other up-to-date clothes, cartons of British and American cigarettes, and various brands of foreign beer and whiskey. There were also plenty of local fresh vegetables and fruits, meats and fish. Rice was selling at six Cambodian riel per kilogram, which was almost a dollar at the official rate (the unofficial, or free market, rate was fifty riel to the dollar). This was three times the normal price, which was the result of severe floods in the eastern and central parts of the country, followed by severe droughts in the northwest. The floods generally were the worst in seventy years, I learned from Kong Somol, the hardworking minister of agriculture (who studied at the University of Georgia and spoke the best English of any Cambodian I met). In a number of provinces, he said, half or more of the rice crop had been destroyed.

Somol as well as other officials said that the combination of natural disasters had created a shortfall of half a million tons of grain. Some spoke of another famine, such as the one that occurred in the period shortly after "liberation" in 1979, but the fact remained that there was probably enough grain available to feed most people minimal rations if it could only be properly distributed. Much of the eastern part of the country was under water, however, and roads and rails almost everywhere were still in disrepair. To make it worse, Somol continued, Cambodia ordinarily needed at least two million draft animals and was already short about eight hundred thousand. Now uncounted additional thousands of animals, mostly buffalo, were missing and many were presumed drowned in the floods—during a drive outside the city I saw several wandering aimlessly in the fields or swimming in the swollen canals. Draft animals perform three-quarters of the agricultural work in Cambodia and the rest is done by hand, with the help of new one-man Japanese gasoline-powered plows, some of which had just been donated by the Food and Agricultural Organization of the United Nations; but there was already a shortage of spare parts which could be obtained only on the black market. Cambodia used to export a variety of agricultural commodities, Somol added, but it was in such a state of ruin that it would take at least five years, barring more disasters, to produce enough rice and maize for regular export again. "We had less than fifty thousand hectares of rubber left after liberation," he said, "but only sixteen thousand have been rehabilitated so far. Vietnamese workers used to run the rubber plantations, with the help of some Cambodians, but not many of our people want to go back there now. Pol Pot killed off the rubber specialists, too, and now the young men and women want education and training in other things. As for light industry, about all we have at the moment is a jute factory and handicrafts. Our sugarcane factories are still broken down. We're terribly short on electricity, and when floods like these come along, the situation gets worse. We have gold, silver, and iron up north but no means yet to develop any of it. Our best hope is that we can build up the rubber plantations in five years or so, but who knows how long it will take to get all these other things started." Somewhat despairingly, Somol pointed out, heavy floods emphasized the need for an efficient water-control system, but neither the Cambodians nor the French ever addressed themselves to this problem rationally; moreover, 60 percent of the country's small irrigation systems, including pumps and drainage facilities, were not working because the Cambodians lacked the basic elementary training in such things as regularly changing lubricants.

The nation remained geographically and politically divided, and demographically and psychologically fragmented as well. Few were the families that had not suffered some deaths and had remained intact. My guide, whose name was Heng, told me that of sixteen families in his native village in the province of Stung Treng, his was one of only two that survived, though his father, a fisherman, died in a work camp. The rest of the family was almost completely dispersed, with only the two youngest of eight children remaining with the mother. The other six children all ended up in different work camps but lived. Heng, who was twenty-four years old in 1975, was sent to Kompong Thom province, where he had to hide the fact that he spoke a little English or he would have been executed. "I worked in the fields as a farmer," he said. "There was never enough to eat and I had a bad case of malaria. I was a bag of bones." During a long morning's ride among several villages near the city, we stopped to talk to two eighteen-year-old girls who were walking along the road. The father and brother of one had been killed, and the guardian aunt and uncle of the other. Both girls originally came from the same village twenty miles away and they now worked together helping other families raise crops collectively on thirty hectares—about seventy-four acres—growing just enough extra rice to feed themselves. At another house nearby, where the remnants of several families were living together, the father of one man, both parents of another, and the older brother of a third had been murdered by Pol Pot's men. They spoke of the damage done to the crops by the floods and of the shortage of small electric pumps lent them by the state, which were being shuttled around from one village to another. At another stop on the road we met the chief of a village of 155 families who was busily overseeing two pumps distributing water through the fields. He had lived here before the war, had gone to Battambang province in the northwest under Pol Pot, and returned to his own village afterward, when he heard the Vietnamese had come. "There is not enough food this year," he said. "We need more pumps, fertilizer, and pesticides. Now we have to work doubly hard to make up for what we have lost in the floods."

At an orphanage ten miles from Phnom Penh we spoke with the director, Som Moeung, who had worked in the Ministry of Justice before Pol Pot took over. He managed to hide that fact and avoided execution, but his parents were killed and one of his five children died of starvation in a camp that originally had five thousand families, only 250 of which were still there in 1979. Some of the others had been moved elsewhere but many had died, either of malnutrition, dysentery, or malaria, or had been killed. After 1979 he was appointed the social action chief of the provincial committee of Kandal to start up the orphanage, where he now had fifty boys and twenty-one girls living in a rectangular building that had been an orphanage previously. The government was providing a hundred and twenty-one riel, about seventeen dollars officially, per month for each child, most of whom attended a nearby school during the day and worked in the rice fields in their spare time. When they reached the age of twenty-one, Som Moeung said, the majority were sent to work at a nearby glass factory, but a few were being sent abroad for technical study, usually in Vietnam or the Soviet Union. I talked to one twelve-year-old boy who said his parents and three brothers and a sister had all been killed and he had then lived in the forest for two years, moving about constantly and eating leaves and berries, until liberation. Two seventeen-year-old girls were the sole survivors of their families. Both hoped to become nurses.

Considering the shortages of food, equipment, medicines, and just about anything one could think of, I thought it astonishing that the country was able to function at all systematically. Yet by now most of the farmers were organized into so-called Solidarity Groups, or Krom Samakki, with each group consisting of twenty to thirty agricultural workers on twenty or so hectares of land, with an average of five pairs of oxen per group. (The government does not recognize private ownership of land.) All the work, performed as much by women as men, was carried on collectively, and the crops were shared. Half the total crop was reserved for children and old people. Those entering the army received an amount equal to the bulk of the share of the best worker in the group. Nurses and teachers were then allotted their portions. Ten percent of the total crop of the solidarity group was set aside for buying seeds, and the rest was divided among the various families according to need. There was nothing compulsory about the system, Minister Somol said, and it all operated rather informally, but the basic aim was to foster as much community cooperation as possible in advancing toward socialism in three stages of collectivization. Those families who wanted to work privately could do so as long as they shared a basic amount of their main crop with their fellow villagers. "The solidarity groups, in a sense, are traditionally Khmer," Somol added, "but they were started up in 1979 mainly because of the shortage of men—there are quite a few more women than men in the country. We're still experimenting with various kinds of groups to find out which are the most effective. In all, there are now more than a hundred thousand solidarity groups in Cambodia."

One of the three American relief agency workers then in the country, Eva Mysliwiec, of Oxfam, gave the Cambodians full credit for coping with disaster, but said emphatically, "What they need here is security, stability, equipment, and a regular source of manpower. So far they have none of these things." The Western economic embargo against Vietnam established after the 1978 invasion, which affected shipments to Cambodia too, made sheer survival extremely difficult, let alone reconstruction and repair of the nation's shattered infrastructure. Miss Mysliwiec, as well as others I spoke with among the fifty or so aid workers from fifteen international agencies, all made the point that they felt shackled by the distinction between humanitarian and developmental aid made by the State Department and by other Western bureaucracies. In the case of the United States, for example, licenses had to be approved by the State and Commerce Departments for the importation of any form of assistance. During emergencies, such as the earlier big famine, these were relatively easy to obtain, but once the worst was over, despite Cambodia's dire need for continuing help, many licenses for equipment and further aid were denied; even when they were granted on appeal, the amounts were limited, and it took months of wrangling with Cambodian officials, who were constantly being transferred, to direct the assistance to where it was most needed. "Spare parts for machinery were usually considered to be developmental, so we couldn't get them once the emergency was over," Miss Mysliwiec said. "The world would rather wait apparently until another famine starts instead of investing at once in more tools to avert one."

Fred Kauffman, a tall bearded man who was working for the Mennonite Central Committee and who had just returned from a three-day trip to the province of Kampot, where he had investigated the possibilities of processing soap from coconuts with simple mechanical oil separation equipment and filters, said, "What we're mainly looking at now is low-key, small projects to which the Khmer adapt better anyway. Some of them still want larger, more modern things, but they're not geared for them and they can't maintain them. The few motor vehicles they have seem to run on paste and spit, and they don't even have enough of those to pick up the garbage in the streets of Phnom Penh, though that's due as much as anything else to the fact that most of the new population are simple villagers with no notion of how to run a city or keep it clean. Most Cambodians are pretty good learners if they're well taught. The main thing I feel about the Khmer now is their sense of insecurity. They've been through so much, and they're not sure of themselves in this strange new situation, with more responsibilities being thrust upon them. Virtually the whole new bureaucracy is inexperienced—the old one is gone, mostly dead. They're vulnerable, and they feel it. The heavy hand of the Vietnamese is still apparent, though it may be less visible than it was at first. No matter what they claim, though, the Vietnamese are here for their own security; they want to make sure that the Cambodians are dependable allies before they will even think about leaving, and that hasn't happened yet. The public's insecurity has also increased because people are still worried about Pol Pot returning to power, especially if the opposition to the regime continues to grow."

During my time in Phnom Penh I sensed this feeling myself time and again. Everyone I spoke with brought up Pol Pot's name almost ritualistically, as if he were an evil spirit whose influence hung heavy over the land and couldn't be dissipated. . . . "In Pol Pot times," people kept saying in somber tones; it was never "the Khmer Rouge," just Pol Pot who was mentioned, whether it was someone recounting his personal experience or the guides who provided the litany of horror stories as they conducted me through such unforgettable places as the mass graves, including the largest site a few miles out of town, where the remains, mostly skulls and other bare whitish-gray bones, of nearly nine thousand victims are neatly piled in rows on wooden shelves in what was once the burial ground of a rich family. A dozen or so skulls had fallen to the ground, but I hesitated to pick them up. This apparently was a major killing site, and most of the bones were found in 130 nearby pits that are slowly being overgrown with weeds. Other remains were brought to the site from Tuol Sleng prison in Phnom Penh, which is Exhibit A for those few foreigners who visit Cambodia and which, with unconscious Orwellian precision, is officially named the Museum of Genocidal Crime.

A high school before 1975, Tuol Sleng was the largest prison in the country "in Pol Pot times." Sixteen thousand prisoners were tortured and killed there, and among the macabre exhibits are racks, iron shackles, hangmen's bars, and other instruments of torture and death. Surrounded by a double wall of cement and corrugated barbed wire, the first two floors of the long building were used as single cells and the top floor as a mass detention center, where the illuminating files of all prisoners are now kept and which is a gold mine of historical information. Biographical accounts include detailed confessions of some of the principal leaders of the Kampuchean Communist Party, about which very little was known until it came to power, in 1975. In the garden in front, white tombstones mark the graves of fourteen persons who were killed on January 7, 1979, just before the Vietnamese "liberated" the city. Inside, the walls of three rooms are lined with photographs of all the prisoners who passed through Tuol Sleng, including old regime officers and officials, teachers and students, doctors and other professional people, Buddhist monks, and anyone who was suspected of ties to the republican government. Among those executed were seven foreigners—five Indians, an Australian, and an

American, James William Clark, who, the caption said, was a CIA agent captured in a gunboat offshore while taking photographs of installations with a telescopic lens.

Even in less ghoulish places, one feels the impact of Pol Pot, mainly because he is mentioned so often. His name came up at least a dozen times during the first afternoon of my visit, when my guide took me to watch people building dikes to hold back the rising floodwaters of the Mekong, which flows through Phnom Penh and into the Tonle Sap, or Great Lake, before it reverses its flow each fall and thus causes flooding under even normal conditions. Because of the abnormally high water, many of the homes on islands in the river were already submerged to their rooftops. The dike building was going on apace, though, typically, the Cambodians had turned this into a festive occasion. There were as many vendors of pineapple and other seasonal fruits, candies, and dried meats and of spinning plastic toys and balloons on sticks as there were dike workers. Hundreds of youngsters scampered back and forth along the riverbank. The guide made a point of telling me that the games they were playing included several in which Pol Pot was the villain.

Though his real name is Saloth Sar, born in Kompong Thom province on May 19, 1928, everyone in Cambodia and elsewhere has always called him Pol Pot, the revolutionary name he adopted at an early age. Whatever his murderous reputation, he surely is one of the more extraordinary revolutionary figures of modern times. Sihanouk, among others, has admitted his charismatic leadership qualities and his legitimate revolutionary credentials, elementary and ideologically fuzzy as they may be. It is no accident that, although the Khmer Rouge killed five of Sihanouk's children and a dozen or more members of his extended family, the prince and his fellow non-Communist leader, Son Sann, who heads the Khmer People's National Liberation Front, remain in tenuous alliance today with Pol Pot against the Vietnamese and their sponsored Cambodian regime directed by Heng Samrin. Not much is known about Samrin's background, either, other than that he is a renegade Khmer Rouge officer who turned against Pol Pot in 1978 in the eastern military zone of Cambodia, near the Vietnamese border. A series of regional revolts against Pol Pot had broken out over the previous year or so, and Samrin's was rather late, possibly because it had been preceded by that of another Khmer Rouge officer in the same zone named So Phim, who was secretly working with the Vietnamese and was mysteriously killed after a series of purges and internecine eastern zone plots. Heng Samrin then, in effect, took his place. The People's Republic of Kampuchea (PRK)—Kampuchea is Cambodia's old Khmer name—was established by the Vietnamese with Samrin as president when they took Phnom Penh in January 1979, a fortnight after their invasion was launched on Christmas Day, 1978. Although incapable of surviving without the material help and guidance of the Vietnamese, by the time of my visit late in 1984 the new government was beginning to function fairly well in its own right, at least in some areas of activity. It had built up a small if inexperienced corps of civilian workers whose Vietnamese advisers were remaining in the background more than they did at first, and its thirty-thousand-man army was starting to take a greater initiative in battle, though the Vietnamese were still very much in charge.

In the late summer of 1985 there were disturbing reports that undisclosed numbers of Khmer recruits were being used as "human mine detectors" after being trained for this suicide duty by Cambodian specialists at a school established by the Vietnamese in Phnom Penh. Visiting Western correspondents were told that some of the graduated students had participated in the Vietnamese dry season offensive of 1984–85 along the border and had been killed in action fulfilling their duties in finding mines and being blown up with them. The desertion rate among army recruits was said to be high. Cambodian civilians as well as some soldiers were also being used to construct ditches and other defensive barriers along the frontier, and hundreds were suffering from severe forms of malaria. Earlier reports submitted by a visiting American human rights committee composed of three lawyers, who had interviewed dozens of Cambodian refugees at border camps, quoted them as claiming that a new systematic campaign of torture of political prisoners in Cambodia was being conducted by the Samrin government at the instigation of the Vietnamese. The report was officially acknowledged by the State Department, which said that it was consistent with its own accounts of "widespread use of torture and other forms of mistreatment by Vietnam and its client regime in Cambodia to extract alleged 'confessions' from persons suspected of opposing the regime installed by Vietnam." One of the three committee members, Floyd Abrams, a well-known New York lawyer and civil libertarian, said that thousands of prisoners had been tortured with electrodes and were regularly and severely beaten. While the new violations of human rights "pale in comparison to the mass murders" of the Pol Pot regime, Abrams added, they "rival those of other nations whose abuses have provoked outcries from the world community." Abrams decried "the absence of a functioning legal process in Cambodia" and concluded, with a note of cynical sadness, "Neglect of the human rights of Cambodians reflects, in part, the view that nothing better can be hoped for people who have suffered as much as they have."

(3)

The group fighting the Samrin government and the Vietnamese is called the Coalition Government of Democratic Kampuchea; Sihanouk is officially its president and, until September 1985, Pol Pot was still "Commander in Chief of the National Army." Whether his announced retirement then was purely cosmetic or not, in point of fact his Khmer Rouge majority faction continues to operate independently of the lesser forces of Son Sann and Sihanouk, about fifteen thousand and seven thousand respectively. (To emphasize how confusing Cambodian politics and names can be, Pol Pot's place was said to have been taken by the Khmer Rouge minister of defense, Son Sen, who is not to be confused with Son Sann.) Other officers, including some of the more competent survivors of the old republican army of pre-1975 days, provide what little semblance of unity exists among the three disparate opposition elements. Almost from the outset, however, constant bickering and, from time to time, some actual fighting among them has occurred, which has caused Sihanouk on several occasions to threaten to resign as the coalition's president. Since mid-1985, a serious rift in the ranks of Son Sann's Khmer People's National Liberation Front has taken place, further threatening the coalition's tenuous cohesion. Son Sann has been accused by his top military commanders and some of his fellow political leaders of refusing, more stubbornly than before, to cooperate with Sihanouk, and, more important, of meddling in military matters. Early in 1986, a breakaway group headed by Suk Sutsakhan, the commander in chief of the KPNLF army, and including the chief of staff, Dien Del, and several regional military commanders as well as members of the Front's executive committee, sought Son Sann's expulsion, or at least a pledge from him to confine his activities to ceremonial and representational duties. The new group called itself the Provisional Central Committee of Salvation. Son Sann denounced its "open rebellion," which he called illegal, and declared it "banned." The internecine struggle was largely responsible for the reduced activity of the KPNLF forces within Cambodia; all but a few hundred of its troops did, in fact, withdraw to Thailand, leaving the Cambodian fighting to the far stronger Khmer Rouge and to about five hundred of Sihanouk's forces. While by April of 1986 a tenuous compromise appeared to have ameliorated the split within the KPNLF, it continued to be regarded as symptomatic of the problems that had all along marked the non-Communist opposition. Sihanouk and Son Sann were at odds on both military and political issues. Cooperation between the Front and Sihanouk's organization was regarded as essential by the Southeast Asian nations and by the United States, which had just begun openly as well as covertly to lend military support to the two coalition members in an effort to strengthen them and isolate the Khmer Rouge. Washington took this step, with some reluctance, believing it might eventually lead to the establishment of a new government in Phnom Penh that would not be altogether dominated by the Vietnamese or, alternatively, to a regime again headed by the Khmer Rouge.

If it proves true that Pol Pot is really taking a backseat, both politically and militarily, which most observers doubt, the important figures in the Khmer Rouge will probably be Son Sen, on the military side, and Khieu Samphan, who is vice-president for foreign affairs of the coalition and prime minister of the Democratic Kampuchea (or Khmer Rouge) faction, which has kept its old name. Despite its claims of having renounced communism and adopted a program of moderate socialism, there also appears little doubt that the Khmer Rouge troops are still committed revolutionaries and are still capable of waging campaigns of terror within Cambodia whenever they find targets of opportunity. Writing for the *Sunday Times* of London, Jon Swain, who remained in Cambodia for a fortnight after its fall in 1975 and who appeared as a central figure in the film *The Killing Fields,* reported, after returning to the

country a few months after my visit, that the Khmer
Rouge soldiers were as ruthless and savage as ever. He
cited an incident that had occurred a few weeks before his
arrival when Pol Pot's guerrillas butchered between a
hundred and fifty and two hundred civilian passengers on
a train near Takeo, forty-seven miles south of Phnom
Penh. Prior to that, Khmer Rouge soldiers had bayoneted
a hundred and fifty people after ambushing a train at
Oudong, only twenty miles north of the capital. The Lawyers Committee for Human Rights report cited above also
referred to continuing abuses of human rights by the
Khmer Rouge forces. The report accused the Pol Pot faction of setting up a brutal system of social control in its
areas, adding that despite its efforts to project a more
moderate image, "Draconian measures were [still] used to
enforce even the image of reform: persons . . . could be
imprisoned for making such comments as 'Things are
being done the way Pol Pot used to do.' " The State Department, without any comment about the apparent contradiction with its continuing support of the Pol Pot
government in the United Nations, underlined what the
report said by noting that its findings "support our belief
that the Khmer Rouge remains a totalitarian organization
determined to dominate completely the lives of persons
under its control." Notwithstanding this appraisal, which
few observers denied, there were growing reports in mid-
1986 of conflicts among Khmer Rouge commanders and
indications that a number of them were carving out their
own reginal fiefdoms much in the manner of old Chinese
warlords. The dominant and most radical figure in the
military hierarchy, it was said, was Ta Mok, whose troops
operated in northern Cambodia near the Thai border and
had the reputation of being the most brutal.

The coalition forces as a whole are incapable of maintaining control of any Cambodian territory beyond some
border area strips and scattered pockets in the interior of

the country, notably in the northwest and in the five provinces around the Tonle Sap (Great Lake). Nevertheless,
the resistance remains sporadically active in most provinces. Sabotage actions have taken place in a number of
districts near Phnom Penh, and a few in Phnom Penh
itself. Coalition troops have also managed to cut Vietnamese supply lines by attacking roads, railways, and water-
ways, and have struck at the administrative apparatus in
villages, communes, and districts, making it more difficult
for the Vietnamese to enlist the support of local Cambodian self-defense guards as well as army recruits. Coalition
officers claim that the big Vietnamese offensive in western
Cambodia in 1984–85, for which Hanoi sent in sixty thousand fresh troops, cost the enemy one-third of the total in
dead and wounded. Overall, despite the internecine struggles, the strength of the guerrilla fighters seems to be
growing, and the war, ironically, has more and more come
to resemble the American effort to combat the North Vietnamese conventionally, with the Vietnamese now cast in
the role of the Americans, complete with helicopters. An
indication that the coalition guerrillas are achieving some
success was the fact that, late in 1985, they prompted the
wholesale arrest by the Phnom Penh goverment of village
and commune officials suspected or accused of collaborat-
ing with the coalition elements.

Legally, though it has no seat of power, the coalition
retains the support and recognition of the six members of
the Association of Southeast Asian Nations (ASEAN)—
Indonesia, Malaysia, Singapore, Thailand, the Philippines,
and Brunei. The UN, ASEAN, and the United States have
all along led the condemnation of Vietnam for having
belligerently invaded Cambodia in 1978, and collectively
they continue to demand the complete withdrawal of Vietnamese troops. Only then, as Washington continues to say,
will any discussion on normalizing relations and possibly
restoring aid to Vietnam be begun. ASEAN diplomats,

notably the Indonesians, have sought to promote compromise approaches that would at least get a dialogue started sooner. It remains unclear just at what point in such talks the Vietnamese might begin the withdrawal of a sizable number of troops. Some progress has been made over the past year, however, in defining the components of a dialogue. It would certainly include the leaders of the Heng Samrin government, notably Hun Sen, who is both chairman of the Council of Ministers, or prime minister, and foreign minister. He is a tough, brash thirty-four-year-old former Khmer Rouge officer who was apparently one of the Khmer Communists close to the Vietnamese in the late seventies, though he goes out of his way to assert his independence, as he did when I spoke with him in Phnom Penh, maintaining, for example, "We need the Vietnamese forces here only to help us defend ourselves until we are strong enough ourselves. If we don't need them, we'll tell them to go, and they'll withdraw. All foreign forces should withdraw from Southeast Asia, including the Americans in the Philippines."

Hun Sen was extremely hard-line at the beginning of our hour and a half conversation, maintaining that Sihanouk and Son Sann were "dangerous allies of Pol Pot and the Khmer Rouge" and that, therefore, there could be no negotiations with them, let alone with Pol Pot, later mellowed to the point of saying that "as we get stronger ourselves, we will offer clemency to those who have been misled, but they will have to accept our new constitution. Sihanouk is temperamentally like a cloud after a rain. What's important is whether he has abandoned Pol Pot and the Khmer Rouge. If he gives up his mistakes, he may come back and live with the people, but we will not invite him. As to his future, the people will have to decide—including me." Hun Sen seemed to leave the door open for reconciliation with other ranking members of the Khmer Rouge and for them to be included in talks. Presumably this would include Khieu Samphan, about whom Hun Sen simply snapped, "We don't speak about him, but we say anyone who admits his mistakes." Samphan goes back a long way and at one point was a member of one of Sihanouk's governments before he turned against the prince and took to the jungle in the sixties. The two men were later reconciled in Peking and he joined Sihanouk's government-in-exile. As a leading member of the coalition, especially if Pol Pot has actually retired, Samphan, as mentioned earlier, would be bound to be included in any coalition talks, along with both Sihanouk and Son Sann. In December 1985 the three coalition leaders met in Peking, under Chinese auspices, and renewed their pledges of unity. Since my conversation with Hun Sen, there have been further signs that he is ready to negotiate, on more equal terms than he originally indicated, with all of the coalition elements. Nevertheless, despite these outward indications of progress, a resolution of the Cambodian situation, either politically or militarily, scarcely seemed imminent in mid-1986.

The basic problem remains the Khmer Rouge, as such, irrespective of its leaders. So far, neither ASEAN nor the United States, having supported the Pol Pot regime in the United Nations, is prepared simply to turn around and recognize the Vietnam-sponsored government of Heng Samrin and Hun Sen. Washington's support of Pol Pot has puzzled a great many people, including ordinary Americans, who cannot understand how we could possibly have stood behind a man accused of having murdered so many Cambodians. Sihanouk himself has partly answered the question. "It is not very clean to be with the Khmer Rouge," he has said. "I feel very uncomfortable . . . but we have to behave like that. Why? Because there is the danger of Vietnamese expansionism and Soviet hegemonism. . . . Those states are very dangerous; we cannot allow them to go further." Unfortunately, as Sihanouk has also pointed out, the Khmer Rouge, with or without Pol Pot, continue to provide the muscle and it is difficult to conceive of any talks that would exclude them as a faction. If the Chinese ceased supporting them and the Thais withdrew their right of sanctuary, Hun Sen told me, "There could be a solution to the problem tomorrow."

There are those, myself included, who believe that because of the shifting world power situation, in which the Chinese and the Russians have been holding their own dialogue to seek a limited rapprochement and to reopen channels of trade and cultural exchange, the Chinese might in time be persuaded to stop backing the Khmer Rouge. The rise to power in the Soviet Union of Mikhail Gorbachev is a vital factor in this projection. Gorbachev is already seeking a new ameliorative role for the Russians in Southeast Asia, possibly so he can concentrate on Soviet domestic problems, and he has urged the Chinese and the Vietnamese to come to terms with each other, something that Hanoi would dearly love to do but for which Peking so far has not shown much enthusiasm. When I was in Hanoi, Vietnamese officials I spoke with all made a point of stressing that the two things they wanted most were peace with China and recognition and help from the United States. If the Chinese can be persuaded to drop or lessen their support for the Khmer Rouge in the interests of peace in Southeast Asia, the United States would in all likelihood have to exert its influence to convince them that it is no longer in the interest of anyone, including the Chinese themselves, to keep Vietnam isolated and bogged down in Cambodia, which is essentially the case despite its military success there. Unfortunately, because of its preoccupation with other foreign matters—in the Middle East, Central America, Africa, and Europe—the Reagan administration has shown only sporadic interest to date in playing a constructive role in the newly evolving situation in Southeast Asia. Its main thrust has been to negotiate with Vietnam over the identification of the twenty-four hundred missing wartime prisoners and to encourage ASEAN to take the lead in any dialogue with the Vietnamese about the problem of Cambodia. The Russians and the Chinese, each for their own reasons, seem content to continue accepting the status quo—a so-called stable war—in Cambodia, despite their joint efforts to reach an accommodation.

When Pol Pot took over Cambodia in 1975 after the defeat of what was left of the Cambodian Republican forces and the withdrawal of the South Vietnamese and the Americans, his image was that of a crude but credible peasant revolutionary leader. He had mistakenly been said to be pro-Vietnamese, but in fact, from the outset, he was more in the Chinese than the Vietnamese camp. Above all, he had a strong bias against the urban elite who had dominated Khmer public life under the French and afterward —the urban-rural cleavages in Cambodia have always existed, although they have often been obscure and somewhat inchoate. Poorly educated himself and surrounded by a small group of Cambodian Communists whose educational qualifications, personal backgrounds, and revolutionary notions and ideas varied considerably, Pol Pot immediately ordered the mass migration from the cities to the countryside. The decision had apparently been taken by the central committee of the Communist Party of Kampuchea a year earlier in the name of a cleansing operation —to rid the cities, especially Phnom Penh, of the worst attributes of the urban way of life, including the profligacy, waste, and corruption of the ruling class and the bourgeoisie, which meant anyone who was educated and held a professional job, from officials and teachers to private persons. What Pol Pot and his henchmen sought to do was to create a national agrarian change or upheaval overnight, dedicated to the planting of rice and other crops that would make Cambodia as nearly self-sufficient as possible and then able to export its surplus to obtain foreign exchange for gradual and limited industrialization. (One of their subsequent errors was to dispose of their "surplus" by overexporting too soon, chiefly to China, which made Cambodian starvation worse.) There is little doubt that the mass exodus from Phnom Penh and the depopulation of other cities and towns was carried out brutally for the most part, and that Khmer Rouge soldiers, many of whom were illiterate boys in their teens, were motivated by blind hatred of urban residents and feelings of anger and revenge. They had been indoctrinated with this hatred since they were youngsters in the jungle, practicing war games with wooden guns before they began to get arms from the North Vietnamese, the Chinese, or on the black market. It is doubtful that any of them had anything more than the most rudimentary knowledge of what communism was all about.

That the revolution got out of hand and by 1977 had reached an unprecedented and virtually uncontrollable level of violence seems by now to be well documented. There were waves of killing that varied from region to region, and that resulted partly from continued internal migrations that were both forced and voluntary as some people fled from one area to another. Lack of food and other bare necessities, above all medicines for stomach ailments and malaria, accounted for many more deaths than executions, though forced starvation as a policy was also a major cause. What was kept up, under duress, was the agrarian scheme to plant more and more crops and build irrigation canals, many of them dug by hand under conditions of forced labor, and part of this network of canals proved lasting and useful. But what was obviously lacking was a basic blueprint, a revolutionary plan of action suitable for the special conditions that obtained in a highly underdeveloped country. Comparisons have been made between what happened in Cambodia and the Great Leap

Forward in China in the late fifties, and there are certain similarities, including the elementary conditions that obtained in both countries and the excesses that took place, partly because of the great mistrust of educated urban intellectuals. There are some indications that Pol Pot and his cohorts, and particularly Khieu Samphan, who wrote a treatise during his days in Paris about agrarian revolution predicated on enforced urban migration to the countryside, used the Great Leap as their later model. Whatever the impetus or inspiration, it certainly didn't work in Cambodia, where the experiment was like a wild leap in the dark. As events got completely out of hand—the killings increased, and disease and starvation grew endemic—the situation quickly degenerated into total chaos. What happened inside Cambodia may have been exaggerated by some observers as an unmitigated phenomenon of death and destruction. In fact, the pattern was uneven, but however one interprets the stories of the early refugees and the late survivors who escaped into Thailand, it was apparent that a national disaster on a grand scale had taken place. Whether one million or two million people eventually died, of whom in either case probably about a third were executed, Pol Pot's peasant revolution obviously was an abysmal and unprecedented failure. As a lesser consequence, the twin myths of Cambodia as a gentle land inhabited by a gentle people had once and for all been laid to rest.

Such, in brief, was the background that preceded the Vietnamese invasion of Christmas Day, 1978, to "liberate" Cambodia. So much has been written about the country in the past decade, though very little based on firsthand observation, and so much happened prior to that which has been fogotten or remains confused and obscure, that the average reader of today's military and political events has every reason to be puzzled. To trace the threads of this complicated situation, in which Prince Sihanouk has played a key role, one should go back to the early sixties, when Cambodia was struggling to get on its feet as an independent nation, which it had become as a result of the Geneva Conference of 1954.

(4)

Cambodia is the only country that I, as a journalist, have ever been officially thrown out of, and the only place where I once performed—or tried to perform—a diplomatic mission. Not surprisingly, Sihanouk was involved in both episodes. In the larger scope of events, they each revealed some of the strange quirks in the prince's behavior that demonstrated his capacity for acting rashly in situations that then get beyond his ability to control. He often responds to these situations in such a way as to enmesh himself further in a position that is contrary to his original or ultimate purpose, which remains the salvation of the Khmer nation. On occasion, when he appears to be most self-defeating and contradictory, he is simply balancing several options at once, which he enjoys doing, even if he confounds himself as much as he confounds others. But invariably his sheer amiability, his sense of historical humor, and his ability to laugh at himself enable him to escape difficult situations, either by conveniently forgetting what he has said or done before or by simply taking a new tack. He is never at a loss for words, whatever he does, and they are usually expressed in a high, squeaky voice which keeps rising the more excited he becomes as he presses his points. There is something at once irrepressible and irresistible about Sihanouk, which, beyond his deep-felt patriotism and sheer enthusiasm, may derive from his passion for playing several roles simultaneously—when he was ruling Cambodia he produced and directed a number of exotic films in which he and his beautiful Khmer-

French-Italian wife, Monique, played the leading or subsidiary parts, and sometimes both. Moreover, the flamboyant prince has never lost his sense of royal prerogative, and he is still convinced that he was predestined to lead the Cambodians, his "children," or "the little people," as he always called them, to freedom and salvation. As he has written in his memoirs, which he is preparing for publication, "In Cambodia, essentially only 'the little people' remained faithful to me," by which he primarily meant the country's poor peasant class. Those who are still alive today undoubtedly are among his strongest supporters.

This is one reason why, in 1985, forty-four years since he ascended the throne at the tender age of nineteen and thirty years since he renounced the title of king, to which he was historically entitled—and despite the fact that a whole new generation has grown up inside Cambodia that has known only pain and sorrow and knows little or nothing about him—he may still prove indispensable. If he is not the only man who can preserve some form of independence or neutrality, he may yet prove to be an important transitional leader, even as a figurehead under some form of Vietnamese patronage or influence, which seems to me unavoidable. It is significant that the Vietnamese themselves, who would prefer to be rid of him, have now accepted the fact that it is difficult or impossible to ignore Sihanouk. The more conversations I had with Vietnamese officials in Hanoi and later in the United States, the more this became apparent. In fact, during the six weeks I was in Vietnam—when the Vietnamese were coming to realize that they would eventually have to make some concessions on the Cambodian issue—the pendulum in their attitude toward Sihanouk visibly veered from official disdain to grudging acceptance of his continuing political presence. As one high official commented, "Sihanouk is like a mosquito who gets under your net at night and won't let you sleep."

My banishment from Cambodia took place late in March of 1964, not long after Sihanouk, in one of his fits of pique, had peremptorily terminated all American military, cultural, and economic aid, totaling about thirty million dollars a year, and ordered his embassy in Washington closed. Over the previous decade, the United States had given the Cambodians about three hundred and fifty million dollars' worth of economic and military assistance, which was considerably more than anyone else gave. Sihanouk himself had described this as "the oxygen that keeps Cambodia alive." But he resented the fact that, unlike the lesser amounts donated by the "flexible" Chinese and by the Russians, American aid was not in the form of outright grants but was conditional and guided by restrictions. Even though United States assistance was designed to "provide us with the framework of a modern state" by helping to build roads, bridges, and so on, Sihanouk complained that it wasn't of much help in satisfying the "pressing needs" of the poor. Moreover, he said, the United States had kept trying to get him to express his avowed support for the West, preferably by backing the Southeast Asian Treaty Organization, so ardently fostered by Secretary of State John Foster Dulles. Anyone who knew Sihanouk at all should have been aware that this was the worst sort of tactic to adopt as he pursued his acrobatic game of neutrality. Not only was he loath to make such pledges, but the net effect, especially after some border incidents involving American advisers accompanying South Vietnamese troops, was to drive him further away from the United States and closer to China.

Sihanouk's flirtation with the Chinese began in 1955 at the historic conference of Asian and African nations held in Bandung, Indonesia. The year before, at the Geneva Conference, the French joined eight other Western and Asian nations in terminating the first Indo-China war by setting up two Vietnams and confirming the independence of Laos as well as Cambodia. In 1953, in fact, worn down by fighting the Vietnamese, the French had succumbed to what Sihanouk called his "Royal Crusade for Independence," which had been a prolonged mixture of bluff and sulk on his part as he moved about from capital to capital on a world tour before settling down at Siem Reap, near Angkor Wat. Having gained France's capitulation, Sihanok held a referendum, a few months before the Bandung Conference, that supported his long fight for independence by a resounding 99.8 percent vote. It was at this point that he surprised his people by announcing his abdication as king at thirty-two years of age. Appointing his father, Suramarit, and later his mother, Queen Kossamak, to replace him, he said he had been too isolated and revered—"I could only see the flowers and hear the lies"—and that he wanted henceforth to help the Cambodian people remove "the injustices, corruption, and exploitation from which they have suffered so long."

At Bandung, he and Premier Chou En-lai hit it off immediately, and Chou remained Sihanouk's friend and benefactor until his death, late in 1975. The prince made repeated state and personal visits to Peking and always received top treatment. Chou gave him a large comfortable house, much less austere than the cold stone palace Kim Il Sung, the Korean dictator, his other benefactor, built for him in Pyongyang, the North Korean capital, where, after 1970, he spent part of his time. From the outset of his friendship with China, in the fifties, Sihanouk typically felt free to criticize the Chinese whenever he saw fit, as he did when he commented that "human life is of no importance there." Even as he began accepting economic aid from Peking and established formal diplomatic relations in August 1958, he remarked cryptically, "I know the Communists are going to cut my throat, but I am ready to die for my country." He kept on accepting American aid too, including modern rifles, machine guns, mortars, half-tracks, and light tanks, but the Cambodians wouldn't take any military advice from the Americans or allow them to go out in the field. The French, with about two hundred fifty advisers in the country compared with sixty Americans, were supposed to do the day-by-day basic training of Cambodian troops, but they didn't receive much cooperation either, and, privately, French and American officers agreed that the Cambodian army would scarcely be able to hold its own in a battle against the Thais, let alone against the South Vietnamese, and at best might be able to handle some problems of internal security.

Given the political shenanigans that were going on during those frantic years in neighboring Thailand and South Vietnam as well as in Cambodia, it is doubtful that Sihanouk's sedentary forces were capable of doing even that. In 1960 and 1961, after a series of plots and conspiracies allegedly directed against him by his two neighbors, Sihanouk broke his formal ties with Saigon and Bangkok. He kept repeating that his two worst enemies were Premier Sarit Thanarat, of Thailand, and President Ngo Dinh Diem, of South Vietnam, and maintained that the United States was their protector and that, in effect, they were American puppets. Moreover, he accused the United States, and specifically the CIA, of being the principal backer of a Cambodian nationalist named Son Ngoc Thanh, who in the past had occasionally collaborated with Sihanouk in the Cambodian struggle for independence from France, but for the most part had been his rival. In the early sixties, Thanh, whom I had come to know in Saigon, where he was leading a quasi-underground existence in the Cholon area, was still the head of the right-wing Khmer Serei (Free Khmer) movement, whose origins dated back to the end of the Second World War. Its armed strength at this time was no more than a few thousand men who mostly operated in the South Vietnamese border provinces of the Mekong Delta, which were populated by Cambodians and Vietnamese peasants and by those of mixed stock. The Khmer Serei had been armed by the South Vietnamese, primarily with old French guns, and were really part of Saigon's paramilitary structure. However, they also had some contact with the CIA and with American Special Forces, and, with the approval of President Diem, who hated Sihanouk as much as Sihanouk hated him, they probably received a small number of American weapons originally given to the Vietnamese.

In the late sixties, Special Forces Green Beret teams made constant forays into Cambodia in what were anti-Sihanouk missions because of his condonation of the use by the Vietnamese Communists of the sanctuaries. Most of these forays were mounted by Vietnamese, Thai, and Chinese mercenaries attached to the Green Berets, but they also included some Cambodians who belonged to the Khmer Serei. In his mood of suspicion of American motives, Sihanouk openly accused the Americans of backing the Khmer Serei, and he specifically charged the CIA with furnishing Son Ngoc Thanh with mobile radio equipment for setting up transmitters in the jungles of South Vietnam, southern Laos, and northeast Thailand to beam propaganda against him to Cambodia. While Washington denied that it was in any way still associated with the Khmer Serei or Son Ngoc Thanh, the Americans, by the mid-sixties, were undoubtedly losing their enthusiasm for the mercurial prince. The situation went from bad to worse when Washington refused to send him armed jets and antiaircraft equipment as part of its military aid. Sihanouk obtained a few modern fighter planes from the Russians instead, but, more important, he drew closer to the Chinese, who also later gave him some planes. In one of his moments of near hysteria, he declared that "without Chinese support I would already have died," and that "it is absolutely impossible for me to serve as a satellite of the Americans and to become an enemy of the Chinese."

After the overthrow of President Diem in November 1963, which had taken place with the approval and support of the Americans, though they had strongly disapproved of Diem's murder, Sihanouk believed he was next on the Americans' "hit list." But when President Kennedy was assassinated two weeks later, Sihanouk's first response was to order three days of national mourning and to send his premier to Washington for the funeral. Anti-American signs on the streets of Phnom Penh disappeared overnight, and the newspapers were ordered to stop their vitriolic anti-American attacks. However, on December 9, 1963, the offical Cambodian radio broadcast an expression of joy over the death of President Sarit, of Thailand, who had died of natural causes the day before, and also over the death of "the great boss of these aggressors." The following day, Sihanouk himself declared in a broadcast that "the three enemies of Cambodia are now in Hell to pursue their SEATO [Southeast Asia Treaty Organization] meetings."

This series of events eventually contributed to the diplomatic break between the United States and Cambodia, though this did not come until May 1965. Meanwhile, early in March of 1964, I received a letter from Sihanouk inviting me to Phnom Penh, and soon after that I picked up my visa in Paris. When I arrived in Cambodia, a ludicrous Graustarkian debate was still going on about what exactly had been said about Kennedy. Sihanouk angrily denied that Kennedy's name had been mentioned in connection with any "rejoicing," which may have been literally true, though the United States had demanded an inquiry of the broadcast incident and had denounced the Cambodians' behavior as "barbaric." Sihanouk, in return, had demanded an apology for that accusation, which Washington had refused to offer. No one any longer seemed to know who should apologize for what.

Overshadowing these histrionic changes was the more difficult issue of defining the vague borders between Cambodia and South Vietnam, a matter that was becoming increasingly contentious and which, along with the alleged violations of the borders, was the main reason for the break with the United States. Part of the argument hinged on whether this should be resolved at another Geneva-type conference or be settled by mixed commissions on the scene. Sihanouk had already announced that, in any event, he was first going to Paris to visit President de Gaulle, who was his hero along with Chou En-lai and who had supported his ideas about a new international conference to safeguard all of Southeast Asia's neutrality, Indo-China's in particular. But now the prince also threatened to fly to Peking to "discuss our problems with our good Chinese friends" and to call upon them to settle Cambodia's border problems with "the ultimate masters of South Vietnam—that is, the goverment of North Vietnam."

Shortly after my March 1964 arrival, as I was settling down in my room at the Hotel Le Royal for a siesta after lunch, I was suddenly roused and summoned to appear at the immigration office of the Ministry of Security. Sihanouk, I knew, had just spoken at a huge outdoor rally of his rubber-stamp National Congress and had said that, because Cambodia was encircled by hostile powers, he might be forced to "renounce neutrality in its present form and negotiate an alliance with certain receptive powers, particularly with the People's Republic of China."

Now, briefly, I was told that my visa had been revoked. Since I had filed no stories so far and was awaiting a promised audience with Sihanouk, I saw no reason for my expulsion, nor did I get any explanation from the sleepy immigration official, who seemed not at all interested when I reminded him that I was in the country at Sihanouk's personal invitation. He simply stamped the visa CANCELED and wrote in red ink alongside that I was to leave as soon as possible. I flew off to Saigon the next morning, while my seven banned cohorts—a Lebanese representing the Associated Press, a Japanese, and a group of five French television journalists—made equally hurried departures for Bangkok, Tokyo, and Peking via Hanoi. It was, I thought, at least a neutral dispersal.

(5)

I did not return to Cambodia until two years later, in July 1966, when relations with the United States, officially by then broken more than a year, had not yet been repaired. By now, however, Sihanouk had begun to show signs of losing some of his enthusiasm for China. In a series of editorials, for example, that appeared shortly after my arrival in the left-wing newspaper *La Dépêche*, with such bold headings as THE GRAND ILLUSION and THE WRONG HORSE, the point was repeatedly made that the real "paper tiger" in Asia might not be the United States, after all, but China, which had reacted to the American bombing of Hanoi and Haiphong that began in 1965 with continued promises of support for the North Vietnamese but had failed to intervene in their behalf, as Peking had previously threatened. When, during this visit, I finally managed to interview the prince, I asked him if the editorials represented his views. He evaded a direct answer by pointing out that the Sangkum, his national political movement, was composed of a left, a center, and a right wing, adding, with a smile that typically ended in a light giggle, that the leftist members "have been deceived in love"—obviously meaning by the Chinese. As for himself, he said, with revealing candor, "I am a nationalist, not a Communist, but I am still a monarchist. I have been useful to Peking. I appreciate the nationalism of others, and I seek respect for mine, and for myself as a human being, but I realize that you cannot change the nature either of men or of states."

It was during this visit that I attempted to carry out the diplomatic mission I have referred to earlier. It was, in fact, a twofold mission, half of which has remained secret until now; the other half was publicized almost at once. The fact that both proved unsuccessful did not detract from the satisfaction I derived from trying to accomplish two seemingly worthwhile aims—to discuss secretly with the Vietcong the possibility of obtaining the release of American war prisoners, and to improve relations with Sihanouk.

In the spring of 1966, on a visit to New York and Washington, I was asked by Averell Harriman, who was then President Johnson's roving ambassador, if I knew Wilfred Burchett, an Australian correspondent who for many years had had a close working relationship with leaders of the Vietnamese and Chinese Communist parties. I had known Burchett since the Second World War, when we were both war correspondents in the Pacific. At this time, in the sixties, he and his Bulgarian wife were living in Phnom Penh. He had been a good source on matters pertaining to Communist strategy and tactics and, since he had spent a considerable amount of time not only in Hanoi but with the Communist troops in the jungle, we had a number of useful conversations and exchanged ideas about the war in Vietnam. Harriman already knew I had received a Cambodian visa, and when I told him I knew Burchett quite well he asked me if I would be willing to undertake a private mission in behalf of the American government and particularly in behalf of Harriman himself, who was devoting much of his time to obtaining the release of prisoners held by the Vietnamese Communists. Because I would be dealing with a humanitarian matter, I agreed, despite some misgivings about a conflict of interest with my job as a correspondent.

The plan Harriman had devised was to approach Burchett and ascertain if he would be willing to arrange a meeting for me with Vietcong officials, who had quasi-diplomatic status, and to introduce me as a personal representative of Harriman with the right to negotiate preliminarily on the prisoner-of-war question. The idea was to offer the Vietcong nonmilitary assistance such as food and pharmaceuticals, which they desperately needed, in exchange for the release of some American prisoners we knew they were holding. We also had in mind the return of some Communist prisoners as part of the bargain, if we could persuade the South Vietnamese to release them. As for Burchett, we knew that he wanted to visit the United States and also to return to his native Australia, from where he had been banned, to see his elderly and ill father. In return for his assistance, I was to tell Burchett that a visa to the U. S. would be forthcoming and that we would try to persuade the Australians to grant him a visa, too.

Before I left, I asked Harriman, who knew Sihanouk and was one of the two Americans Sihanouk liked most— Mike Mansfield, the Senate majority leader, was the other —if he would write me a letter to the prince, which he did. A week or so after our meeting at the State Department I left for Paris, with instructions to check in with our embassy in France before I returned to the Far East, and with further instructions to keep in touch with Harriman via diplomatic cable, using the communications facilities of the Australian Embassy in Phnom Penh, since the Australians were representing our interests in Cambodia following the break in American-Cambodian relations the year before. Harriman's letter to Sihanouk was formal and brief, but before I left New York I received a phone call from him during which he suggested that I make a special point of giving Sihanouk his warm greetings and telling the prince that he would welcome the chance to see him again. Now, in Paris, in the office of John Gunther Dean, who was handling Indochinese affairs at the American Embassy and would later become our ambassador to Cambodia, I received another message from Harriman, telling me to go further in my efforts to reestablish a relationship with Sihanouk and to suggest directly that Harriman pay him a visit.

The first two people I saw in Phnom Penh were Noel St. Clair Deschamps, the Australian ambassador, and Burchett. I found Burchett, by now a roly-poly man in his fifties with a gruff but pleasant manner, who obviously enjoyed behind-the-scenes conspiracies and, I suspected, was not inexperienced as an intermediary, surprisingly willing, if not eager, to help out. He immediately agreed that the humanitarian aspects of the prisoner proposition were reason enough for us, as reporters, to involve ourselves, but I also felt that he was particularly attracted by the personal quid pro quo we offered him. He promised to make an approach to the Vietcong and to get back to me as soon as possible.

As for Deschamps, he was completely cooperative from the outset, not only in permitting me to use his communications facilities whenever I wished, but in helping me on my major task as a correspondent in Cambodia, above all explaining Sihanouk's political gyrations and the growing political predicament in which the prince was finding himself. Having been in Phnom Penh for a number of years, the portly Australian diplomat had become, along with the French ambassador, the most trusted Western representative among the many diplomats of varying persuasion who used Cambodia as a listening post. They allowed themselves, in turn, to be used by Sihanouk in the strange game the prince was playing, utilizing the issue of accepting the borders he outlined on *his* maps as the definitive ones and granting diplomatic status in various grades, including some new ones he invented, according to their degree of compliance. This made for a peculiar collection in which divided countries like Korea and Germany, not to mention Vietnam, vied with each other on the map issue. Sihanouk enjoyed every moment of this semantic contest, especially since he was the sole judge or referee. Deschamps enjoyed watching him and interpreting his actions, which he did extremely well, with mixed admiration and humor. His acceptance by the prince as a friend was apparently not hindered by the fact that the Australians were also representing the United States. Whether they suspected that I was up to anything extracurricular was something I never found out, but, at any rate, neither Sihanouk nor anyone else ever said anything to me about this aspect of my mission. On the other hand, it was hard to keep secrets in Cambodia.

I had cabled Harriman about my successful first meeting with Burchett and I had received added instructions to ask the British Embassy to deal with him in case I had to leave Phnom Penh before we received any answer from the Vietcong—my visa was good only for two weeks. As it turned out this wasn't necessary. In a day or so, Burchett suggested I write a letter to Tran Buu Kiem, one of the ranking Vietcong officials who came to Cambodia periodically from the jungle and was in town at the moment. I wrote the letter immediately, explaining my mission in general terms and adding that the United States was prepared to do what we could to return some prisoners if the Vietcong released some that they held; I also alluded to further offers we were willing to make and expressed the hope that Kiem would grant me an interview. Burchett delivered this letter the same day, and then we heard nothing for four or five days. Kiem apparently had left the city to return to his jungle headquarters, and to discuss my letter with his superiors there. When he returned, I received, through Burchett, a page-long polite letter signed by Kiem in which he thanked me for my letter and agreed that the issue of war prisoners was indeed a humanitarian one but that it would have to be determined as part of a larger political settlement, in accordance with the basis for negotiations that had been suggested separately by both the National Liberation Front and the Hanoi government. This was more or less the answer we had expected, and while disappointing, it may have opened a door in Hanoi by letting the Vietnamese know we were willing to engage in prisoner exchanges.

(A year later, in the fall of 1967, I happened to be back in Phnom Penh and at the airport the day that Tom Hayden, the antiwar activist, arrived by plane with three American sergeants in his custody who had been prisoners of the Vietcong and whose release he had managed to obtain while visiting Hanoi as a member of a peace delegation. Hayden came up to me and remarked quietly, "Tell your friend Harriman that this works better." Although he later did see Harriman on the prisoner issue, he had arranged for the freeing of the three, the first such release that took place, without making any prior contact with American officials. Thereafter, the Communists released two or three prisoners at a time, usually on national holidays, to other leaders of the American antiwar movement who visited Hanoi. Interestingly enough, though, about this same time, a captured Vietcong agent named Sau Ha told his South Vietnamese interrogators in Saigon that he had instructions to contact the American Embassy and to suggest a prisoner exchange, and he specifically listed a dozen or so top Vietcong leaders whose release was sought. Ha also mentioned talks about "other matters," and a number of American officials in Saigon and Washington jumped at the bait and interpreted it as a possible opening for larger peace negotiations. The State Department gave the name Operation Buttercup to this secret initiative. A reply was sent to the Communists via the channels Sau Ha had suggested, expressing interest, and the Americans also sought to persuade the South Vietnamese to release some prisoners on Ha's list as a token of good faith, hoping to get some back from the

Vietcong. But, again, Hanoi's answer was the same one I had received the year before—the prisoner issue was part of a larger political solution and could be settled only in accordance with the formal points outlined by the Front and Hanoi. Operation Buttercup thus died out, one of many such peace initiatives, some real and some phony, that came to nought during the long war. In February 1968, however, shortly after the start of the Communists' big Tet offensive, the South Vietnamese did turn over three prisoners to American officials, two of whom had been on the Communists' Buttercup list, and the three were subsequently released to the Vietcong without publicity through secret channels. Sau Ha, who may have been bona fide or may have started the whole Buttercup affair on his own, was also released after Tet.)

When I went to visit Sihanouk at the palace in mid-July of my 1966 visit, he gave me a warm welcome and launched immediately into a frank conversation, part of which I have already quoted. It was apparent that he had by now become emotionally committed to the border issue, and he emphasized that reconciliation with the United States could take place only when we recognized Cambodia's "existing borders" and ended all "military action against my country." The fact that Secretary of State Dean Rusk had already made it clear that we did support the "neutrality and territorial integrity of Cambodia" was not enough—the prince wanted us to initial those lines he had drawn on his old French maps, or at least make a sufficiently strong symbolic gesture toward them. But when I gave him Harriman's letter and expressed the special greetings I had been asked to extend, as well as Harriman's desire to visit him, Sihanouk beamed and said, in his excellent French, that he liked Harriman "very much" as one of the "few Americans who understands us," and that he would indeed like to see him in Phnom Penh. He had just finished hosting an elaborate three-day state visit from President de Gaulle and his wife, which the prince ' had supervised personally down to the last detail, including importing a chef and a maid from the Hotel Crillon in Paris and directing a floodlit historical pageant under the stars at Angkor Wat. De Gaulle had been vastly impressed. He had responded by agreeing to Sihanouk's demand that the Americans withdraw from Vietnam and, at the conclusion of the visit, he and Sihanouk signed a joint communiqué calling for the neutralization of all of Indo-China.

Now, however, sensing another opportunity to make a diplomatic coup, Sihanouk was almost agog at the prospect of a visit from Harriman. Having sent the bad news to the State Department about my failure to get very far with the Vietcong on the matter of prisoners, I was able to give Harriman the good news about the proposed visit. I left for Saigon, carrying a small silver bonbonnière Sihanouk gave me and feeling that I had at least done some good during my brief diplomatic foray. Harriman's trip was arranged within a week or so, and a date was set. Alas, at the end of July, a couple of weeks before Harriman was due in Phnom Penh, two American planes dropped some bombs on the Cambodian village of Thlok Trach, only a thousand yards from the Vietnamese border on the ill-defined maps, and two days later two similar incidents took place just as several foreign diplomats were inspecting the area. There was some suspicion that the bombs were dropped on purpose by American officers who were against Harriman's coming to Cambodia in the first place. In any event, the Americans expressed regret but foolishly noted that *their* maps had shown the villages to be in South Vietnam. Not unexpectedly, Sihanouk furiously canceled or at least postponed the Harriman visit, declaring that the United States first had to recognize that "Cambodia is a country that has frontiers." Harriman never did make the trip, although perhaps I had at least helped create a thaw. Not long after, Chester Bowles, who had been ambassador to India and was a liberal Democratic Party leader, paid the prince a visit; but it was not until July 1969, four years after the break with the United States, that Sihanouk accepted a small American mission headed by a chargé d'affaires back in Phnom Penh. (Significantly, in 1985, during my long conversation with Sihanouk in New York, he admitted he now felt that, among his mistakes, had been allowing the diplomatic break with the United States to go on so long.)

(6)

In March 1969, shortly before we resumed relations with Sihanouk, the United States had begun the secret B-52 bombing of North Vietnamese border sanctuaries in Cambodia, which a year later, in April 1970, led to our invasion of the country following Sihanouk's sudden overthrow. It seemed to me then, as it seems to me now, that the temporary military benefits we derived from the bombing and the invasion, which so drastically widened the scope of the war, were never sufficient reason for wreaking such terrible damage on Cambodia and further damaging our own moral prestige. The fact that Sihanouk did not protest the bombing and, without any seeming contradiction, had condoned the use of the sanctuaries by the North Vietnamese and the Vietcong for four years, since 1965, made little or no difference. In his desperate efforts to maintain his posture of neutrality, although he detested the Communists, Sihanouk was astute enough to realize that the North Vietnamese and the Chinese, whoever ultimately came out on top in Indo-China, would outlast the Americans, whose friendship and staying power he had decided he could not depend on anyway. In a typical example of his ambivalence toward the United States, Sihanouk has written in his memoirs: "In the sixties

I never ceased . . . warning Khmer opinion that the acceptance of American aid would bring the extension to our territory of the Vietnamese war. The Americans, in fact, give nothing for nothing. They consider those who are under an obligation to them as their allies at the military level, i.e., they see them in the long run as a relatively inexpensive cannon fodder which will economize the precious life of their 'boys.' "

Sihanouk's last hope for China was that his friend Chou En-lai would prevail in the Cultural Revolution that was already creating havoc—those momentous events were reflected in demonstrations by radical Chinese youth in Phnom Penh, but Sihanouk could do little about those beyond making a few arrests. Nor was there anything he could do to stop the Vietnamese Communists from stepping up their activity in the sanctuaries—establishing their main headquarters there for prosecuting the Vietnam war, using jungle depots for storing new supplies that had either come down the Ho Chi Minh Trail or had been shipped northward into Cambodia from Sihanoukville, and basing at least four regular North Vietnamese divisions and as many as one hundred thousand additional ‛Hanoi and Vietcong troops at a time in a string of bases that reached from southeastern to northeastern Cambodia. Sihanouk also undoubtedly knew that Hanoi was encouraging the Khmer Communists—the Khmer Rouge —in their guerrilla activity; in response he had sentenced three of their leaders, including Khieu Samphan, to jail in absentia, but there was little he could do beyond that, either. His acceptance of our secret bombing without protest had, in fact, been foreshadowed by his comment to Bowles, who had visited him in January 1968. Sihanouk had told Bowles, "We don't want any Vietnamese in Cambodia. . . . We will be very glad if you solve our problem. We are not opposed to hot pursuit in uninhabited areas. . . . For me only Cambodia counts. I want you to force the

Vietcong to leave Cambodia. In unpopulated areas, where there are no Cambodians—[in] such precise cases I would shut my eyes." Two months after the bombing began, at a press conference in Phnom Penh he said that he had not issued any protest because, among other reasons, "I was not in the know, because in certain areas of Cambodia there are no Cambodians."

It was doubtful that Sihanouk didn't know what was going on, but it served his interests, just as it served the different interests of Hanoi, Peking, and Moscow, to say nothing about the secret bombing. But when it soon began to leak out in the press in Washington, the issue exploded and, along with the subsequent invasion of Cambodia, more than anything else gave fresh impetus to the antiwar movements culminating in new demonstrations in Washington and other cities and in the tragic killing of four students at Kent State University. The debate about the wisdom of the bombing and then the invasion also caused new deep divisions in the troubled Washington bureaucracy that reached all the way to the White House and that ultimately led to the resignation of three of the top aides to Henry Kissinger, President Nixon's national security adviser. In the first of his two-volume memoirs, *The White House Years*, Kissinger admitted he had some initial doubts himself about the wisdom of the bombing but at length decided that it was warranted because it "saved American and South Vietnamese lives." The attacks were "undertaken reluctantly, as a last resort, as a minimum response," he wrote, "when we were faced with an unprovoked offensive killing of four hundred Americans a week" in South Vietnam. The only alternative considered, Kissinger noted, was to resume the bombing of North Vietnam. The bombing had been temporarily suspended because of the secret peace talks Kissinger had begun with the North Vietnamese in Paris, which had struck several snags and were at a standstill. About all that Kissinger would admit about the bombing of the sanctuaries was that "We were wrong, I now believe, not to be more frank with Congressional leaders."

Self-serving as Kissinger's memoirs are, they are fair in revealing the often deep-seated differences that existed among the top policymakers in Washington, including those on his own staff who disagreed with some of his judgments. They are also revealing in disclosing the constant vacillation and irrationality President Nixon displayed in dealing with major issues and decisions, especially as the Watergate scandal began to impinge on everything he did. This certainly included many of his decisions on Cambodia. In rereading the Kissinger sections on Cambodia, I was struck by the evidence I found to substantiate two of my long-held convictions. The first concerns our handling of Sihanouk. Whatever his many contradictions, his often brilliant but also bewildering efforts to play too many games at once—to set Peking off against Hanoi, Moscow off against Peking, Washington off against all three, and so on—there was never any doubt about his deep concern for Cambodia and for saving it from being swallowed up by one Communist power or another. This is something, it seems to me, we should have kept in mind far more consistently, and it would have served us better, and surely Sihanouk, if we had foregone our often petty niggling and haggling attitude and approach and accepted his demands on border recognition, for example, which would have included tacitly acknowledging the existence of his beloved century-old maps. It would also have meant expressing more forceful apologies for the inevitable but obvious border violations that took place (as in the bombing of the village that caused Harriman's trip to be canceled, for which we issued an ill-couched apology followed by a second one, too late, that still wasn't strong enough). Moreover, we ourselves should have taken greater initiative in reestablishing relations with Cambodia far sooner than we did and not maintaining the four-year hiatus that took place; we should have given Sihanouk more military and economic aid without strings, which was a foolish and petty habit we demonstrated time and again in dealing with other countries too, invariably to our own ultimate detriment. Finally, and most important, we should have done much more than we did to forestall the coup that overthrew Sihanouk in mid-March 1970, and that led at the end of April to our two months' ill-advised invasion, to which I shall return in a moment.

In all likelihood, none of these things would have prevented an eventual Vietnamese takeover of Cambodia, perhaps even before 1979, though it is conceivable that a neutral Cambodia under a pliant Sihanouk would have been accepted by Hanoi, at least for some years, as may yet turn out to be the case under somewhat different circumstances now, in the mid-eighties. My second feeling on rereading what Kissinger has to say about Cambodia has to do with the timing—or mistiming—of our military actions throughout the Vietnam war. This is something that is part of the new revisionism the American military establishment is now displaying. Top officers, for example, now acknowledge that we should have taught the South Vietnamese both conventional and counterinsurgency tactics and let them fight their own war far sooner and, one might have hoped, far better. Many of our ground casualties among the fifty-eight thousand killed and more than one hundred thousand wounded we suffered in the war resulted from such major encounters as Iadrang, described in the previous chapter, though just as many or more were the result of small firefights by squads and platoons, during which, invariably, the Communists knew what we and they were up to much better than we did.

In any case, there is still a strong feeling among both military and political experts that we should never have entered a war we were not determined to win. Almost everyone who spent any length of time in Vietnam had to agree eventually with this; it is an argument quite apart from defending or opposing our involvement in the war in the first place. Having myself believed in our initial political commitment, I was skeptical about and then opposed to putting half a million troops into the country. But once committed, there is no doubt that we misused our troops just about as badly as we misplayed our political hand, which is saying a lot. The sanctuaries in Cambodia, with which we are concerned here, were a major case in point. If we were going to go into them at all, we should have done so far sooner than we did, long before the North Vietnamese started to build them up and install concrete bunkers and underground hospitals and storage depots in a whole string of border bases, and before they started constucting the elaborate network of the Ho Chi Minh Trail, including the many extensions they used so artfully from 1969 on. We probably should have cut off the trail as best we could at the top along the Demilitarized Zone and western Laos. And, finally, we should have blockaded and mined the harbor of Haiphong, which I doubt would have elicited any significant response from China or the Soviet Union. All of this, if done earlier and in coordination, and if sustained, in all likelihood would have been far more damaging to the North Vietnamese than the limited bombing of the north, which we began in 1965, and for which we were widely and justifiably criticized both at home and abroad. In 1971, I summed up my own feelings when I was called on to testify before the Senate Foreign Relations Committee, then headed by Senator William Fulbright, the outspoken Arkansas Democrat, who was among those who had turned against the war at an early date. "Having fought the wrong kind of war," I said, "we didn't even fight the wrong kind of war right."

To return now to Sihanouk and to the March 1970 coup that ousted him, which caused him to commit perhaps the biggest blunders of his dexterous and daredevil political career; which then led the North Vietnamese to move deeper inside Cambodia and helped prompt the American cross-border invasion—all in the space of two months. This has always seemed to me as important and as disastrous a period as any in the long war. It marked the end of Cambodia's and Sihanouk's thirty-year struggle to remain neutral and independent. The tragic events that ensued—above all, the victory and reign of terror imposed by the Khmer Rouge; the Vietnamese invasion of 1978; what is happening today, and what might happen next—can all be dated from that brief catastrophic span of time.

The stage for this sorry sequence of events was set early in January 1970, when Sihanouk and his wife, Monique, and an entourage of eleven left Phnom Penh for the French Riviera, where every year or two he went to "take the cure" for his obesity and various ailments, real or imagined. He left behind a pile of domestic economic and political problems he felt he could handle from abroad. This was his first miscalculation. For a number of months, and perhaps for as long as two or three years, Prime Minister Lon Nol and First Deputy Prime Minister Sirik Matak, who was Sihanouk's cousin, had been conspiring against him. They chiefly objected to his connivance with the Vietcong and the North Vietnamese, which had allowed the Communists to continue using the sanctuaries militarily and enabled those around Sihanouk in the palace—and some of the top military men (including Lon Nol himself, according to Sihanouk)—to siphon off profits from the shipment of arms and rice to the Communist hideouts through the port of Sihanoukville and two smaller ports. Once Sihanouk was gone, Lon Nol and Sirik Matak moved quickly and effectively to clip his wings. Tax receipts were ordered to be channeled directly into the government treasury instead of into the palace, and a gambling casino in Phnom Penh that had been a major source of profit for the palace was ordered closed. A number of state enterprises Sihanouk had set up were dismantled, and both foreign and domestic trade restrictions were eased. A series of demonstrations inspired by Lon Nol and Sirik Matak against the North Vietnamese and the Vietcong took place, culminating on March 11 in a huge one in Phnom Penh in front of both Communist embassies—Sihanouk had granted them separate recognition. The two embassies were sacked and over the next few days anti-Vietnamese demonstrations in the city reached riot proportions. An order was issued for all Communist troops to leave the country by March 15, which the North Vietnamese and the Vietcong naturally ignored.

Sihanouk, having been released from the hospital in southern France in good health, had returned to Paris, where he had an audience with President Pompidou. When he heard the news of the Vietnamese embassies' being attacked, he cabled his mother, Queen Kossamak, that "I am sure this grave event was willed and organized by individuals who wish irremediably to destroy the friendship of Cambodia with the socialist bloc and to throw our country into the arms of an imperialist capitalist power." He accused these persons of having taken advantage of his absence to pursue "their personal and family interests" as well as "to carry out their designs," and he added that he would return at once to Phnom Penh, to rally support for his cause or alternatively, if the people so willed, to resign. On March 12, however, he received a message from Sirik Matak informing him that Prince Kantol, another cousin of the prince and a sometime prime minister, was being sent to Paris as a special emmisary. Sihanouk replied that he would refuse to meet with Kantol. As he told me the story in 1985, "They wanted me to stay in Paris while they, Matak and Lon Nol, handled the problem. They were ready to offer me sixty thousand francs a month. Nothing was said about my remaining head of state. I refused to see Kantol because no one could buy me off."

Sihanouk told me further, "I knew, by this time, that if I went back I would be arrested and assassinated. I had learned this from the royal police who had previously warned me that I would be deposed unless I obtained foreign aid, if not from the Americans then from the Communist powers. There were two contingency plans, to arrest me at Phnom Penh if I arrived there, or, if I went to Siem Reap, to take me off into the forest near Angkor Wat and kill me. So it was not a mistake for me not to return, as people have said. My mistake was in misjudging the hearts and minds of my army officers because they always wanted the United States to be with them. They had this nostalgia for American aid. I had tried to get a resumption of aid from Washington in 1969, after relations were reestablished. I also wanted to persuade the United States to use me as intermediary with Hanoi in the cause of peace, to serve as a bridge. I wanted Cambodia to avoid war at any costs, and I wanted to play a role. It wasn't a matter of pride, it was a practical proposal, to buy enough time. But when the American chargé d'affaires, Mr. Lloyd Rives, arrived in Phnom Penh, he was very reluctant to discuss any of this with me and he said he had to wait for an ambassador to come. But the clock was running out. So I felt I had to go to Moscow and Peking to try to get aid or obtain the help of the Communist powers in at least reducing the North Vietnamese presence in Cambodia. It wasn't very skillful or wise of me, perhaps, but I felt I had no choice."

By this time Sihanouk was in a state of near panic. There are those who still feel that, despite the warning against his life, he should have taken the chance of returning to Phnom Penh, where he enjoyed sufficient prestige and popularity to regain control over the situation and avoid the coup that took place on March 18; or that, at least, he should have stayed in Paris. But on March 13, the prince suddenly flew off to Moscow, where he met with Leonid Brezhnev, Alexei Kosygin, and Nicolai Podgorny, the three top Soviet officials. "I told them that I neeeded a lot of aid at once to let my army know I was trying," Sihanouk said to me. "The Russians agreed to give me some jeeps, weapons, and tanks but said it would take five months for anything to reach Cambodia. That was too slow. I also told Prime Minister Kosygin that the Vietnamese Communists should be called out of the sanctuaries because I could no longer close my eyes to what was going on. Kosygin refused to intervene, saying that to do so would be to stab the Vietnamese in the back. I thought this was nonsense. President Podgorny advised me to return at once to Phnom Penh instead of going on to Peking. He said a special Soviet plane was ready to fly me home. The president appeared to be put out and a little disappointed when I refused. I wondered if his disappointment was due to the fact that I had escaped the trap laid by my enemies." While in Moscow, Sihanouk received a delayed telegram from the queen, his mother, warning him not to return to Phnom Penh. "For my mother to have acted in this way, there must have been a grave threat hanging over me," Sihanouk later wrote in the memoirs. On March 18, after five days in Moscow and with no positive results, he left for Peking. As he was driving to the airport, Prime Minister Kosygin informed him that he had just been deposed as chief of state by the unanimous vote of ninety-two members of the Cambodian National Assembly. For once Sihanouk was silent.

In Peking, Chou En-lai gave Sihanouk the usual warm welcoming hug in front of virtually the entire diplomatic corps that had turned out at the aiport to greet him. Chou assured the prince at once that, as far as China was concerned, he was still Cambodia's chief of state rather than Cheng Heng, the Assembly chairman, who had been designated by Sihanouk as interim chief but had now been chosen by the rebellious Assembly to replace him. Then Chou settled Sihanouk and his entourage in a complex that had once belonged to France and had been taken over by the Chinese Foreign Ministry. Sihanouk later described it as "a bourgeois village right in the center of Peking, a few hundred meters from the famous Tian An Men Square. My private residence was a vast luxurious dwelling, with numerous servants, a brigade of talented cooks, a well-equipped secretariat, and all the services of a royal palace, car park, maintenance personnel for the buildings and gardens, sporting installations, cinema, etc. . . . The fact is that the more I found myself dependent on Chinese generosity, the more I felt embarrassed and humiliated. Before March I was the equal of Chou and Mao, for I was the leader of a very proud and very independent nation. Henceforth, I was no more than a fictive Head of State, a 'landless Johnny' sponging on a state which was very friendly, certainly, but foreign."

Kissinger, who had been accused of being the architect of the secret bombing and the invasion of Cambodia, virtually professes ignorance in *The White House Years* of the events taking place in Cambodia at this time. He refers to the "bravado" of Lon Nol and Sirik Matak in courting disaster by challenging the "far superior forces of the North Vietnamese and the Vietcong." Writing of Sihanouk's crucial week of hesitation in Paris, he says, "The United States also believed and preferred that Sihanouk's bold reentry into Phnom Penh to face down his opponents would have turned the tide of events and was in everybody's best interest." Had he returned, Kissinger adds, the United States would have supported his resumption of his careful balancing act, which Kissinger described to Nixon as "placing himself deliberately on the extreme left wing of the right wing." Let alone having nothing to do with planning the coup—which was in accordance with everything I was able to find out—the United States, Kissinger afterward wrote, "was hardly as purposeful as some imagine, or as effectual as others pretend." Perceptions of what was going on inside Cambodia, where the United States as yet had no intelligence personnel, lagged far behind events, he adds, and "we did not even grasp its [the coup's] significance for many weeks. . . . The motivations of the principal actors in Phnom Penh were quite obscure to me. . . ."

All this odd mea culpa may be true, which makes our diplomatic performance all the more pitiful, but it hardly excuses the failure of the United States to do anything to persuade Sihanouk to go back to Phnom Penh from Paris or remain in France, instead of dashing off in pell-mell flight to Moscow and Peking. A routine effort was made, I later heard, to get the French to try to convince him to stay in France, but obviously it wasn't very forceful or effective. The fact of the matter was we no longer had much influence over Sihanouk, and had no real or firm opinion about him. We had long tended to regard him as an interesting maverick or a nuisance but had never understood his real patriotism or his predicament. We were dismayed at his propensity for courting disaster as a result of being inconsistent, willful, and opportunistic, all of which he could be. For the most part, though, given his delicate and dangerous geopolitical location and position, he was extremely astute, he was fully aware of what he was doing, usually had good reasons for doing it, and more often than not he got away with it. On this occasion, however, at this critical juncture, he did not. He felt double-crossed, let down, cornered, and frightened, and he lost his grip, his nerve, and his sense of judgment. More than ever he needed guidance and friends who were willing to stand by and help him, and this is something, despite all its brave talk about Cambodia, the United States was never seriously willing to do. When the opportunity came, we were ready, as usual, to go along with right-wing generals like Lon Nol and his miserable and corrupt brother, Colonel Lon Non, who also came to play a part in the ultimate Cambodian dénouement. Sihanouk's loss was accordingly our loss too, except that it was *his* country, not ours, that was going down the drain. The fact is, we let him down badly, as he had predicted we would. As a consequence, if he acted like an unguided missile once he arrived in Peking, the United States must shoulder a large part of the blame.

As was his way, the now deposed prince began his sojourn in Peking with a series of frenzied and contradictory statements. First he said he had "absolutely no intention of seeking to resume power." Then he pledged to participate in "the sacred struggle our people will wage from inside and outside the country to obliterate this coup d'état and restore legality and democracy." He bemoaned the fact that "I am an unlucky man with a bad destiny." He condemned the United States as "the principal and sole culprit responsible for the war and political instability in the three countries of Indo-China" and he called on his fellow Cambodians to join the resistance forces in the jungle, that is, the Khmer Communists. Finally, with Chou En-lai's approval, he established a New Revolutionary Movement, including Khieu Samphan and two other former Cambodian leaders he had previously denounced and sentenced to death, and announced the creation of a National Liberation Army to overthrow the Lon Nol government. In the last week of April, he organized a "summit" and miraculously managed to arrange the attendance of Prince Souphanouvong, the head of the Laotian Patriotic Front; Nguyen Huu Tho, chairman of the National Liberation Front of South Vietnam; and Pham Van Dong, the premier of North Vietnam; and sizable delegations accompanying each. Unfortunately, the well-organized Communists at the meeting quickly took it over and Sihanouk found himself somewhat in the role of the host who became the odd man out.

By this time, events in Cambodia had already proved the weakness and the inability of the Lon Nol government to cope with the new situation. The Americans realized, too late, that the coup had been a mistake and that they should have tried harder to avoid or preempt it. As North Vietnamese troops moved deeper into the country, the government not only proved incapable of holding them back but the situation got out of hand when the public reacted by massacring hundreds and then thousands of local Vietnamese residents. The Communist troops stepped up their attacks and by the third week of April 1970 controlled a good part of the nation, including "liberated areas" around Phnom Penh, where they were joined by some Khmer Rouge troops—a rehearsal for what was to take place five years later. The Americans and South Vietnamese thus faced the sudden prospect of the fall of Cambodia, with Sihanouk returning to Phnom Penh astride a Red horse, and the whole process of Vietnamization in South Vietnam and the scheduled withdrawal of American forces jeopardized. The stage was thus set for the American invasion of Cambodia, which was falsely presented in heroic terms instead of as the act of desperation it was.

(7)

After a long and painful debate in Washington that included top officials at the White House and their staffs and leading members of the cabinet, the decision was made to invade Cambodia up to a distance of twenty-one miles. The attacks on two key Cambodian areas, the Parrot's Beak and the Fishhook, began on April 30, 1970, and were later expanded to a number of other base areas. There is no need here to go into the details of the invasion, which from the outset was limited to two months, until June 30. It succeeded to the degree that it disrupted the North Vietnamese supply bases, costing Hanoi a substantial amount of war material and forcing it to move its mobile headquarters, the Central Office for South Vietnam, deeper into the country. The invasion probably set back the North Vietnamese timetable in South Vietnam a few months, temporarily bolstered the process of Vietnamization, and saved some American lives. But it scarcely encouraged Hanoi to negotiate a broader peace, including Cambodia as well as Vietnam, as Nixon and Kissinger had hoped, and simply postponed the date of reckoning for the weak and ineffectual Lon Nol regime in Phnom Penh. Kissinger still maintains that the decision to invade was "not a moral issue" but a tactical choice, and that had we not gone into Cambodia it would have fallen to the Communists in 1970 instead of 1975. But at the same time he admits that "Cambodia was ultimately the victim of the breakdown of our democratic political process" and that the debate over the invasion precluded "any coherent strategy." He also admits that from a "mélange of North Vietnamese determination, Cambodian rivalries, and American internal conflicts, everything followed with the inevitability of a Greek tragedy until there descended on that gentle land a horror that it did not deserve and that none of us have the right to forget." Not a moral issue?

As much as anything else, the invasion of Cambodia stimulated the growth and development of the Khmer Rouge, which the North Vietnamese encouraged once their forces spread farther westward into the country. Within a matter of months, the Cambodian Communists were able to take over a greater share of waging the war,

much sooner than they had anticipated, and though the
North Vietnamese continued to play an important role,
they were able to withdraw their main offensive units back
eastward to the sanctuaries and concentrate once again on
their campaign in South Vietnam. There remains little
doubt that the widening of the war in 1970 stemmed from
the overthrow of Sihanouk, which might have been prevented, and that the American invasion then increased
rather than deflated Hanoi's determination to gain control
over Cambodia as well as Laos. The fact that the invasion
probably also made it easier for the Khmer Rouge to come
to power, which proved to be to Hanoi's disadvantage
when the Cambodians introduced their reign of terror
and then made the Vietnamese the principal object of
their xenophobia, can be evaluated in various ways, depending on how one views the situation in Cambodia
today. Whether Sihanouk had he remained in power, or
in a power-sharing position, could have avoided or at least
ameliorated the worst depredations of the Khmer Rouge
is difficult to judge. Over the short run he might have;
over the long run the answer is probably not. The Communists might have killed him at the outset, without fear
of the consequences, or they might have used him for
their own purposes, as they did anyway, both before and
after he returned to Phnom Penh from Peking in September 1975.

The history of Cambodia between 1970 and 1975 is full
of obscurities, misunderstandings, lost opportunities, and
further distress as the country drifted deeper into chaos
and collapse. For the Americans and their new Chinese
allies, jointly seeking a peaceful solution with Sihanouk as
the proposed centerpiece of a new coalition government,
it was a period of frustration and failure. The Russians
and the North Vietnamese simply sat back and adopted a
hard, no-compromise position. The major beneficiaries
were the Khmer Rouge, moving swiftly toward a military

victory with the help of Hanoi's troops, and the prime victims were the Cambodian people. They could do so little to control the political maelstrom they were caught in, which they scarcely comprehended, and while their suffering was nothing compared to the murder and mayhem that lay ahead, they were already being severely punished by the continued American bombing, the spreading ground fighting, and the political repression at the hands of Khmer Rouge and North Vietnamese forces in the countryside who impressed them into troop or work brigades as the Communists captured more territory. Once again, during these five fuzzy years of uncertainty and incipient doom, the elusive thread remained Sihanouk, the perennial survivor. His behavior and performance continued to confound and bewilder both his friends and his foes, but as always he managed to avoid death or oblivion—the latter would have been far more awful for him to contemplate. Peking gave him the perfect vantage point for his maneuvers, which he was able to carry on under the protection of his friend Chou En-lai.

During these five critical years I was in and out of Cambodia a dozen times, and each time it seemed to me that the situation had either remained in dead center or had deteriorated. The Cambodian national army had grown to a size of two hundred and fifty thousand, at a claimed rate of a new battalion a week, and despite cutbacks by Congress, it was still receiving nearly two hundred thousand dollars' worth of American aid per year; but the troops lacked initiative and spirit. Complacency was abetted by nepotism and corruption, and the Cambodian civilian government was in an equally bad state. As in South Vietnam, there was no clear-cut military strategy or tactics, and the war had become far too fluid and confused to enable any kind of village reconstruction program. A typical argument took place about whether to send young cadets to the United States for training in conventional and/or unconventional warfare at Fort Benning, Georgia, or else-where. Colonel Jonathan Ladd, who had served as a Special Forces officer in Vietnam and was now the politi-cal-military counselor at the embassy in Phnom Penh, put his finger on the problem when he commented to me, "The Cambodians have got to clean up their own backyard first, and they're not going to learn how to do that in America. We have to accept them for what they are rather than what they ought to be, and one thing they're not going to do is march through Belgium."

Despite sporadic American efforts to promote a cease-fire on the ground, accompanied by a halt to our bombing, so that negotiations to end the war and establish some sort of compromise government could be started, the Com-munists were confident enough of victory by now to refuse to cooperate. As a result, the American bombing contin-ued, and once again became a source of bitter debate, this time over the accuracy of our targeting. Although it was officially denied, a secret communications center at the American Embassy in Phnom Penh coordinated the at-tacks by acting as a relay point. American officers at the embassy used a radio-telephone system linking the Cam-bodian general staff, the American Seventh Air Force based in northern Thailand, and battlefield command-and-control planes, including forward air spotters near the target areas in Cambodia's eastern and northeastern provinces. In the second volume of his memoirs, *Years of Upheaval,* Kissinger vehemently denies that the B-52 op-erations were conducted "sloppily" and insists that the Seventh Air Force controlled them with the utmost care, relying on "up to date photographs, precision radar, and infrared sensors." He admits there were "tragic accidents" but only "two serious ones" and no "systematic bombing of civilians." The story was much more serious than that. I was in the embassy in Phnom Penh when two staff mem-bers of the Senate Foreign Relations Committee spent five frustrating days trying to find out what the actual role of the embassy was. Only after cabling Senator Stuart Symington in Washington did they finally obtain enough cooperation from embassy officials to ascertain that the Americans in Phnom Penh were indeed playing a key role in planning the attacks and that, as Cambodian civilian witnesses had been telling correspondents for some time, the casualty rates were high because the targeting was often way off. With about sixty B-52 sorties a day taking place, the use of maps that were several years old and on a scale of fifty to one could not possibly provide adequate identification of all the villages that were hit. Besides, in many cases, the peasants and their families had fled, seeking refuge in other villages five or ten miles away that were often unmarked on the maps but were indiscriminately bombed.

Ambassador Emory Swank grew increasingly critical of our Cambodian policy, including the bombing, which was actually supervised by the chief of mission, the number two man, Thomas Enders. Enders was primarily an economist and he was one of Kissinger's favorites. He was more than six and a half feet tall, and I remember vividly how he towered over the Cambodians, many of whom were less than five feet in height. Somehow, whatever his talents— and they were considerable—it always seemed to me a mistake in the first place to send a man of his awesome proportions to Cambodia. Aside from a tendency to be overbearing, he was overwhelming and way out of the average Cambodian's reach or ken. There should, I recorded in my notes, be a rule of diplomatic dimensions, to include physical measurements. Brawn as a negative as well as a positive factor should be considered along with brains among the standards in the selection process.

Beyond the issue of the bombing, and the by now almost hopeless situation of the Cambodian government forces, Sihanouk himself, unfortunately, posed some of the big-

gest problems. From the moment he had arrived in Peking
from Paris and Moscow after the coup against him, he had
insisted that a Communist takeover was now the only solution in Cambodia. Kissinger maintains, in retrospect,
that "whatever desire Sihanouk may have had for conciliation, he was himself a prisoner of the Khmer Rouge and
of his own 1970 declaration of total war against the Cambodian government." Even after the Paris peace accords
of January 1973, the prince intransigently declared that
he would never make a deal with Lon Nol, and that Cambodia's future would be determined by "the resistance operation in the interior," by which he meant Khieu
Samphan and the handful of other leaders who had returned to Cambodia and were leading the resistance in the
jungle. Even when Sihanouk visited a "liberated zone" in
northern Cambodia for a few days in March 1973, the
Khmer Rouge cleverly utilized the trip to exploit his standing abroad while undermining it at home and refused to
disseminate what he said inside Cambodia. At the same
time, realizing that he retained a wide following in the
country, they conducted a systematic purge against all
pro-Sihanouk elements.

None of this pleased Chou En-lai and the Chinese, who
felt that Sihanouk was still the best bet to help them rather
than to allow Hanoi to dominate Cambodia. Accordingly,
the Chinese kept urging Sihanouk to cast his lot with the
Khmer Rouge. As for the Americans, Sihanouk continued
to be ambivalent, as he had so often been before. In a
retrospective interview in February 1985 with two American scholars of Cambodia, David Ablin and Marlowe
Hood, he admitted he had made his mistakes but maintained that as early as 1972, when the American-Chinese
"honeymoon" had just begun and the Khmer Rouge were
still relatively weak, Chou and the North Vietnamese
"wanted me to go back to Phnom Penh in order to preside
over a tripartite national reconciliation government with

Sihanoukians, Lon Nolians and the Khmer Rouge." In New York, in my 1985 discussion with him, Sihanouk told me, "Chou suggested to Kissinger in 1972 there be negotiations. Hanoi favored the idea at the time because the Vietnamese felt themselves spread too thin throughout Indo-China. But Kissinger said no. He said the Americans were going to Peking for bilateral negotiations and didn't want to see Sihanouk." Kissinger says nothing in his book about this earlier ploy. In any event, by early 1973, Kissinger makes clear that he and Chou En-lai were working closely to bring about Sihanouk's return to Cambodia, and that the strongest card in the Sino-American hand then was the continuing American bombing that was preventing a Khmer Rouge victory. But when Congress began moving in May to halt the bombing by the end of August and cease American military operations throughout Indo-China, the whole deal fell apart. Despite Le Duc Tho's adamant refusal to include a Cambodian cease-fire in his private peace talks with Kissinger about Vietnam, Kissinger wrote that a halt to the fighting in Cambodia seemed imminent, to be followed by Sihanouk's return to deal with "existing political forces so as to give himself room to maneuver between them and the Communists. We nearly made it," he adds, "with all that it would have meant for Cambodia's future. But our inability to maintain domestic support was to doom our proposal and Cambodia—and to shake Chou En-lai's position at home to its foundation." He concludes by saying, "The Congress doomed Sihanouk as surely as it did the Phnom Penh government."

In my view, aside from Kissinger's underestimating domestic dissent, it was far too late by then to mount the sort of diplomatic offensive in Cambodia that he had in mind. Once again, the United States had missed the boat. If Sihanouk had compounded his early mistake of not returning to Phnom Penh, and aligning himself too closely with the Khmer Rouge, Kissinger should have moved sooner than he did to help Sihanouk. By early 1973, the Khmer Rouge and the North Vietnamese were already riding too high toward victory to be receptive to any compromise involving Sihanouk and the Americans. Some seventy Communist battalions were within a forty-mile radius of Phnom Penh and were sporadically subjecting the city, as well as several nearby provincial capitals, to rocket barrages. The end was clearly in sight for the republican regime of Lon Nol in Cambodia as well as for South Vietnam. Interestingly enough, at this point Son Sann, Sihanouk's now shaky ally in the current opposition to the Vietnamese in Cambodia, was in Phnom Penh trying to establish contact with Khieu Samphan and four other leaders of Sihanouk's government-in-exile, who were in the jungle. But Son Sann got nowhere, and time kept running out.

Sihanouk made another near-fatal mistake in September 1975, when, five months after the victory of the Khmer Rouge, he returned to Cambodia as a figurehead chief of state. As the terror mounted and the internal killing increased, the Khmer Rouge, or Democratic Kampuchea, had to make sure that Sihanouk would keep silent and out of sight. Undoubtedly there were some Cambodian Communists who would have preferred to kill him and get rid of him once and for all. As he had earlier realistically said, when the Khmer Rouge took over they would "spit me out like a cherry pit." But whatever moderate voices there were prevailed, perhaps including Khieu Samphan, or, for his own reasons, Ieng Sary, the foreign minister of Democratic Kampuchea, who had earlier been designated to shadow Sihanouk whenever he left Peking. The prince and his family were kept under house arrest in Phnom Penh, first in his old palace and then in a guesthouse. Now and then he was trotted out to make an official statement of one kind or another, and he was allowed to travel to the United Nations, soon after the Vietnamese invasion, to speak in defense of the overthrown Pol Pot government, still recognized by the UN as "legitimate." When I later saw Sihanouk in New York, he maintained that his return to Cambodia after the Khmer Rouge took over was not a mistake. "I went back because I didn't want to be in exile," he said. "I requested the Khmer Rouge to let me come home the very day they entered Phnom Penh. I got Chou En-lai to intervene in my behalf. The Chinese wanted me to be head of state. But the Khmer Rouge, though they gave me the designation, wanted to hide many things from me, I discovered. In April 1976, I resigned voluntarily. I saw what was happening to my country, to my people, with all their liberties gone. I was put under house arrest and I was punished, and my relatives were killed or arrested. But I don't regret going back. It was my duty."

When he was asked, in another 1985 interview, why the Khmer Rouge acted so cruelly after their takeover, Sihanouk cogently pointed out that no one had expected them to be such "monsters" but that they were "very Stalinian" and were "maniacs," who from the outset had been determined to "liquidate all the enemies of our country" in order to save it. They acted as they did, he explained, out of "much pride" and because they felt they were defending "the poor class." They were also determined "to reach total communism in one leap forward," to be more extremist than the leaders of the Cultural Revolution or the Gang of Four, and to become the one Communist Party to achieve communism "without a step-by-step policy, without going through socialism."

Sihanouk's description of the Cambodian Communists' behavior and the reasons for it was close to the mark. But the history and development of the several factions of the Communist Party, or parties, in Cambodia remains highly complicated and confusing. This is due in large part to the lack of hard information, though a handful of scholars who read and speak Khmer have slowly been obtaining access to original source material over recent years, including the records and confessions now available on the top floor of Tuol Sleng prison in Phnom Penh. Even so, the murder or disappearance of so many top leaders as a result of purges and intraparty feuds over the years has left huge gaps in knowledge that may never be filled. Another reason for the paucity of information is the obsessive secrecy that has characterized the lives of virtually all Cambodian Communists. To a considerable degree, this was the result of their vast mistrust of their Communist neighbors, especially the Vietnamese, but it was also a product of their deep mistrust of one another. In his useful book *Cambodia—1975–1982,* Michael Vickery, who first went to Cambodia in 1960 as an English language teacher in provincial high schools and has maintained an almost constant interest in the country ever since, reaches the conclusion that the excesses of the period after 1975 "lay in the very nature of a peasant revolution, which was the only kind of revolution possible in Cambodia." It was "a working out of strictly local contradictions," Vickery adds, by a small zealous vanguard leadership that, "perhaps out of shock," quickly and meekly gave up whatever ideological goals it had set once it seized power. In a provocative paragraph, Vickery writes, "It is certainly safe to assume that they did not foresee, let alone plan, the unsavory developments of 1975–1979. They were petty bourgeois radicals overcome by peasantist romanticism and serve as a perfect illustration of Lenin's target in his strictures against 'petty-bourgeois revolutionism, which smacks of anarchism . . . and easily goes to revolutionary extremes, but is incapable of perseverence, organization, discipline, steadiness.' "

Vickery cites other scholars, such as Eric Wolf, to bolster the Marxist argument that a peasant revolution "without outside leadership" is bound to fail. The net result in Cambodia under Pol Pot after 1975 was that the petty bourgeois intellectuals, including those who had studied abroad—like Pol Pot and Khieu Samphan, in France—were pulled along and eventually pulled down by the very peasants they professed to lead. Rather than make use of the revolutionary potential of the cities, as Wolf notes, the Cambodian revolutionaries murdered the urban intellectuals, including innocent teachers and professional leaders, and destroyed the cities themselves, in accordance with the desires of the peasant rebels for whom "the state is a negative quantity, an evil to be replaced . . . by their own 'homemade' social order." Since landlordism was not a particularly serious problem in Cambodia and most peasants were of a middle rather than poor level, their anger was directed not at rural landlords but at the network of usurers in the towns and cities—a point perhaps purposely ignored by Sihanouk in his analysis. The only external force to propel the revolution along, in Wolf's analysis, was the Vietnam war and American intervention, which by spilling over into Cambodia encouraged the peasants to liberate themselves from their constraints in their own vindictive way.

In this analysis, then, which I find generally convincing, the peasant revolution in Cambodia, with apparent populist motivations and characteristics, simply ran amok and carried its inexperienced and unprepared leadership with it. The excesses, accordingly, as Vickery points out, "did not spring forth from the brains of Pol Pot or Khieu Samphan" or from whatever revolutionary theory these two leaders and others acquired in Paris, but were due primarily to the basic, simple contradictions and cleavages between Cambodia's rural and urban society. Khieu Samphan's Paris dissertation about agriculture being the necessary basis of development, deserving of special initial emphasis, may have had something to do with the rapid forced exodus from the cities that took place in 1975; but this does not deny the fundamental thesis of Vickery,

Wolf, and other scholars. What Vickery describes as the "homemade" quality of Democratic Kampuchea, which is what the Pol Pot faction in the antigovernment coalition and the coalition itself is still called, led to some strange twists and turns both before and after Pol Pot and his group took over the country in 1975. Vickery points out that in April 1977, "When Ieng Sary told the ASEAN group of nations that 'we are not communists, we are revolutionaries' and do not 'belong to the commonly accepted grouping of Communist Indochina,' he was being absolutely truthful," in his own fashion. Since 1979, as Vickery adds, the Democratic Kampuchean remnants have moved closer to "the Asian capitalist countries," and have even renounced socialism in favor of a free market economy and a pluralistic parliament. This may simply represent more cynicism and opportunism on Ieng Sary's part, but it prompted Vickery to conclude by attributing at least equal cynicism to the United States. By careful taking note of what Sary had said, and realizing that Democratic Kampuchea might yet prove a useful partner in the effort to put a halt to Vietnam's drive for hegemony in Indo-China, Vickery notes that "the U.S. treatment of Democratic Kampuchea, like its reaction to the Indonesian massacre of 1965 and the policy pursued in El Salvador, shows that mass murder is tolerable so long as it is on the right side—the bloodbath is then benign."

The United States has not gone that far in condoning the actions or accepting a role for Pol Pot, who may or may not have taken himself out of the picture by his announcement, early last September, that he was giving up his role as commander of Khmer Rouge troops and would henceforth simply serve in an advisory capacity and as head of a new college of national defense. The immediate reaction of Sihanouk and most foreign observers was to greet the statement with caution and skepticism and to describe it as cosmetic; but there was some hope that it represented a real concession, on the part of the Chinese in particular, who have been the chief backers of the Khmer Rouge. The Vietnamese and the Heng Samrin regime in Phnom Penh have, until recently, continued to demand the total removal of Pol Pot *and* the Khmer Rouge as one of the chief conditions for the holding of any peace talks to end the Cambodian war and establish a new coalition government. By late 1975, however, Samrin and Hun Sen seemed less insistent on eliminating *all* elements of the Khmer Rouge. The fact that the Chinese hailed Pol Pot's retirement as "conducive to unity" in the struggle against the Vietnamese seemed significant. It could indicate an awareness on the part of Peking, perhaps privately stimulated by Washington as well as by Moscow, that it has achieved about as much benefit as possible from supporting Pol Pot and that it consequently is ready to reach some sort of accommodation with Vietnam. This is what Mikhail Gorbachev has specifically urged on both countries since he took over the reins in the Soviet Union. The Chinese have responded by sticking to their guns—literally on the Sino-Vietnamese border, where artillery attacks on Vietnam, in late 1985 and early 1986, were particularly heavy —but at the same time Peking has toned down its anti-Vietnamese propaganda, and there have even been some diplomatic niceties exchanged with Hanoi.

(8)

In real or feigned retirement, Pol Pot remains as mysterious and enigmatic a figure as ever. Scholars, notably Ben Kiernan, an Australian who has spent a number of months in Cambodia since 1979 and is the author of *How Pol Pot Came to Power,* published in 1985, are still trying to piece together the story of his life and his revolutionary career, much of which has remained obscure, as Kiernan points out, because "his rise . . . took place in a climate of uncertainty and terror." Although his name at birth was Saloth Sar, as mentioned earlier, he has never admitted to it. He was the youngest of seven children. His father, who owned twelve hectares of rice and garden land in a small village in Kompong Thom province, was a well-off peasant and the family's red-tiled-roof house next to a river was the best in the area. At the age of six he spent a year as a novice in a Buddhist monastery in Phnom Penh and then six years at a private Catholic school. At fourteen, having failed an entrance examination to a Phnom Penh high school, he attended the Norodom Sihanouk High School in Kompong Cham province, and then, after a year of studying carpentry in Phnom Penh, he went to France in 1949 on a technician's scholarship. Fellow Khmer students in Paris, including many who became leaders of the revolution afterward, described him as gentle and shy with a "retiring personality." He took part, but not actively, in a Khmer student group called the Marxist Circle, which had loose ties to the French Communist Party, though in fact it was more antiroyalist and nationalist than Socialist or Communist, as attested by the fact that its particular hero was the earlier mentioned Son Ngoc Thanh, probably the best-known Khmer nationalist figure of the day, who, far from ever being a leftist, would later collaborate with both the South Vietnamese and the Americans. Saloth Sar was a poor, or lazy, student, in Paris, though he wrote several articles for left-wing publications which he signed "Original Khmer." In the summer of 1950, he spent a month in Yugoslavia, where he joined a work brigade and was impressed by the Yugoslavs' policies independent of the Soviet Union.

When he returned to Cambodia early in 1953, the nation was in turmoil. Sihanouk had just declared martial law and dissolved the National Assembly, and was about to launch his Royal Crusade for Independence as a commoner rather than as a king. It was about this time that Saloth Sar adopted the revolutionary name of Pol Pot. He became the protégé of Tou Samouth, the leader of the Cambodian branch of the Indochinese Communist Party established by the Vietnamese in 1951. From the outset, Pol Pot resented Vietnamese domination of the party, even though, after a period working in the rural areas, he became Tou Samouth's personal secretary back in Phnom Penh and played an important part in holding the party's small urban structure together at a time when Sihanouk was cracking down on all opposition and many Khmer Communists either defected or fled to Vietnam. In the fall of 1960, meeting secretly in a room at the Phnom Penh railway station, a score or so members of the Khmer People's Revolutionary Party adopted the temporary name of Workers Party of Kampuchea. Pol Pot was chosen the number three man in the hierarchy, which was composed of an odd mixture of antiroyalist French-trained intellectuals and leftists, others who had remained in Cambodia all along and had retained their respect for Sihanouk as a bona fide nationalist, and a few home-grown dedicated Communists who later became the nucleus of the Pol Pot regime.

In July 1962, Tou Samouth was killed after being seized in his safe house in Phnom Penh—some believe that Pol Pot was involved in the kidnapping and murder. In any event, he became party secretary of what by then was called the Communist Party of Kampuchea and he at once set a course that was as independent as possible of the Vietnamese while at the same he constantly increased his own power position. After 1963, when he left Phnom Penh and took to the jungle, he traveled about constantly, and in 1964 he went up the Ho Chi Minh Trail to Hanoi, where he remained several months. He held discussions with top Vietnamese officials, apparently including Le Duan, who was number-two man to Ho Chi Minh. The

Vietnamese urged him to adopt a go-slow revolutionary policy and to wait for a Vietnamese victory to precede a Cambodian one. Pol Pot's response was not recorded, but he was certainly aware by now that, like it or not, he was almost totally dependent on Vietnamese military aid and that the Vietnamese also represented the greatest threat to his own continued leadership. From Hanoi, Pol Pot traveled to Peking, where he also spent several months. According to Ben Kiernan's account, he was unaware, when he arrived, that Sihanouk was also there, and Sihanouk was unaware of Pol Pot's coincidental presence. (Sihanouk himself confirms this.) Pol Pot held several long talks with Deng Xiaoping, the Communist Party secretary, who, like the Vietnamese, though for different reasons, urged him to hold back on his armed rebellion against Sihanouk but at the same time to encourage Sihanouk to crack down on certain "legal" left-wingers in and around his government. Apparently not knowing how Pol Pot already felt about the Vietnamese, the Chinese, for their own reasons, wanted to cause a rift between the two Indochinese parties—Vietnam's and Cambodia's. At the end of their stay in Peking, the Cambodians were honored at a sumptuous banquet given by Mao Zedong. Pol Pot was as secretive about his Chinese trip as he was about everything (though he did not try to keep his visit to Hanoi secret), and even years later he said nothing about traveling to China, nor did the *Livre Noir,* a semiofficial Party history, ever mention it.

In the latter half of the sixties and the early part of the seventies, and particularly after the coup that overthrew Sihanouk in the spring of 1970 and the follow-up American invasion, the power of the Khmer Rouge under Pol Pot and his small group of revolutionary zealots, including several who were already acting like regional warlords, continued to grow as they tightened their hold on the countryside. As they became stronger, the Khmer Rouge also grew more ruthless and moderation gave way to extremism. In rural areas the "Democratic Revolution" began to have a wider effect, including the organization of families into small work groups, the introduction of collectivization programs marked by the confiscation of crops and, in some cases, enforced communal eating, which became prevalent later. Those suspected of counterrevolutionary activities were punished, or simply disappeared, or sometimes were executed on the spot; these included some of the thousand or so survivors from among the original several thousand Khmer cadre who had spent years of training in Hanoi, the last of whom had begun to straggle back to Cambodia. The old easy ways of conducting trade and commerce in a country where food, especially rice and fish, had always been plentiful were slow to be eradicated, which prompted the Khmer Rouge to move even more stringently to introduce their "new system," without regard for local customs. In Kiernan's words, "Popular approval of relatively moderate policies became an excuse for extremist ones," which overnight led to the establishment of monopolies by the state over rice, salt, fuel, and cloth. Private ownership of land in many places was abolished, and the state moved "to control everything." But there was nothing remotely resembling a cohesive plan to make these measures feasible or even comprehendible to the average peasant.

Ironically, the heavy American bombing of 1973, which destroyed a significant number of Communist troop-units while also driving fresh village volunteers into the ranks, played into the hands of the extremists and helped seal the moderates' doom. Kiernan goes so far as to suggest that only the bombing "prevented what would otherwise have been an inevitable insurgent victory in 1973," at a time when the Party's policy on both domestic and foreign affairs was, in fact, still not generally accepted in the revolutionary movement. In various regions, especially in the eastern zone bordering Vietnam, it was regarded as too harsh and extreme. But had the revolution actually triumphed in 1973, Kiernan adds, the cities might never have been evacuated as they were two years later, and the revolution, with all its ensuing horrors of murder and starvation and death from disease, might not have got out of hand so catastrophically. Moreover, Sihanouk, with much of his urban as well as considerable rural support still intact, might well have been able to return once Lon Nol was removed, his position perhaps more secure than before, even under some sort of Khmer Rouge dispensation. This seems unlikely to me, though it is true, as Kiernan says, that the extremists were by no means sure enough of themselves yet to be in absolute control. What is intriguing is the suggestion that Lon Nol's defeat at the earlier date of 1973, and Sihanouk's return, would have worked better than the plan being hatched by Kissinger and Chou En-lai to bring him back to replace Lon Nol under a republican aegis—the failure of which Kissinger blames on the bombing halt ordered by the United States Congress. Had the Khmer Rouge extremists been restrained by victory, it is possibly true, as Kiernan also points out, that the Khmer people could have been spared much suffering; that is, the revolution, had it lost momentum, might not have moved toward greater violence and its own ultimate destruction. But I doubt that an earlier Communist victory would have avoided the inevitable clash with the Vietnamese. In fact, as Kiernan himself admits, the Khmer Rouge "did not wish to win in such a fashion," that is, in a moderate climate, because "they stood to lose too much in an open political atmosphere."

In any case, with the dwindling help of the Americans, who over a five-year period had given the Cambodian government about a million dollars a day in military and economic aid, and spent a total of seven billion dollars more on aerial bombardments, Lon Nol managed to hang on until mid-April 1975. By mid-1974, though, the Khmer Rouge decision to launch the final offensive was taken by the Party's Central Committee. By then it was clear that, far from coordinating their offensives, the Vietnamese and the Cambodians were going their separate ways. Once Pol Pot had succeeded in overthrowing the Lon Nol regime, and the Americans had left in far smaller numbers but almost as ignominiously as they were soon to flee Vietnam, at the end of April 1975, Pol Pot became more anti-Vietnamese than ever. He and other Khmer Rouge leaders, particularly his closest fellow extremists, had hopes of seizing the Kampuchea Krom areas in Vietnam's delta bordering on Cambodia, which the Cambodians had long coveted and still claimed were theirs historically—in fact, they laid claim to eighteen provinces in South Vietnam, including Saigon—but no one, least of all the Vietnamese, paid much attention to that. Nevertheless, emotions were high enough to convince the Cambodians that the Vietnamese, in turn, had their own plans to capture Saigon and then march on Phnom Penh, all of which accounted for the increasing tension between the two countries. There was some justification for the Cambodians' fears, though not enough to account for their too precipitate response, which soon cost them dearly and brought them more trouble than good. Pol Pot and the other ultra-chauvinistic Khmer leaders might have opposed the Chinese just as vehemently had Peking interfered in Cambodian affairs as blatantly as the Vietnamese had all along, but the Chinese were too smart for that. They were playing a much more subtle and longer-term game. Quite a few Khmer who had studied in Hanoi and had then gone on to China for extended periods may have sensed the direction of the future, and comprehended the broad role in Southeast Asia the Chinese had in mind; but there was far less fear of, and indeed more basic admiration for, the Chinese Communists than of the heavier-handed Vietnamese, who from the outset had not hidden their intention to dominate all of Indo-China. They had already taken over the more docile Lao, whose leaders in fact were members of the Vietnamese Laodong (Workers') Party, which became the Communist Party of Vietnam. This, along with the age-old enmity between the Vietnamese and the Khmer, who, far from docile, were as tough as or tougher than the Vietnamese, was reason enough for what happened next.

As soon as the Khmer Rouge captured Phnom Penh, a special meeting of all new cabinet ministers and regional and zonal chiefs was summoned by Pol Pot. In addition to ordering the evacuation of all cities and towns, the abolition of markets, and the dismantling of the old regime in every way possible—including execution of all Lon Nol officials—Pol Pot, in the name of the new Angka Loue ("Organization on High"), declared that all Vietnamese "are welcome to return to their homeland." At the same time he gave orders for as many troops as possible to proceed to the Vietnamese border. Between two and four hundred thousand resident Vietnamese, some of whom spoke Khmer, crossed the border and established themselves in camps or went farther into Vietnam, some of them as far as Saigon. (Many of them would later return to Cambodia in what has become a new contentious issue involving charges of "colonization" by the Vietnamese.) As early as May 1975, Cambodian troops rocketed and mortared the Parrot's Beak region and invaded several islands off the southern coast of the Mekong Delta, including the strategic island of Phu Quoc. These were all places the Cambodians had long claimed were theirs, and the more ambitious of Pol Pot's commanders also wanted to seize as much of the mixed heritage Khmer Krom border area as possible before the Vietnamese Communists moved in. But the Vietnamese struck back swiftly, first drove the Cambodians off the islands, and then set up border patrols. By early June, Pol Pot told visiting Vietnamese leaders that "ignorance of local geography" had been the reason for the Cambodian attacks, but this was purely an excuse for the Cambodians to beat a temporary tactical retreat.

Though most of the subsequent fighting along the Cambodian-Vietnamese border consisted of quick thrusts and counterthrusts, or shelling attacks, the Cambodians held their own and frequently were the aggressors. Their troops followed Pol Pot's orders to cause the Vietnamese as much damage as possible, and to punish civilians as well as troops. As early as the fall of 1975, it was apparent how seriously China viewed the burgeoning war in an anti-Vietnamese context. Peking announced in September that it was extending Cambodia a billion dollars' worth of military and economic aid, interest-free, plus a twenty-million-dollar gift. This was said to be the largest amount China had ever made available to another nation at one time. The Cambodians were obviously encouraged to sustain their attacks. With a tough, brash army whose morale, at this juncture, was probably higher than that of the war-weary Vietnamese, they fought tenaciously and well. Hanoi made at least one serious effort, after the initial round of fighting, to negotiate a peaceful settlement to the border disputes, including the establishment of a ten-kilometer demilitarized zone and the creation of an international supervisory body, but the cocky Phnom Penh government, with Peking's strong support behind it, rebuffed the offer. By early 1977, however, the Vietnamese outnumbered the Cambodians by seven or eight to one. Furthermore, Khmer morale dropped as the internal situation in Cambodia grew worse, and under grueling conditions, soldiers as well as civilians began fleeing to Thailand. The tide had begun to turn. Hanoi's strategy and tactics accordingly were simply to grind away at Pol Pot's forces, driving them deeper into Cambodia with each successive attack or counterattack, and these meat-grinder tactics more and more took their toll.

At the same time, Pol Pot was encountering increasing domestic trouble as his precarious house of cards, built on terror, began to fall apart. There were a number of regional revolts beginning in 1976, which he put down with his customary ruthlessness, but he paid a price. By the end of that year, or certainly by 1977, at least half of the original hard-core Communist leaders who had been with him throughout the revolution had either been murdered or had disappeared, as had a majority of the so-called old Khmer Rouge rank-and-file members. Moreover, two or three coup attempts—including one in 1976 in the Siem Reap region, where an effort was reportedly made to poison Pol Pot and his party of friends at a banquet—had taken an added toll of lives after the plots were discovered. More rebellions took place in 1977, and each time the unity of the Khmer Rouge was further shattered and its ranks further depleted. Early in 1978, a significant rebellion occurred in the Western Zone, which led to more executions. Some students of contemporary Cambodia, including an American named Steve Heder, who was in the country in 1979 and later, doubt that there were that many rebellions against the Pol Pot regime. Instead, he believes that scattered preemptive measures were taken within the Party and the armed forces as a result of unpopularity of local leaders who, for the most part, were acting on their own, and whom the Party did not trust. If so, this was the inevitable product of nearly four years of dislocation, disorganization, and dispersal of the population. As Heder noted, "So the purgers were always able to establish a temporary united front with the population against the local Party leaders. The Party center could say, 'These guys are a bunch of traitors. If you can just help us get rid of them, all the promises we've made are finally going to come true.' The population was, unfortunately, naive enough to believe that."

Pol Pot apparently believed it himself, and, like so many tyrants before him, maintained that his basic policies were sound, that he was being betrayed by disloyal friends and saboteurs. (In 1981, according to Heder, he told a small group of intellectuals meeting near the Thai border that "I was too trusting of others," which in effect was saying that he should have struck sooner and harder against the enemies around him, real or imagined.) Estimates of the number of persons eliminated in the purges run as high as two hundred thousand, but even if the total was half of that, it was high enough, given the many problems the Khmer Rouge had imposed upon itself of controlling the residual population and maintaining any loyalty at all after having already killed a million or a million and a half people. In the spring of 1978, following the rejection by the Cambodians of another Vietnamese offer to settle the border disputes through negotiations, the internal revolts came to a head in the Eastern Zone, where the most likely opponent of Pol Pot, the popular long-time leader So Phim, was Party chief. After several weeks of fighting and frenzied intra-Party skirmishing, So Phim was killed under mysterious circumstances, and several thousand of his armed supporters fled across the border into Vietnam with Heng Samrin, the young but not nearly as popular Khmer Rouge officer who would soon become head of the new regime installed by Hanoi.

A month or so after the Eastern Zone rebellion subsided, the climactic Vietnamese attack began on Christmas Day. There was no doubt by now that the Vietnamese intended to subjugate Cambodia, but they probably would have preferred to grind away at Pol Pot's weakening forces and hope that his regime would fall apart on its own. It seems likely that Hanoi's decision to go all out instead was prompted by the refusal of the Chinese to rein in the Cambodians and to give them still more military aid while encouraging them to continue attacking across the Viet-

namese border. The Chinese determination to let the
Vietnamese bleed as much as possible in Cambodia had
already been proved. Now they increased the buildup of
their own forces along the border with Vietnam in the
north, which would result in China's seventeen-day invasion of Vietnam in February and March 1979, in response
to Vietnam's takeover in Cambodia the month before. Militarily, the Vietnamese were far more successful during
this initial main phase of what has justifiably been called
the Third Indo-China War. It took them twelve days to
capture Phnom Penh, with relatively slight losses, while
the Chinese, though causing considerable damage to factories in northern Vietnam and a fair number of casualties, suffered many more casualties themselves and
scarcely proved their point about "teaching Vietnam a lesson." The Chinese managed to hide their embarrassment
after their 1979 failure—which they simply claimed was a
victory—and they could offer all sorts of excuses for their
refusal to attack Vietnam a second time, in 1984–85, as
Sihanouk's coalition government urged, including the pri-
macy of their economic reforms. They could still also fall
back on the advantage of geographic safety, or conve-
nience, and could claim that, from a revolutionary standpoint in Cambodia, time was still on their side, though that
could no longer be assumed. The Vietnamese had been
able by this time to entrench themselves in Cambodia and
to consolidate a regime that had begun its shadowy existence under dismal circumstances after Phnom Penh was
taken. Seven years later, in 1986, the People's Republic of
Kampuchea certainly had not prospered, but it had en-
dured and had slowly established some identity of its own
that at least furnished a feasible alternative to the dreaded
return of the Khmer Rouge, with or without Pol Pot.
Much of the population by now felt that the Vietnamese
and the Heng Samrin government represented the lesser
of two evils.

(9)

The question of whose side time actually favors in Cambodia today remains a valid one, and, like everything else in that still stricken country, is highly complicated. Despite the apparent success of Vietnam's dry season offensive ending in the spring of 1985, and the likelihood that another big attack might once more disrupt the scattered coalition forces, the war has now changed into what is primarily a guerrilla contest waged in the interior of the country. As stressed in an important article by General Le Duc Anh, the commander of Vietnamese forces in Cambodia and a member of the Politburo, that appeared in December 1984 in the Vietnamese army magazine, "The inland front . . . is the final place for deciding the success of the Cambodian revolution," while the so-called border front with Thailand affords points of entry and infiltration corridors "to pour forces and weapons inland for guerrilla and sabotage activities, seizing land, controlling the population, building counterrevolutionary forces, and so forth." Anh described the fighting within the country as "a fierce revolutionary struggle" which could prove "long and complicated."

Coming from General Anh, this can be read as a virtual admission of failure, and one wonders what the Vietnamese senior army staff had originally expected of the Cambodians, whose capabilities for resistance they should have known, especially when forced to the wall. It is worth recalling that, at the outset of the serious fighting in Cambodia, as mentioned earlier, General Vo Nguyen Giap, who was no longer in favor and was about to be retired, privately warned that it would take longer to subdue the Cambodians than some of the brash new young officers of the Vietnamese army trained in the Soviet Union supposed. For reasons of political disunity, it has taken the opposition coalition all these years of repeated setbacks on and near the Thai border to become fully aware of the importance of the inland front; and the ability of the fragile coalition to build up and then sustain a guerrilla army remains seriously in doubt. Even so, the coalition elements, particularly the Khmer Rouge, show no signs of giving up the fight.

After their defeat in January 1979, the Khmer Rouge forces, then totaling about twenty thousand and still led by Pol Pot, had retreated to the Thai border, where they set up camps in the north and southwest hills and began the difficult task of trying to recreate a new revolutionary image for themselves. This was all the more difficult after the long years of harsh treament to which they had subjected the Khmer people. Now, even for those who had managed to survive, the Khmer Rouge was scarcely able to provide those two basic necessities of food and security. The result was that, between the fall of 1979 and the spring of 1980, about a third of the civilian population in the border areas controlled by Democratic Kampuchea disappeared. The Vietnamese captured or "liberated" some; others were killed by Vietnamese shelling or bombing; and, surprisingly, more fled voluntarily to Vietnamese-controlled zones than to an unknown future as refugees in Thailand.

Despite a fair amount of international economic aid during the 1979–80 period, especially food and medicines, most of which came in through Thailand, and a strengthening by the Chinese of the Khmer Rouge forces by about a third, to thirty thousand, Democratic Kampuchea's prospects remained poor. Few believed the claims made by the defeated government that a new line of moderation was to be adopted. Heder, who toured the border region at this time, quoted a Communist Party official who had been expelled from the Party in 1977: "The cadre who were responsible for the ulta-left line and the killings still grasp all the power. Now they suddenly say they've changed a hundred percent. They could change back just as suddenly. . . . They don't accept any criticism or admit they were wrong. They blame everything on others. How can you trust them?" The hated security apparatus and killer squads of the Khmer Rouge were still all around the camps and a traumatic fear existed that there would be more killings and purges. As another man told Heder, perhaps the worst was yet to come and everyone would be "beaten to death and disposed of—except Pol Pot." Heder's own estimate of the situation was that, in spite of its regaining a certain amount of armed strength, support for Democratic Kampuchea was waning and, "As a result, in August 1980, the prospects for an increase in the effectiveness of its resistance seemed dim to nonexistent."

It was at this juncture that the wheels within wheels in Indo-China's—and indeed in all of Southeast Asia's—ever complex political mechanism began to spin with even more than their usual velocity. Since then, though very little has been settled, the diplomatic wheels have kept on spinning.

The Vietnamese were still uncertain about what course to adopt, which was one reason they had sought to negotiate a solution to the border crisis as far back as 1975. When they invaded Cambodia in 1979, they were not eager to become the overseers of a ravaged country, to adopt the fractious Khmer as wards, at least not before they had set their own house in order. This disinclination had nothing to do with their long-term, unaltered aim of including Cambodia, along with Laos, in what they used to describe as an Indo-China Federation, though they now preferred to call the relationship one of "unity and cooperation among three like-minded socialist nations." Initially, Hanoi's Politburo sent its top members, its best army leaders and technical experts to Phnom Penh in the early months. One of the first to arrive was Le Duc Tho, the

number-two man in the Politburo. When I spoke with Tho
in Hanoi five years later in the fall of 1984, he said, graphically (reminding me, incidentally, that he was a poet and
had written a number of poems about Cambodia), "The
first day I came to Phnom Penh, I could see no one, the
city was deserted. There was no barking of dogs, no cack-
ling of poultry. Then, slowly, there were long lines of people, returning. They were all in black pajamas and thin,
like a line of ghosts." Le Duc Tho went on to say, with
some degree of truth, that the Vietnamese had invaded
Cambodia reluctantly because of the "perfidious and
wicked policy of the Chinese," who had refused to let the
Khmer Rouge government negotiate over the border dispute. He insisted that Hanoi "had no other choice—we
were obliged to wage a new war to save Cambodia from
further genocide at the hands of Pol Pot and his Chinese
masters." Ambassador Ngo Dien, who had been with Tho
on that early trip, recalled, when I spoke with him in 1984
in Phnom Penh, that they had been "taken aback by what
had happened, the look of the place, the look of the people. The destruction was everywhere. It was like a forest,
a jungle. There was nothing to eat. There was just nothing. So we felt we had to help. It was a practical matter,
nothing ideological. Something had to be done."

One of the first things the Vietnamese had to do was
establish credibility, not only for themselves but for their
surrogate Khmer. This was not easy, and the dour, laconic
Heng Samrin was scarcely a well-known or charismatic
figure around whom to build a new regime. Hanoi's original choice was a man named Pen Sovan, who was a bona
fide nationalist they had groomed to become head of the
new Kampuchean People's Revolutionary Party they reestablished, using the old name they first selected back in
1951. Sovan was named Party secretary, as well as vice-
president and defense minister of the new government.
As one of the few survivors of the early group of old

Hanoi-trained cadre, many if not most of whom Pol Pot had killed, he was not welcomed by the other new leaders, whose ties with the Vietnamese were not as close. The Soviet Union was known to have given Sovan its blessing, which did little to enhance his support among the independent-minded Khmer. At any rate, after an inner power struggle about which not much is known, Sovan suddenly disappeared from the picture. Poor health was given as the reason for his withdrawal. He is believed to have gone to Moscow, though other reports say he is back in Hanoi. It was apparent during my stay in Hanoi that no one among the Vietnamese leaders wanted to talk about him, and mention of his name seemed to embarrass them.

The position of ASEAN, the group of Southeast Asian nations, took on new importance almost as soon as Vietnam overran Cambodia. Originally created as an economic organization two decades ago, ASEAN took a long time to get off the ground partly because of the many racial and cultural as well as social and political differences in the backgrounds of its five original members. Economically, despite all the talk about cooperation, these developing nations, now totaling six with the addition of Brunei, each with its own considerable resources, have been competitors rather than collaborators, and they also have had frequent disputes, including political ones, over seemingly trivial matters. Nevertheless, as individual nations they prospered rapidly and, led by Singapore, achieved surprisingly high growth rates. The war in Vietnam and its aftermath served better than meetings or communiqués to politicize the organization and, ironically, give it more purpose and cohesion. Of the five initial members, the one most concerned with the Vietnam war, for geographic reasons alone, was Thailand, which the United States had used as an airbase and supply center. Once the war was over, the Thais, in effect, needed a new patron to replace the Americans, who continued to profess their friendship and give the Thais considerable aid but were no longer as concerned as they had been with the country's security. The Thais faced an internal problem of a northern and northeastern Communist insurgency supported by the Chinese, who were also backing insurgency movements in Burma and Malaysia and had been the major outside supporter of the powerful Communist movement in Indonesia, which culminated in the failed coup of 1965 and the collapse of Sukarno.

The ASEAN nations, both singly and collectively, thus had many reasons for being concerned about their powerful northern Communist neighbors, Vietnam and China. Except in Burma, China gradually withdrew its support for the various Southeast Asian insurgencies, which simmered down. But Thailand became more immediately vulnerable to spillover attacks by the Vietnamese across its borders, and also had to shoulder the main burden of caring for scores of thousands of new Cambodian refugees. As a result, the Thais soon drew closer to the Chinese, with whom they now shared an interest in holding the Vietnamese in check. Thailand became ASEAN's new "frontline" nation, though there were some key differences of attitude within the group toward Vietnam. Indonesia and Malaysia tended to be the most conciliatory, while Singapore joined Thailand in being the most skeptical and worried about the dangers of a larger war. Diplomatically, ASEAN's chief problem was the embarrassing one of maintaining support for Pol Pot's Democratic Kampuchea in the United Nations against Heng Samrin's People's Republic of Kampuchea, backed by Hanoi. Most of the UN, including the United States, held to the traditional view that no matter how wicked and horrible Pol Pot's rule had been, the Vietnamese had invaded Cambodia illegally and had overthrown an "established government." This is still the view of a vast majority in the UN today, and Democratic Kampuchea retains its seat. For the non-Communist elements in the coalition, therefore, the problem after Vietnam's takeover in Cambodia and ever since has been one of broadening Democratic Kampuchea's base and diminishing the bloody image of its main military arm, the Khmer Rouge, thereby projecting a more legitimate alternative to Vietnam's surrogates in Phnom Pehn. At the same time the campaign to persuade the Vietnamese to withdraw from Cambodia has continued, and the combined diplomatic and military contest has now lasted seven years. If there are some signs of possible resolution, including Vietnam's expressed willingness to reach a compromise on certain aspects of the problem and an equal desire on the part of most of ASEAN to make some sort of accommodation, the solution is still a long way off, as everyone concerned agrees. And the key to it is still held by China, and to a lesser extent by the United States and the Soviet Union.

The creation of the coalition opposing the Vietnamese and the Samrin government in Phnom Penh dates back to 1976, when a small group of former neutralists calling itself the Association of Overseas Cambodians was formed in France to help Sihanouk. According to one of its founders, "We were convinced he could not stay for long with the Khmer Rouge once he realized their true nature." Seeking someone responsible other than Sihanouk, who was still in Peking, as its president, the association turned to Son Sann, who was then already sixty-four years old and living in exile in Paris. (Many years earlier, before joining several of Sihanouk's governments, he had been the young prince's tutor.) Reluctantly, since he had always avoided the limelight, the former financial expert and cabinet member accepted. This was the start of what became the Khmer People's National Liberation Front, of which Son Sann became the head and which now has an armed strength of almost fifteen thousand. When it was created, in the fall of 1979, it could muster only two thousand men, combining five small and rebellious resistance groups that had previously spent most of their time fighting each other or smuggling precious stones and other goods across the borders of Thailand, Burma, Laos, and Cambodia. As the new group began to obtain the support of Thailand and other nations, including the United States, Democratic Kampuchea and its Khmer Rouge forces responded by renouncing communism in favor of a free market economy, though it didn't alter its authoritarian ways. By the end of 1980, Son Sann was welcomed in Peking and was promised some military aid, though the Chinese continued to give most of their support to Democratic Kampuchea. In 1981, at a secret meeting in Bangkok between Son Sann and Prime Minister Khieu Samphan of Democratic Kampuchea, Samphan offered Son Sann his job, but Sann held out for more power in a new coalition government. Wise in the way of negotiations, Sann commented, "Before I walk into the tiger's cage, I need a big stick."

As for Sihanouk, he had tried, during the Carter administration, to get the Americans to help him raise an army of a hundred thousand men, but he was rebuffed. Aware that only the Chinese would be willing to contribute military aid, and only to a group aligned with the Khmer Rouge, the prince announced in the spring of 1981 that he was willing to form a new united front with the Khmer Rouge; and he also said he was creating a new political party, the United Front for an Independent, Neutral, Peaceful and Cooperative Cambodia, with headquarters in Peking. Son Sann responded by angrily claiming that Sihanouk was trying to divide the opposition and he refused to recognize the prince's new party. A meeting between the two men in France, at which Sihanouk proposed a federation of the two nationalist movements, failed because of the anti-Sihanouk feelings of some members of Son Sann's entourage. Meanwhile, in July 1981, after bitter preliminary arguments between the Chinese and

ASEAN representatives, a conference sponsored by the United Nations and attended by eighty-three nations unanimously approved a declaration calling for Vietnamese withdrawal from Cambodia and the establishment of a UN peacekeeping body and UN-sponsored elections. The Chinese resolutely supported Pol Pot against ASEAN's efforts to undermine him and reach their own compromise with the Vietnamese. The United States sought to be impartial but seemed to favor a formula that would be acceptable to the Chinese as well as to ASEAN. The conference ended with the Vietnamese disavowing it and accusing the United States and China of "using ASEAN as their instrument."

Six weeks after the end of the United Nations conference, the next act was played out in Singapore, with a meeting among the three coalition factions represented by Sihanouk, Son Sann, and Khieu Samphan. Little progress was made either there or at subsequent ad hoc meetings in Bangkok. Each group sought to project its own demands and protect its own authority rather than express a willingness to compromise on a workable coalition government. Singapore saved the day, or at least everyone's face, by suggesting a new format for each faction to "retain its identity and be free to propagate its own distinctive program and philosophy for the future of Cambodia." The Singaporeans also simplified the proposals for a new government by suggesting a small ruling body of a president, a prime minister, a deputy prime minister, and three ministers representing each of the three movements. Its immediate function would be to avoid further clashes between the Khmer Rouge and the forces of Son Sann and Sihanouk, which had begun to take place fairly frequently along the Cambodian-Thai border and inside Cambodia.

As projected, the pro-tem coalition government would be dissolved after a Vietnamese withdrawal, pending elections to establish a new permanent government. Democratic Kampuchea would thereby lose its interim legal status, which the UN conference, with China's backing, had endorsed—pledging that it would remain the legitimate government until *after* free elections took place. Both Sihanouk and Son Sann objected to the proposal set forth in the Singapore compromise of working closely with the Khmer Rouge, even on a temporary and quasi-legal basis, but they reluctantly conceded the point, and the new agreement, which was described as "a shotgun wedding," went into effect in 1982. None of the three parties has chosen to challenge or test it. Moreover, sporadic battles among the three component forces continued and sometimes resulted in considerable casualties. Sihanouk kept issuing new threats to resign as the coalition's president, while Son Sann seemed to veer between outbursts of anger against Sihanouk or members of his own faction who took issue with him and sullen fits of apathy, during which he appeared to lose interest. In the fall of 1985, he warned that by the time the coalition forces prevailed inside Cambodia, if they ever did, it would be too late because "so many Vietnamese will become Cambodian citizens that they will be in charge," even if the Vietnamese troops did withdraw. This was an exaggeration based on the number of Vietnamese who had allegedly returned to Cambodia from Vietnam; estimates ran as high as seven or eight hundred thousand, but, in fact, the more realistic approximation was somewhere between two and three hundred thousand. Despite the inability of the two non-Communist coalition leaders to get along with each other, they both acted on the assumption, and expressed the fear, that the Khmer Rouge was getting stronger and was operating in most or all of Cambodia's provinces, while their own smaller armies, despite more aid from the Chinese and a little more from the Americans, were having a hard time keeping up their strength. In one of his not infrequent moments of despair, Sihanouk, toward the end of 1985, said, "The day the Vietnamese go home, the Khmer Rouge will wipe out our nationalist forces and there will be no reason for them to step down. If we win the war, I would rather be in France than in Phnom Penh with the Khmer Rouge."

Despite these pessimistic statements and the two leaders' deteriorating relationship, as well as Son Sann's internal problems in the liberation front, non-Communist supporters of the coalition point out that the Khmer Rouge have their own morale problems, and that the coalition's very existence is important to maintain leverage against both the Khmer Rouge and the Vietnamese. This has been ASEAN's point of view as well. During the second half of 1985 and the early months of 1986, a number of diplomatic developments took place that gave impetus to the possibilities of progress and the hope for some sort of eventual solution in Cambodia. The ASEAN group sought to promote so-called proximity talks, or indirect negotiations, whereby Vietnam and the opposition coalition government would discuss solutions through intermediaries who would move back and forth between the two main parties. This idea, floated by Malaysia, did not seem to make much headway, but both sides appeared willing to consider it as a means of getting a dialogue started. At the same time, Indonesians began playing a more active role as mediators, suggesting various formulas and timetables for the gradual withdrawal of Vietnamese forces from Cambodia, the introduction of peacekeeping forces and observer groups, and the holding of supervised elections to include all political groups within the framework of "national reconciliation." These ideas were surfaced during the United Nations General Assembly late in 1985 by Dr. Mochtar Kusumaatmadja, the Indonesian foreign minister, who has had a number of conversations with his Vietnamese counterpart, Nguyen Co Thach. The Vietnamese, as has been their habit, kept issuing contradictory statements and blowing hot and cold on all peace proposals. On the one hand, they spoke of the "irreversibility of the situation in Cambodia" and "the great achievements" of the Heng Samrin regime, and on the other hand they called for "joint discussions between the two groups of countries to settle all problems raised by each side." These contradictions, beyond propaganda, appeared to reflect the continuing differences within the Hanoi Politburo between the "hawks" eager to prosecute the war to a finish, and the "doves" favoring a political resolution.

Nevertheless, acting out of a growing desire to end their isolation and possibly at the instigation of the Soviet Union, the Vietnamese, as already noted, professed to be more willing than before to talk directly to the Cambodians on the coalition side, if Pol Pot was really out of the picture. For example, in mid-1985 Foreign Minister Thach told three visiting American correspondents in Hanoi that, if the Chinese ceased their aid to the Khmer Rouge and the Thais stopped offering their sanctuary inside Thailand, the Vietnamese would simultaneously begin to withdraw their troops from Cambodia. The Heng Samrin government and Sihanouk's coalition could then "negotiate on the basis of the sharing of power," Thach said. "It is their affair. We will support the right of self-determination of the Khmer people and a Khmer reconciliation on the basis of the elimination of Pol Pot." This was further than Thach or any other Vietnamese official had gone before, at least in public, in offering a settlement through negotiations on an equal basis, but his conditions still left it up to the Chinese to open the door and the Russians to push it. But when the Chinese tried to open the door, the Vietnamese failed to respond. Early in 1986, Peking hosted a meeting among Sihanouk, Son Sann, and Khieu Samphan, during which an eight-point offer was made to discuss peace with the Phnom Penh regime.

Hanoi accused the Chinese of "rigging" the proposal and said it reflected "the hostility of China."

Indonesian Foreign Minister Kusumaatmadja had put the situation in a nutshell in his United Nations aide-mémoire when he had said: "Another point which should be realized is that the Cambodian problem is a manifestation of the conflict between two competing strategies in Southeast Asia, namely the Chinese strategy implemented through the Pol Pot regime and the Soviet-backed Vietnam strategy championing Heng Samrin as the 'real' government of the Cambodian people. It is this particular aspect of the Cambodian conflict, being the fulcrum of two competing strategies for the hegemony or domination of Southeast Asia, which makes the Cambodian problem an intractable one. Any attempt to solve the Cambodian problem without recognizing this basic fact is bound to fail as the two contending parties have the will and endurance to continue the conflict indefinitely." A number of international observers and commentators who have followed Indo-China events carefully felt, by 1986, that, despite all the peace maneuvers, the "relatively stable" war in Cambodia would continue precisely because it still served the special interests of the major powers, including the United States as well as the Soviet Union and China. At the same time, they admitted that the course of events inside Cambodia, both military and political, could determine the tide of events. The Vietnamese could step up their offensive tactics and, taking advantage of the long-term handicaps of the opposition, prosecute the war to victory or at least to the point where the opposing forces would be reduced to a "nuisance." Conceivably, an opposite development would find the Khmer Rouge becoming stronger as the non-Communist elements disintegrated, with Son Sann and/or Sihanouk fading from the picture.

Writing in *Indochina Issues* in December 1985, Donald K. Emmerson, who directs the Center of Southeast Asian

Studies at the University of Wisconsin, suggested that "even the less fanciful of these domestic scenarios is less likely than a continuation of the status quo. The near-term prospect is for stalemate not checkmate. The insurgents are unable to rid their country of Vietnam's troops and clients, but the Vietnamese and their Khmer collaborators have also proven themselves unable to assure their own permanent security in occupied Cambodia. . . . However strikingly American, Chinese, and Soviet policies toward Cambodia differ, they share a common principle of balance: to honor commitments to friends without risking general war. According to this principle, the war is worth continuing and limiting." Emmerson pointed out that the Chinese "at minimal risk to themselves" were able to go on tying down their Soviet and Vietnamese rivals by letting the war go on, while prosecuting their program of Four Modernizations at home. The Russians, on their part, were able to keep Vietnam dependent on them and continue enjoying the use of their new naval base at Cam Ranh Bay in Vietnam, without risking a wider war and still keeping open their diplomatic bridges to China, the United States, and to ASEAN. As for the Americans, Emmerson said, there was no reason for them to outreach either China or ASEAN in seeking a solution to a war that "drains Vietnamese and Soviet resources at minimal cost to Washington, and does not threaten regional stability." Toward the end of his paper, Emmerson did concede that "There are signs the United States, China, and the Soviet Union are all reconsidering their policies—toward Indo-China, toward each other, or both. The likelihood of the impasse in Cambodia being broken by diplomacy from the outside is greater than the chance of resolution through conciliation from within. But the core struggle in Cambodia, rooted as it is in the ethnic histories and national identities of its Khmer and Vietnamese protagonists, will continue."

My own feeling is that the moves toward a resolution of the Cambodian problem that have taken place in the past year or so are genuine, and that they have received, and are receiving, continuing impetus and encouragement both from the parties immediately concerned *and* from the major powers. For whatever reasons of their own, including above all a desire to end their isolation and be less dependent on the Soviet Union, most Vietnamese leaders, as they indicated as far back as 1984 when I was in Hanoi, are more eager to conclude the war through negotiations than to continue it militarily. Either way, they figure, they will retain their paramount position in all of Indo-China, although a compromise in Cambodia might delay the process a few years. The non-Communist coalition in Cambodia and the slowly maturing and somewhat more independent government of Heng Samrin are willing or eager to find a solution. The Khmer Rouge are less so, and of all the parties concerned would probably favor a fight to the finish, but they would not find it easy to go it alone indefinitely in a hostile internal climate, and without unlimited help from China. There is little doubt that the ASEAN countries are anxious to bring about an end to the war and foster their pet project of turning all of Southeast Asia into a zone of peace, independence, and neutrality, as well as prosperity.

As for the major powers, while it is true that over the past six and a half years the Cambodian war stalemate has brought them certain compensations, if not benefits, this is no longer so much the case. The Russians, under Gorbachev, are increasingly aware that their popularity in Vietnam is diminishing, that it would cost them less to let other nations, including Western ones, help bear the burden of restoring Vietnam economically, and that they could still keep Cam Ranh Bay while making new friends in the rest of Southeast Asia by promoting peace. Contending with the Chinese in the area does not interfere with the Soviets' desire to reach an accommodation with Peking on other issues, as they are seeking to do. The value of Vietnam and Cambodia, as pawns for both Communist powers, is no longer as great as it was, and these other issues have become more important. The Chinese, as long as their present leadership lasts, are determined to concentrate on their Four Modernizations and to reduce external friction wherever possible. Peking's willingness to entertain Hanoi's overtures, while maintaining its historic attitude of imperiousness, is a sign of this, though the more important manifestation is its own sincere desire to further its rapprochement with Moscow. As Richard Solomon, of the State Department's Policy Planning Committee, has pointed out, the Chinese are also seeking to sustain their new balance between the Soviet Union and the United States, "to have better relations with each than they have with each other." As for the Americans, while still preoccupied elsewhere in the world, their desire to accommodate ASEAN and to reenter the Southeast Asian arena has brought them to the point where they are more willing than they were a year or two ago to take an active part in prosecuting a Cambodian solution. But whether they are willing to play a major role remains doubtful.

At the moment, more than the usual number of intangibles and imponderables continue to confound the issues. Is Pol Pot really moving aside, or was his resignation statement pure subterfuge? Would the Chinese seriously consider eliminating or at least cutting back their support for the Khmer Rouge, and would they then be prepared to support or condone the establishment of a neutral transitional government in Cambodia headed by Sihanouk? What kind of international guarantees could be given and enforced to secure such a government and then supervise free elections for a permanent regime? Will the Vietnamese be serious about withdrawing all their troops from Cambodia by 1990, or even sooner, as they have indicated, leaving the forces of the new Cambodian army and perhaps some of the non-Communist coalition elements to defend a new joint regime? Or would the Vietnamese insist, as they have in Laos, on leaving at least thirty or forty thousand of their own troops in the country indefinitely, and how would a new Cambodian government, the ASEAN countries, and the Chinese react to that? Can Vietnamese migration back to Cambodia be kept at the present level, below the flash point of inspiring fresh outbursts of anti-Vietnamese nationalism on the part of the Khmer, and what rights of citizenship and other privileges will these returning or new Vietnamese settlers be given? How can the elimination of the Khmer Rouge elements be assured, even if the Chinese reduce or eliminate their support, and will Democratic Kampuchean leaders such as Khieu Samphan actually be allowed to participate in the new government? Will the Russians continue to encourage the Vietnamese to reach a settlement and really be willing to loosen their tight strings with Hanoi? Is the United States, beyond its gesture of support to the forces of Son Sann and Sihanouk—several million dollars, which can be used for military aid—truly willing to foster a solution in Cambodia and reach an accommodation with Vietnam, and will it use its power and prestige to bring about a settlement within the larger framework of regional peace and security? And if so, would it best act alone or in concert with China and perhaps with the Soviet Union?

It seems more than ever apparent that there can be no Cambodian settlement of any kind without some sort of international commitment and leadership, including the participation of the three major powers. The United Nations and ASEAN, together or separately, could play a useful role in implementing an agreement, but the basic guarantors would almost have to include the big powers, acting, as Sihanouk has suggested, under the umbrella of another Geneva-type agreement. If the possibilities of an agreement seem somewhat better today than at any time in the previous seven years, it is primarily because the major players are at least more willing than they were before to consider one, or say they are, but there have been no firm commitments as yet, and the situation on the ground could quickly change. Therefore, both the timing and the time-span involved are tricky and tenuous, while the factor of damage control remains unpredictable. If several more major rounds of fighting take place during the coming dry and wet seasons, through the end of 1986 and beyond, the level of guerrilla combat inside Cambodia may reach new heights of violence and further destroy a country already so hurt and shock-ridden that major international assistance on a sustained scale for a number of years is required.

The best time to seek a settlement, assuming both sides are willing to talk, is between the heavy fighting of the dry seasons. This seasonal interval is also the logical time for the outside world to bring what pressure it can for a settlement. To raise the Cambodian crisis once more to the necessary level of the world's conscience and understanding will be no simple task, given the long and dreadful history of the past two decades and the fact that people everywhere have become so inured to disaster, death, and destruction that statistics and even photographs or television segments no longer have much meaning. It would still appear, however, that the man who is in the best position to provide the leadership needed during this crucial period is Norodom Sihanouk, who, despite his sporadic pessimism, is still waging his own crusade for the preservation of the Khmer people. More than ever before, he would require the loyalty and support of the five million or so "new Cambodians" who constitute the population of the country today, many of whom hardly know him, while the memories of those who do are clouded over by so much pain and misery that they can scarcely comprehend each other. These are the tragic remnants of those he used to call his "children" or "the little people." He still uses these terms with affection and respect, and without any condescension, arrogance, or paternalism on his part. In 1981, in an earlier short sketch called *Bittersweet Memories,* he wrote: "Emotionally and politically, I have always been much closer to the genuine, hardworking, loyal and faithful people than the Khmer politicians of the past, most of whom were corrupt, disdainful schemers or, like Pol Pot's pseudo-'democrats,' cold-hearted ideologists who sentenced those who would not obey them to a rapid or slow death. . . ." That closeness has passed the test of time and has been reciprocated. Whether it still exists, given the added tragedies that have been heaped on Cambodia, and whether it would again be a positive factor if Sihanouk gets another chance to play a role, is impossible to predict. But the affection and sincerity on his part are real and enduring, and they will survive as long as he does.

Epilogue

The mildly optimistic note at the end of the final chapter is not meant to belie my title, *Bitter Victory*. Whatever happens in Cambodia, whether Sihanouk prevails or not, cannot expunge the dismal record of death and destruction wrought by the Khmer Rouge that has made the saga of this unfortunate country one of the greatest tragedies in world history. The Vietnamese can take credit for overthrowing the Khmer Rouge, and even a limited ultimate "victory" by them—to the extent that they achieve their goal of dominating Cambodia as they dominate Laos—may satisfy their compulsion to secure their borders and their expansionist aims in the Indo-China area. But it will surely not meet the aspirations of the Cambodian or the Lao people, who deserve their full independence as nations in their own right.

North Vietnam's victories over the French and over the Americans and the South Vietnamese were classic and unique in military terms, but they have remained hollow if not bitter as far as the Vietnamese people are concerned. Life for the average Vietnamese today is no better than it was three or four decades ago, and in some respects it is worse. The colonial master is gone, along with the American dispenser of mixed bombs and bounty, but the country is steeped in poverty and much of it still lies in ruins. Oddly enough, both the French and the Americans, as people, are regarded with more esteem and admiration nowadays than the Russians, who gave so much to the war effort and remain Vietnam's biggest benefactors.

It is more the fault of the Vietnamese than anyone else that their victory has not been savored and that they are still struggling to achieve peace, let alone prosperity. If the new economic programs of liberalization are auguries of a better future, they will require years to implement, and other nations, particularly the United States and Japan, will have to extend the sort of assistance that the Communist countries cannot offer, notably light industrial equipment and consumer goods. But in the final analysis, it will be up to the Vietnamese themselves to realize the fruits of their wartime success and refashion their shattered national economy.

Perhaps even more important, if the inheritance of bitterness that has marred the past and still scars the present is to be altered, will be the ability of a new generation of Vietnamese leaders to transcend their narrow nationalism, to reach beyond their natural pride and their passionate patriotism. This may prove the hardest challenge, above and beyond economic reform and political compromise, for it involves changes in outlook and, in the final analysis, a change of heart and mind. Whatever justification may lie in the legacy of bitterness the Vietnamese feel, subjugated as they were for so long by the Chinese and the French, they will not find peace and contentment until they confront themselves in their convoluted historical mirror and regard other nations, especially their neighbors in Southeast Asia, with less suspicion and mistrust. If this is a two-way street, the main burden is on Vietnam, if only because it is one of the world's strongest military powers. It may be too much to expect Vietnam to demilitarize itself, but it is not too much to hope that the ingenious people who built the Ho Chi Minh Trail to wage war will finds ways to build similar paths for peace that will benefit the whole region. Therein lies the road away from bitterness to the better life the Vietnamese people, who have given and suffered so much to achieve victory, deserve.

Index

Ablin, David, 260
Abrams, Floyd, 214
Africans, 25, 148, 194
Agent Orange, 34
Agriculture, Cambodian, 204–205, 207, 222–224, 271
Agriculture, Vietnamese, 67, 71, 81–86, 88–92, 97–99, 112, 136, 139,168; in central Vietnam, 118, 119–120
Amerasians *(con lai)*, 24–26, 132
Americans: and retreat from Saigon, 1, 16, 19; and Vietnam war, 2, 142, 177; Vietnamese attitudes towards, 51, 192, 299; missing in action, 52, 59–62, 222; in Cambodia, 211–212. *See also* United States
American-Vietnamese war: and U.S. withdrawal, 1–2, 47–48, 56, 186, 189; effects of, 11, 68, 74, 299; and Vietnamese cities, 14, 15, 121, 123–124, 131; destructiveness of, 43, 45, 50, 88, 117, 119, 139, 140; U.S. performance in, 44–45, 166–169, 175–177, 179, 180–181, 188, 193–195; and French war, 48, 148, 156, 167, 170–172, 193–195; U.S. involvement in, 55, 171–174, 181–182, 190; veterans of, 71, 72; and China, 81–82, 135, 167, 169, 184, 185, 187, 234, 246; U.S. view of, 142–143, 176–187; Vietnamese view of, 143–144, 148, 175–176, 181–182, 187–195; and 1973 agreement, 146–147; political aspects of, 147–148, 176–177, 186, 189; military aspects of, 176–185, 187–188, 245–246; negotiations during, 185, 234–238; and Cambodia, 196, 197, 218, 240, 242, 243, 265, 268. *See also* Ho Chi Minh Trail

Angka Loue (Organization on High), 274
Angkor Wat, 197, 240
Anh, General Le Duc, 57, 93–94, 279
Annam, 77. *See also* Vietnam, central
Apbac, battle of, 172, 173
Association of Southeast Asian Nations (ASEAN): and Cambodian-Vietnamese war, 56, 218–220, 222, 266, 283–287, 289, 292–295; and Vietnam, 57, 59, 137
Australians, 44, 211, 235, 236, 237, 267

Bam, Brigadier General Vo, 149, 150, 151, 153, 163
Bandung Conference, 227, 228
Banmethuot, battle of, 145, 147, 178, 187, 193
Big Victory, Great Task (General Vo Nguyen Giap), 182
Binh, Mme Nguyen Thi, 10, 125
Binh, Archbishop Nguyen Van, 130
Binh, Pham, 137
Binh Gia, battle of, 173
Binh Xuyen sect, 35–36
Bittersweet Memories (Norodom Sihanouk), 297
Black market, 28, 67–68, 82, 205; in currency, 27, 80, 105, 122, 133, 139
Boat people, 20–21, 29, 52, 133. *See also* Refugees
Bowles, Chester, 240–241, 242
Brezhnev, Leonid, 250
Britain, 78
Brunei, 56, 283. *See also* Association of Southeast Asian Nations
B-2 front, 144, 163, 190
Buddhism, 8, 9, 11, 120, 126–128, 211
Buddhist Church, Unified Vietnamese, 126, 127

Burchett, Wilfred, 234, 235, 236, 237
Bureaucracy, 32–33, 66, 100, 102, 103, 136, 210
Burma, 284, 286

Cambodia, 196–297; and France, 1, 197, 206, 222, 227–229, 236, 285; atrocities in, 7, 20, 49, 198, 205–207, 210–211, 213–214, 223, 272; and U.S., 59, 189, 231–235, 240–245, 247, 252, 254–259; and American-Vietnamese war, 143, 163–164, 168–169, 196, 246, 247; Vietnamese occupation of, 198, 213, 219–221, 224, 282; effects of war on, 203–207, 209–210, 282, 299; foreign aid to, 203, 209, 227, 249, 280; opposition coalition in, 212, 215–218, 284–286; under Pol Pot, 222–224, 274–277; and Geneva Conference, 225, 227–228; communism in, 263–266. See also Pol Pot; Sihanouk, Norodom
Cambodia—1975–1982 (Michael Vickery), 264–265
Cambodians, Association of Overseas, 285
Cambodian-Vietnamese war, 274–279; and Vietnam's domestic problems, 2, 65–66, 68, 81–82, 99; negotiations concerning, 3, 49–50, 200–203, 292–296; and Vietnam's foreign relations, 39, 48, 52–54, 56–58, 61, 107–109, 134–138, 141; Vietnamese policy on, 94, 184; and ASEAN, 283–285, 287, 289
Cam Ranh Bay, 107, 108, 292, 293
Canh, Trinh Van, 129
Carter, Jimmy, 52
Castro, Fidel, 125
Catholicism, 11, 77, 128–129
Catholics, Committee for the Solidarity of Patriotic Vietnamese, 130
Cedar Falls, battle of, 44
Central Highlands (Tay Nguyen), 22, 145. See also Vietnam, central
Chanh, Le Quang, 38
Chau, Thich Minh, 127
Chiang Kai-shek, 135
China, People's Republic of: and reunified Vietnam, 3, 39, 54, 64, 107, 109, 136–138; and war with Vietnam, 22, 56–57, 82, 92, 133–134, 139–140, 278; historical relations with Vietnam, 48, 55, 167, 300; and negotiations on Cambodia, 49–50, 135, 201, 203, 220–222, 256, 260, 285, 290–295;

and Pol Pot, 50, 56, 141, 222–224, 270, 273, 282, 291; and U.S., 52, 59, 243; and Cambodian opposition, 56, 57, 199, 286, 288; and Khmer Rouge, 57–58, 200, 267, 280, 290; economic reforms in, 57, 67, 101, 106; and Soviet Union, 58, 88, 106, 108; aid to Vietnam from, 66, 81, 82, 167, 184, 196; as model, 76, 106, 187; and American-Vietnamese war, 81–82, 135, 167, 169, 184, 185, 187, 234, 246; and Southeast Asia, 87, 284, 287; compared to Vietnam, 114, 130; and Sihanouk, 197, 227–228, 230, 232–233, 241–244, 249–253, 256–263, 278
Chinese, ethnic, 29, 30, 86, 97, 133–134, 140
Chinh, Truong, 83–85, 91, 93, 180, 183, 187
Chou En-lai: and Sihanouk, 228, 232, 242, 250–251, 253, 257, 263; and negotiations on Cambodia, 260, 261, 272
Christmas 1972 bombing, 168, 181, 189
Clark, James William, 212
Cochin China, 9, 77. See also Vietnam, South
Collectivization, 45–46, 84, 85–86, 120, 122–123, 208, 271. See also Cooperatives
Committee for the South (COSVN), 171
Communism: Vietnamese, 9, 18, 55, 76–77, 86–87, 116; Cambodian, 216, 223, 233, 263–264, 266, 268, 286. See also Marxism; Socialism; Vietnam, Communist Party of
con lai. See Amerasians
Consumer goods, 38, 80, 99, 109, 111, 300; availability of, 28, 71, 91, 204
Conthien, 117, 125
Cooperatives, 36, 40, 76, 79, 90, 91. See also Collectivization
Cu Chi district, 43, 45, 46
Cu Chi tunnels, 43–45
Cultural Revolution, Chinese, 87, 242, 263
Currency, 99, 102, 104, 105, 133; black market in, 27, 80, 105, 122, 133, 139; exchange rate for, 27, 80, 122; Cambodian, 204

Dai, Mme Nguyen Phuoc, 29–30
Danang, 50, 107, 125, 145, 146, 148, 174; impressions of, 117, 131–132

Dang, Tran Bach, 40
dau tranh. See Political struggle
Dean, John Gunther, 235–236
de Gaulle, Charles, 232, 240
Del, Dien, 215
Deng Xiaoping, 108, 270
Desbarats, Jacqueline, 19
Deschamps, Noel St. Clair, 236, 237
Diem, Ngo Dinh, 8, 35, 78, 128, 129, 172, 231; and Cambodia, 229, 230
Dien, Ngo, 282
Dien, Nguyen Kim, 129
Dien, To Vinh, 170
Dienbienphu, 1, 16, 140, 147, 155–156, 169–170, 193, 194
Dieu, Nguyen, 155
Dong, Pham Van, 9, 63, 93, 105, 114, 135, 253; on education, 65, 69–70; and American war, 174, 185
Dongha, 117, 123–124, 150, 163
Duan, Le, 3, 32, 49, 86, 100, 141, 153; death of, 5*n.*, 105*n.*; on economy, 21, 98, 99, 101, 110; and pragmatists, 67, 93, 102; on foreign policy, 106, 108, 109, 136, 137, 269
Dubris, Jean Pierre, 81
Dulles, John Foster, 227
Dung, Mme Nguyen Ngoc, 41–42
Dung, General Van Tien, 93, 95, 137, 180; and Cambodia, 57, 184; on American war, 143, 145, 157, 163

Eastern Europe, 26, 39, 68, 101, 109, 111, 135, 137
Eastern Europeans, 30, 108
Easter offensive (1972), 181, 185
Economic reforms, 102–106, 116; failures of, 3, 101; in agriculture, 8, 67, 89–91; and ideological disputes, 18, 67–68, 87, 93, 100, 105, 135; and socialism, 42, 86, 93, 101, 104; implementation of, 96–97, 300
Economy, Vietnamese: development of, 2, 109–113; U.S. influence on, 12, 78; and north-south differences, 19, 40, 77; service sector of, 27, 79–80, 112; capitalist sector of, 37–38, 87, 91, 101, 105, 122–123, 133, 135; and socialism, 38, 42; and foreign aid, 39, 66, 81–82, 103, 107–110, 134, 137; and Cambodian war, 66, 107, 134–135, 141, 201; and education, 68–70; state sector of, 97, 99, 111, 122; and energy supply, 105, 109–110; and debts, 106, 107, 109, 111–112; of central Vietnam, 118–123, 131–132. *See also* Agriculture,

Vietnamese; Free market economy; Industry
Education, 65, 68–70
El Salvador, 266
Emmerson, Donald K., 291–292
Enders, Thomas, 259
Exports: Vietnamese, 97–98, 99, 111, 112–113, 118; Cambodian, 205, 223

Facing the Sea (Nguyen Manh Tuan), 32
Famine, 54, 204, 209
Fatherland Front, 41–42
Flags, battle of the, 186, 192
Fonda, Jane, 126
France: Vietnam under, 1, 16, 77–78, 84, 121, 128, 300; and Cambodia, 1, 197, 206, 222, 227–229, 236; influence on Vietnam of, 39–40, 64; and Vietnamese economy, 39, 109; communism in, 116, 125, 137, 268; and Sihanouk, 248, 250, 252; Cambodians in, 265, 268, 269, 285. *See also* French-Vietnamese war
Free market economy, 42–43, 79, 119–120; and economic reforms, 90, 91, 96–97, 99, 100, 103–104, 135; in Cambodia, 266, 286
French-Vietnamese war: end of, 1, 55, 134, 227; veterans of, 9, 31, 33, 71, 72, 150, 169, 180, 193; effects of, 14–16, 25, 121, 139, 299; evaluation of, 48, 143, 170; and Vietnamese mentality, 68, 74; and American-Vietnamese war, 147–148, 149, 156, 167, 170, 171–172, 193–195; and Cambodia, 197, 228
Fulbright, William, 246

Garwood, Robert, 62
Geneva Conference, 1, 55, 149, 170, 171; and Cambodia, 225, 227–228
Germany, 236
Giap, General Vo Nguyen, 93, 180, 182–185, 187, 279
Giau, Tran Van, 9
Gorbachev, Mikhail, 58, 106, 108, 109, 221, 267, 293
Group 559, 150–151
Guam, 158

Ha, Sau, 238, 239
Haiphong, 79, 82, 133, 155, 246
Hanoi, 1, 2, 21, 168; impressions of, 28, 50–51, 70–71, 73, 114–115, 117; people of, 33, 70, 129, 133; economy of, 79–80, 111

Harriman, Averell, 234, 235, 236, 237, 238, 239, 240, 244
Hayden, Tom, 238
Heder, Steve, 276, 277, 280, 281
Heng, Cheng, 251
Highway 9, 123, 150, 151, 153, 154, 163, 188, 189
Hoa. See *Chinese*, ethnic
Ho Chi Minh, 121, 170; associates of, 9, 84, 102, 269; and communism, 55, 94, 134, 187; legacy of, 65, 114–116; and youth, 72, 115
Ho Chi Minh Campaign, 144–145
Ho Chi Minh City, 7–8, 10, 38, 41, 50, 117; impressions of, 13–14, 26–31; people of, 20, 24–26, 130, 133; character of, 21, 23, 27–28; economy of, 79, 86, 97, 98, 105. *See also* Saigon
Ho Chi Minh Trail, 148–149, 149–169, 180, 182, 188–189, 194, 246, 300; and Cambodia, 196, 242, 269
Hong Kong, 17, 131, 133
Hood, Marlowe, 260
Hope, Bob, 44
How Pol Pot Came to Power (Ben Kiernan), 267–268
Huan, Bui Tuong, 9
Hué, 8, 50, 120, 125, 126, 129, 145; impressions of, 117–118, 131
Human Rights, Lawyers Committee for, 214, 217. *See also* Political criminals
Hung, Pham, 94, 171
Hungary, 93
Huu, To, 93, 105
Hu Yaobang, 138

Iadrang, battle of, 175–178, 182, 188, 245
Ideologues: and economic reforms, 67, 87, 91, 93; and pragmatists, 94, 98, 100, 105; and foreign policy, 135, 136
India, 137, 201, 211
Indo-China, 16, 25, 55, 292; and Vietnam, 169, 202, 266, 274, 281, 293, 299
Indochina Issues, 69, 291
Indo-China war, first. *See* French-Vietnamese war
Indo-China war, second. *See* American-Vietnamese war
Indo-China war, third, 278. *See also* Cambodian-Vietnamese war
Indochinese Communist Party, 269
Indonesia, 57–59, 137, 219, 266, 284, 289. *See also* Association of Southeast Asian Nations

Industry: light, 38, 71, 82, 98, 109; growth of, 68, 92, 109–113, 118; and economic reforms, 88–89, 97, 98–100, 105; destruction of, 88, 168; Cambodian, 205, 223
Inflation, 93, 102, 104, 133
International Monetary Fund, 103, 111
Iraq, 111
Iron Triangle, 44

Jackson, Karl D., 19
Japan, 9, 87; and Vietnamese economy, 39, 66, 98, 111, 131, 135, 300
Johnson, Lyndon, 173, 174, 183, 189, 234

Kampuchea, Coalition Government of Democratic, 214–220, 278–280, 284–291, 293, 295
Kampuchea, Communist Party of, 211, 222, 263–264, 269, 276
Kampuchea, Democratic, 216, 262, 266, 280–281, 284–286, 288, 295. *See also* Khmer Rouge
Kampuchea, People's Republic of, 200, 213, 278, 284. *See also* Cambodia
Kampuchea, Workers Party of, 269
Kantol, Prince, 248, 249
Kauffman, Fred, 209–210
Kennedy, John F., 231
Khai, Nguyen, 31, 32, 33
Khanh, General Nguyen, 174
Khanh Ly, 5
Khesanh, 150, 188
Khmer Krom border area, 273, 274
Khmer people, 197, 208. *See also* Cambodia
Khmer People's National Liberation Front (KPNLF), 212, 215–216, 285–286, 289
Khmer People's Revolutionary Party, 2, 269, 282
Khmer Rouge: atrocities of, 7, 49, 212, 217, 223, 272, 280–281, 299; and war with Vietnam, 53, 57, 84, 135, 198–199, 203, 280; and China, 56, 58, 200, 267, 282, 290, 294; and Pol Pot, 198, 210, 213, 266, 276–277; and peace negotiations, 201, 221, 293, 295; and opposition coalition, 215, 216, 219, 220, 285–289, 291; and North Vietnam, 219, 222, 242, 273; regime of, 247, 257, 270–271, 274, 278; and Sihanouk, 253, 260, 261, 262, 263; and U.S., 255, 256, 261

Khmer Serei movement, 229–230
Kiem, Tran Buu, 237
Kiernan, Ben, 267–268, 270, 271, 272
Kiet, Vo Van, 39, 40, 90, 91, 93, 97, 105
The Killing Fields, 216
Kim Il Sung, 228
Kissinger, Henry: and Vietnam, 47, 49, 88; and Cambodia, 243–245, 251–252, 255, 258, 259, 260, 261, 272
Kontum, battle of, 145, 185
Korea, 228, 236
Korean war, 185
Kossamak, Queen, 228, 248, 250
Kosygin, Alexei, 250
Kublai Khan, 140
Kusumaatmadja, Mochtar, 58–59, 289, 291
Ky, Nguyen Minh, 122, 123

Ladd, Colonel Jonathan, 258
La Dépêche, 233
Lam Son 119, 189
Land reform, 76, 82, 84
Langson, 138–140
Laodong (Worker's) Party, 144, 171, 274
Laos, 1, 87, 228, 230, 286; Americans missing in, 59, 60, 62; and Vietnam, 123, 134, 153–154, 198, 256, 274, 281, 295, 299; and American-Vietnamese war, 124, 150, 163, 164, 168, 246; revolution in, 153–154
Laotian Patriotic Front, 253
The Last Meeting in the Year (Nguyen Khai), 31
Lenin, 104, 264
Libya, 111
Lien, Pham Sy, 111
Literacy, 68–69
Literature, 28, 31–33, 34, 51, 80, 142
Livre Noir, 270
Long, Nguyen Phi, 140–141
Lon Nol, 168, 247–249, 251–254, 260–262, 272–273, 274
Lon Non, Colonel, 253
Lottery, government, 112, 133
Luong, Nguyen Van, 118–119, 120
Luong, Tran, 149–150, 153

Ma Bap, 46
McNamara, Robert, 124
Malaysia, 56, 57, 284, 289
Man, Major General Tran Cong, 193
Mangold, John, 44
Mansfield, Mike, 235

Mao Zedong, 135, 187, 251, 270
Marchais, George, 125
Martin, Graham, 193
Marxism, 67, 98, 101, 136, 187. *See also* Communism
Matak, Sirik, 247, 248, 249, 251
MIAs (Americans missing in action), 52, 59–62, 222
Military: Vietnamese, 87, 92, 95, 103; Soviet, 107. *See also* American-Vietnamese war; Cambodian-Vietnamese war
Minh, General Duong Van, 194
Minh, Thich Thien, 127
Minnich, Bob, 29
Minority ethnic groups, 140, 153, 165, 171, 194. *See also* Chinese, ethnic; Van Kieu tribe
Moeung, Som, 207
Mok, Ta, 217
Mysliwiec, Eva, 209

National Liberation Front (NLF), 10, 182, 197, 238, 239, 253; and North Vietnam, 18, 41, 95, 164, 173, 177, 180. *See also* Khmer People's National Liberation Front
Navarre, General Henri, 170, 194
Netherlands, the, 78
New Economic Zones, 20, 113
New Revolutionary Movement, 253
Nghiep, Thich Chanh, 126, 127, 128
Nghiet, Cao Van, 45, 46
Nguyen Hue campaign, 185
Nhan Dan, 40, 71, 72, 104, 193
Nixon, Richard, 186, 189, 243, 244, 251, 255
Nosavan, Phoumi, 153

On Strategy: A Critical Analysis of the Vietnam War (Harry G. Summers), 176
Operation Buttercup, 238, 239
Orderly Departure Program, 23–24, 25, 29
Our Great Spring Victory (General Van Tien Dung), 143, 163

Page, Tim, 29–30, 34
Paris peace negotiations: and Kissinger, 47, 49, 243; and 1973 agreement, 146–147, 168, 186, 189, 192, 260; and Vietnamese strategy, 181, 184, 185
PAVN—People's Army of Vietnam (Douglas Pike), 179
Penycate, Tom, 44
Philippines, the, 56, 219
Phim, So, 213, 277

306   Index

Phnom Penh, 196, 203–204, 210; and
   Vietnamese, 200, 213, 218, 262,
   278, 282; and Khmer Rouge, 222,
   223, 274
Phoenix program, 94
Phuc, Kim, 46
Phuong, Brigadier General Hoang,
   148, 169–175, 182, 184, 188–190
Phuong, Nguyen Dinh, 28–29, 48,
   79, 125
Phuong, Dr. Nguyen Thi Ngoc, 34–
   35
Phuong, Tran, 92, 93, 100–101, 105
Pike, Douglas, 179–187
Pleiku, battle of, 145
Pleime, battle of, 175, 177, 178
Podgorny, Nicolai, 250
Pol Pot, 212, 267–270; atrocities
   under, 7, 49, 198, 205–207, 210–
   211, 214; and China, 50, 56, 141,
   222–223, 270, 273, 282, 291; and
   Cambodian-Vietnamese war, 53,
   199, 273, 274–277, 280; retirement
   of, 53, 215, 216, 220, 266, 290,
   294; and negotiations with
   Vietnam, 201, 202, 284, 287, 290;
   and opposition coalition, 212, 215,
   216, 219, 220, 266; and Sihanouk,
   212, 266–267, 270; regime of, 213,
   222–224, 263–265, 274, 276; and
   Khmer Rouge, 217, 221, 278, 281,
   283
Politburo, Vietnamese, 96; and
   Cambodia, 3, 201, 281–282;
   factions within, 18, 67, 86, 135,
   180, 183–184, 186–187, 190, 290;
   and South Vietnam, 21, 149, 164,
   177; members of, 32, 47, 57, 83,
   90, 93, 94, 279; and foreign policy,
   58, 63, 137, 138; and economy, 97,
   102, 105, 113; and American war,
   144, 146, 181. See also Vietnam,
   Communist Party of
Political criminals, 19–22, 63, 214
Political struggle (dau tranh chinh tri),
   147, 176–177, 179, 185, 186, 188;
   and armed struggle, 180, 181, 183,
   184, 187
Pompidou, Georges, 248
Population growth, 90, 92, 114, 115,
   128–129
Pragmatists: and economic reforms,
   67, 87, 91, 93, 101; and ideologues,
   94, 98, 100, 105; and foreign
   policy, 135, 136
Prices, 80, 100; of crops, 42–43, 84,
   97, 119; and economic reforms, 90,
   91, 103, 104, 105, 106

Production contract system, 36, 40,
   89–91, 92
Protestant missionaries, 153
Provisional Central Committee of
   Salvation, 215
Provisional Revolutionary
   Government (PRG), 10, 95, 125,
   164

Quang, Thich Tri, 8–9, 126, 127
Quangtri, 50, 117–119, 125, 145, 189
Quinn-Judge, Paul, 85
Quinn-Judge, Sophie, 69

Rationing, 80, 103, 105
Reagan, Ronald, 49, 221
Refugees: after 1975, 17, 20–21, 29,
   52, 133; and U.S., 22, 23–25, 60,
   62, 127; during American-
   Vietnamese war, 119, 125;
   Cambodian, 199, 207, 214, 224,
   280, 284
Relief agencies, 209–210
Religion Incarnate, 130
Rives, Lloyd, 249
Rusk, Dean, 239
Russians, 26, 30, 51, 108, 299. See also
   Soviet Union

Saigon: retreat from, 1, 5–6, 16, 17;
   and Ho Chi Minh City, 13, 23, 117;
   changes in, 14–15, 26; and French,
   16, 35, 77; capture of, 83, 143–147,
   178, 187, 190, 193, 194; and
   American war, 78, 85, 131, 155;
   and Cambodia, 273. See also Ho Chi
   Minh City
Samouth, Tou, 269
Samphan, Khieu: and peace
   negotiations, 200, 290, 295; and
   opposition coalition, 216, 262, 286,
   287; and Sihanouk, 220, 242, 253,
   260; and Pol Pot, 224, 265
Samrin, Heng: and Vietnam, 49–50,
   53, 200, 213, 277, 282; government
   of, 56, 214–215, 219, 220, 278,
   285; and peace negotiations, 201,
   267, 284, 290, 291, 293
Sang, Pham, 44
Sangkum movement, 233
Sann, Son: and Vietnam, 49, 53, 199,
   200, 219, 290; and opposition
   coalition, 56, 57, 212, 215–216,
   220, 262, 285–289, 291, 295
Sar, Saloth, 212, 268, 269. See also Pol
   Pot
Sarit, Thanarat, 229, 231
Sary, Ieng, 262, 266

Sau, Vo, 36
Second September Engineering
    Cooperative, 36–38
Sen, Hun, 219–220, 221, 267
Sen, Son, 215, 216
Senate Foreign Relations Committee,
    246, 258
Siem Reap, 228, 249
Sieu, Thich Thien, 126
Sihanouk, Monique, 226, 247
Sihanouk, Norodom, 224–226, 299;
    and peace negotiations, 49, 200–
    203, 219–220, 226, 254, 290–291,
    294–297; and Cambodian-
    Vietnamese war, 53, 54, 197–198,
    199, 245; and opposition coalition,
    56–57, 216, 260, 285–288, 291;
    and American-Vietnamese war,
    196, 240, 243; abdication of, 197,
    226, 228, 268; and U.S., 197, 227,
    230–231, 234, 236–237, 239–242,
    244–245, 256–262, 295; and
    China, 197, 227–228, 230, 232–
    233, 241–244, 249–253, 256–263,
    278; and Pol Pot, 212, 266–267,
    270; and Cambodia's foreign
    relations, 229, 232, 236–237; coup
    against, 247–253, 256, 270, 272;
    and Khmer Rouge, 256, 260, 262,
    263, 265, 269, 289
Sihanoukville, 196, 242, 247
Singapore, 133, 283; and Vietnam,
    39, 97; and Cambodia, 56, 204,
    284, 287, 288
Socialism, 33; in South Vietnam, 18,
    21, 38, 84–85; as goal, 37–39, 42–
    43, 83, 86, 89, 104; obstacles to,
    75–76, 83–84, 87; Vietnamese, 93,
    101, 136; in Cambodia, 208, 216,
    263, 266, 268. See also Communism
Solidarity Groups (Krom Samakki),
    208
Solomon, Richard, 294
Somol, Kong, 204–206, 208
Souphanouvong, Prince, 153, 253
Southeast Asia: and Vietnam, 2, 64,
    87, 281, 300; and major powers,
    88, 273, 294; and Cambodia, 201,
    203, 216, 219, 221, 232, 291, 293.
    See also Association of Southeast
    Asian Nations
Southeast Asian Treaty Organization
    (SEATO), 227, 231
Sovan, Pen, 282–283
Soviet Union: Vietnamese
    dependence on, 3, 39, 52, 54, 55–
    56, 87, 107–108, 135; training in,
    9, 68 116, 207, 279; Vietnamese

attitudes towards, 48, 108, 136–
    137; and Cambodian-Vietnamese
    war, 56, 220, 227, 230, 243, 267–
    268, 283; and China, 58, 88, 106,
    108, 109; influence on Vietnam of,
    76, 106, 113; aid to Vietnam from,
    81, 82, 109, 110–111, 167, 168,
    184; compared to Vietnam, 101,
    134; and American-Vietnamese
    war, 169, 185, 187, 246; and
    negotiations on Cambodia, 201,
    203, 221–222, 256, 285, 290–295;
    and Sihanouk, 244, 250, 252, 260.
    See also Russians
Sukarno, 284
Summers, Harry G., 176, 177, 179
Suramarit, King, 228
Sutsakhan, Suk, 215
Swain, Jon, 216–217
Swank, Emory, 259
Sweden, 111
Symington, Stuart, 259

Taiwan, 133, 135
Tan, General Le Trong, 95
Tang, Truong Nhu, 164, 165
Taxes, 27, 30, 37–38, 79, 89, 112,
    122
Tet offensive, 118, 121, 239;
    planning of, 44, 182, 188; and
    Vietcong, 85, 157, 180, 183, 189,
    191; analysis of, 181, 183, 188–189,
    190–191
Thach, Nguyen Co, 25, 54, 57, 63,
    138, 201, 289–290
Thailand: and Vietnam, 22, 158, 159;
    and Cambodia negotiations, 49,
    201, 221; and Cambodian-
    Vietnamese war, 53, 56, 199, 200,
    216, 283–284, 286, 290; and
    Cambodia, 197, 204, 229, 231; and
    Cambodian refugees, 224, 275,
    280; and U.S., 230, 258, 283–284
Thanh, Son Ngoc, 229, 230, 268
Thi, Mme Ba, 42–43
Thi, Nguyen Dinh, 33, 195
Thien, Major General Dinh Duc, 148,
    155–162, 166–168, 188
Thieu, Nguyen Van, 128, 135, 146,
    192
Tho, Le Duc, 3, 47–50, 148, 155; on
    domestic problems, 32–33, 85, 88,
    93; on Cambodia, 47, 49–50, 53,
    201, 261, 281–282; and foreign
    policy, 63, 136, 137–138, 185
Tho, Nguyen Huu, 10, 253
Thuan, Nguyen Van, 129–130
Tin, Bui, 71–72, 73, 193–194

Tonkin, 77. *See also* Vietnam, North
Tonkin Gulf incident, 173–174
Tra, Lieutenant General Tran Van, 144, 145, 163, 188, 190–193
Trinh Cong Son, 5–8, 13
Tuan, Nguyen Manh, 32
Tu Duc, Emperor, 120–121
Tung, Hoang, 72, 73, 96–97
Tuol Sleng prison, 211, 264
Tuyen, Nguyen Phi, 25

Unemployment, 26, 66, 82, 131, 132
United Front for an Independent, Neutral, Peaceful and Cooperative Cambodia, 286
United Front of Patriotic Forces for the Liberation of Vietnam, 22
United Nations: and Vietnam, 2, 24, 41, 114, 138; and Cambodia, 54, 200–202, 205, 217, 218, 220, 262, 263; and ASEAN, 284, 287, 288, 289, 291, 295
United States: and South Vietnam, 1–2, 23, 78, 84, 146, 147, 172, 174; and reunified Vietnam, 3, 20, 22, 49, 52, 54, 58–64, 107, 137; influence on Vietnam of, 12, 28, 39–40, 72, 78, 85; and human rights, 20, 214; and refugees, 24–26, 133, 199; and Cambodia negotiations, 50, 201, 218–219, 221–222, 285, 287, 291–295; and international agreements, 55, 146, 154; aid to Vietnam from, 82, 109, 110, 119, 300; invasion of Cambodia by, 189, 222, 241, 243, 245, 247, 254–256, 265, 270; and Sihanouk, 197, 227–231, 235–236, 239–240, 244–245, 260–262; and Cambodian opposition coalition, 200, 216, 286, 288; aid to Cambodia from, 209, 227, 228–229, 242, 249, 257; and Pol Pot, 217, 220, 266, 267, 273, 284; and Southeast Asia, 219, 283–284; and break with Cambodia, 231–232, 233, 244–245; bombing of Cambodia by, 242–244, 258–259, 260, 261, 271, 272; and Cambodian coup, 251–252, 253, 254. *See also* Americans: American-Vietnamese war
Urban-rural dichotomy: in Vietnam, 69; in Cambodia, 222–223, 265, 272, 274

Van Kieu tribe, 150, 151, 152
Vickery, Michael, 264–265, 266
Vien, Le Van (Bai Vien), 35

Vietcong: recruits to, 10–11, 36; and American war, 35, 43, 44, 46, 94; and Tet offensive, 84–85, 157, 180, 183, 189, 191; and North Vietnam, 92, 149, 157, 171, 173–174, 177–178, 180, 189; negotiations with, 234–240; and Cambodia, 241, 242, 243, 247, 248, 251
Vietcong: The Organization and Techniques of the National Liberation Front of South Vietnam (Douglas Pike), 179
Vietcong Memoir (Truong Nhu Tang), 164
Vietminh, 9, 195; and French war, 1, 15, 16, 43, 85; recruits to, 31, 33; and North Vietnam, 149–150, 153, 171, 189
Vietnam, central, 77, 117–141
Vietnam, Communist Party of, 40, 72, 94–96; factions within, 18, 86, 135, 192; and South Vietnam, 21, 83, 85; and foreign relations, 88, 274; and economic reforms, 90, 104; leaders of, 102, 114, 187. *See also* Politburo, Vietnamese
Vietnam, Democratic Republic of, 172
Vietnam, under France, 1, 77–78, 121. *See also* French-Vietnamese war
Vietnam: History of the Bulwark B-2 Theatre (Tran Van Tra), 144
Vietnam, North: and Saigon's fall, 1, 6, 83, 144; and Geneva Conference, 1, 55, 170; victory of, 3, 11, 12, 144–147, 187–189; rule of south by, 13, 17–21, 77, 83–85, 94–95, 116; and American war, 15, 55, 238, 239, 299; history of, 16; and peace agreement, 47–48, 146, 185–186; land reform in, 76, 82, 84; aid to south from, 92, 149, 157, 171, 173–174, 177–178, 180, 189; strategy of, 144, 147–148, 158, 166, 169, 174–184, 187; and French war, 147, 299; and Laos, 153–154, 274; and China, 185, 187, 233, 246; and Cambodian sanctuaries, 196, 230, 241, 242–244, 246, 250, 255; and Pol Pot, 223, 269–270; and Cambodian negotiations, 232, 256, 261, 262; and Sihanouk, 236, 245, 247, 248, 249, 251, 254, 260; and Khmer Rouge, 255–256, 257, 272, 273. *See also* Ho Chi Minh Trail; Politburo, Vietnamese

Vietnam, north-south differences in: and northern rule, 17–19, 21, 77, 83–85, 94–95, 116; cultural, 27, 32, 71; economic, 39–40, 66, 89, 91, 101; psychological, 74, 75, 193; and central Vietnam, 118, 123
Vietnam, reunified: problems of, 2, 3, 300; and China, 3, 39, 54, 64, 107, 109, 136–138; changes in, 7, 21; U.S. influence on, 12, 28, 39–40, 72, 78, 85; and Laos, 123, 134, 198, 295, 299; and Catholics, 128–130; invasion of Cambodia by, 198–200, 207, 210–211, 224, 247, 263, 278, 281–282; and Cambodian war, 200, 213–214, 274–281; and Cambodian negotiations, 201–203, 219, 221–222, 290–294, 295; and Indo-China, 202, 266, 274, 281, 293, 299; and Cambodian opposition, 212–218, 220, 226, 264, 267, 283, 285, 299; and ASEAN, 284, 287. *See also* Economy, Vietnamese
Vietnam, South, 9, 16, 77; U.S. support of, 1–2, 78, 172, 174, 186, 245; and American war, 11, 15, 55, 124–125, 144, 152–153, 183, 185, 235, 238–239; northern rule of, 17–21, 77, 83–85, 94–95, 116; defeat of, 47, 145–147, 179, 187–188, 192, 194, 262, 299; youth of, 72, 73; agriculture of, 92, 113; Buddhists in, 127–128; and Cambodia, 196, 222, 227, 229–230, 232, 236, 254, 256–257, 268, 273. *See also* Ho Chi Minh City; Saigon; Vietcong; Vietminh
Vietnamese, 73–75, 113–114, 143–144, 167, 274, 288, 295
Vietnamization, 186, 189, 254, 255
Vinh, Major General Nguyen Van, 149, 150

Wages, 37, 80, 102–105, 112, 113, 135
Watergate scandal, 186, 244
Wolf, Eric, 264, 265, 266
Women, 7, 41, 77–78, 95, 129, 149, 208
Wu Xueqian, 138

Xuanloc, battle of, 146, 162

Youth, 26, 41, 94, 131, 165; attitudes of, 39, 70, 71–73; education of, 65, 68, 69, 70
Yugoslavia, 268

Zurich agreement (1961), 153

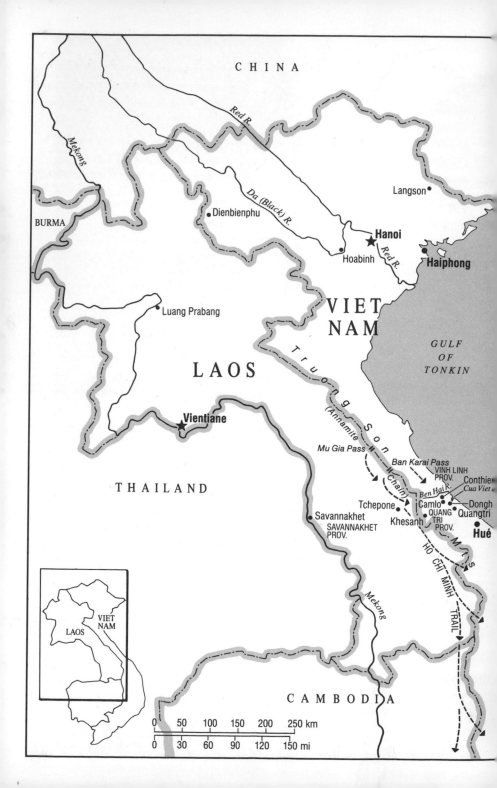